What readers are saying about Bill Eddy and "It's All Your Fault!" 12 Tips for Managing People Who Blame Others for Everything

"We all experience high conflict people in our daily lives. This book gives us both an understanding of the personalities that are prone to blame us for everything and simple tips to manage these unpleasant interactions. It really works."

Stephen Heidel, M.D., M.B.A.
C.E.O., Heidel and Associates, La Jolla, CA

"This book is really on the mark! If enough people use these simple tips with difficult people, it could reduce the level of conflict and risk of violence in families, in the workplace, and in our communities."

Bonnie Dumanis, District Attorney
San Diego, CA

"A practical guide for dealing with high-conflict people in everyday life. As a professional educator I have followed Bill Eddy's step-by step process for years with great success. This book will transform your approach to problem-solving with difficult people."

Dennis Doyle, Ph.D.
Superintendent, National School District, National City, CA

"As both a therapist and attorney, Bill Eddy is uniquely qualified to write this critically needed book. He has an astounding talent for taking complex psychological information and showing readers, point by point, how to avoid the pitfalls of dealing with high conflict personalities and create win-win situations for everyone involved."

Randi Kreger, Co-Author
Stop Walking on Eggshells, Milwaukee, WI

"Bill Eddy's techniques work even when the parties involved in a situation are not "high conflict people." As a mediator, I find that people under stress may exhibit (temporarily) some of the highly charged traits described in this book. By giving them my EAR and using the CARS method to de-escalate their emotions, they are more able then to negotiate constructively for themselves. This is a great book for mediators—or anyone!"

Barbara Filner, Director
Training Institute, National Conflict Resolution Center, San Diego, CA

"This is an excellent book for anyone who works with challenging clients. The 'Tips' help you understand more about these types of people, but more importantly, they also give practical knowledge on how to work with them. It is easy to read, as Bill has done a great job of sharing his life experiences in a great format. Thank you!"

Scott Clarke, Certified Financial Planner
Collaborative Neutral, Dallas/Ft. Worth, TX

"Bill Eddy has provided readers with an essential guide to understanding and managing the most difficult and conflict-prone individuals we are likely to encounter in everyday life, whether at work or closer to home. Eddy has harnessed the knowledge and wisdom that his multidisciplinary background and years of experience have allowed him to accumulate, and distilled that learning into an insightful and commonsense approach, delivered in an interesting and eminently readable book. As a consultant in workplace conflict and violence prevention, I expect "It's All Your Fault!" will become an indispensible desktop compendium for me, as it will for anyone who deals with "high-conflict personalities" in either their personal or professional lives."

Hy Bloom, LL.B., M.D., F.R.C.P.(C.)
Author, The Workplace Risk Assessment-20 and
The Employee Risk Assessment-20, Toronto, ON

"Learning how to handle high conflict people is like learning how to drive defensively. Except harder. We hire police to arrest bad drivers, but no one arrests high conflict people. Instead, it's up to us—to read "It's All Your Fault!" This book is written incisively and insightfully. It's not a one-size-fits-all book. You'll discover the person behind the personality type. And as you do, you find more of the human in yourself. So read "It's All Your Fault!" If you don't, well—"It's All Your Fault!""

Warren Farrell, Ph.D.
Author, Women Can't Hear What Men Don't Say, Mill Valley, CA

"A new generation of potentially High Conflict People is emerging from the academically and socially-competitive cauldron that high school has become. Mr. Eddy has provided a framework and practical strategies through which students, parents, teachers and administrators can become empowered to confront the very issues that prevent the flowering of our nation's greatest resource—our people. On a personal note, the book is brilliant and I fully intend to teach these precepts to my students of psychology. And to live them in my life."

Austin Manghan, M.Ed.
Psychology and History Teacher, Longwood High School, Middle Island, NY

"It's All Your Fault!"

12 Tips for Managing People Who Blame Others For Everything

Other Books and Courses by Bill Eddy

New Ways for Families in Separation and Divorce:
  Professional Guidebook (2009)
  Parent Workbook (2009)
  Collaborative Parent Workbook (2009)
HCI Press

High Conflict People in Legal Disputes (2006, 2008)
HCI Press

Managing High Conflict People In Court (2008)
HCI Press

The Splitting CD: An Interview with Bill Eddy (2006)
Eggshells Press

Splitting: Protecting Yourself While Divorcing a Borderline or Narcissist (2004)
Eggshells Press

Working with High Conflict Personalities (2004, 2006)
(A Six-Hour Internet Course for Mental Health
Professionals at www.continuingEdCourses.net)

"It's All Your Fault!"

12 Tips for Managing People
Who Blame Others For Everything

By Bill Eddy
Attorney, Mediator and Therapist

PRESS

"It's All Your Fault!"
12 Tips for Managing People Who Blame Others for Everything

Bill Eddy
Attorney, Mediator and Therapist

Names and information identifying private individuals have been changed to preserve anonymity. Many quotations have been modified to protect confidentiality and to demonstrate the principles of the book. Some examples are slight alterations of real cases, while other examples were inspired by real cases but are completely fictional. Quotes from Court cases and news publications are accurate and names are real. Appellate case citations are provided for interested readers who wish to review the original published opinions.

Eddy, Bill, 1948-
It's all your fault, 12 tips for managing people who blame others for everything / by Bill Eddy. Includes bibliographical references.
ISBN 978-1-936268-02-3

First printing: April 2008
Second printing: November 2009 by HCI Press

Editor: Danielle LeClair Rakoz
Book design: Pierpoint-Martin

Publisher:
Published by HCI Press
www.hcipress.com

P R E S S Printed in the United States of America

For my mother,
Margaret Eddy (1917-1971)
who taught me from the age of 5 that we
don't judge people—we try to understand them.

TABLE OF CONTENTS

A NOTE OF CAUTION

TO THE READER

This book addresses issues of High Conflict People and their high-conflict personalities. Knowledge is power. The information I provide is intended to help you be more successful in your interactions with people in everyday life: neighbors, co-workers, family members, and even strangers.

However, this personality information can also be misused and can inadvertently make your life more difficult. Therefore, I caution you not to openly label people in your life, nor to use this information as a weapon in personal relationships. Before you go further, I ask that you make a commitment to use this information with caution, compassion, and respect.

My explanations and tips address general patterns of behavior and may not apply to your specific situation. You are advised to seek the advice of a therapist, an attorney, or other conflict resolution professional in handling any dispute.

The author and the publisher are not responsible for any decisions or actions you take as a result of reading this book.

Bill Eddy

Publisher's Note

In 2009, HCI Press acquired the rights to publish this book and other books by Bill Eddy. The text remains unchanged from the previous printings. HCI Press is a subsidiary of High Conflict Institute, LLC, which was co-founded in 2008 by Bill Eddy and Megan Hunter. We are excited to be expanding into book publication as well as providing seminars, program development, consultation and training DVDs. For more information about HCI Press, please see our website at www.hcipress.com. For more information about High Conflict Institute, please see our website at www.HighConflictInstitute.com.

INTRODUCTION

As far back as I can remember I have been interested in other people's conflicts. My first job after college was in New York City. This was in 1970, after the gang wars, made famous just a few years earlier in the movie West Side Story, had settled down a bit.

I was a youth social worker for a neighborhood teen lounge, which had a pool table, a ping-pong table, a record player, and a small basketball court. Twenty to 30 teenagers would hang out there after school. There were rumors that one of the young adults in the neighborhood had killed a man a couple of years earlier, and I suspected that several kids carried knives.

One day one of the kids said, "Bill, there's a fight in the pool room!" My boss was out, so I was in charge. In the pool room were about a dozen regulars, mostly Eastern European kids whose parents had come to the U.S. and were struggling to move out of the run-down apartments in our area. There were also about five African American teenagers I'd never seen before.

The room was silent. Everyone was standing around the pool table. Facing each other, a boy from each group waved a pool cue in the air, looking ready to start another gang war. Because I'd worked as a student a couple of summers before at an African American recreation program outside Philadelphia, I wasn't going to make any racial assumptions about who was at fault.

I didn't have time to think. I naively walked right in between the two boys waving their cues, and I put my hands up to keep them apart. I remember saying, "Okay. Nobody move. Here's what's going to happen. I'm going to close the lounge. Right now, I want you five kids to leave while everyone else stays right where you are. In 10 minutes, the rest of you kids are going to leave."

To my amazement, everyone did exactly what I'd said. I don't remember consciously deciding to say or do anything. I just did it. Afterwards I was in a state of shock at the risks I'd taken standing between two groups of angry 16- and 17-year-olds with pool cues (and maybe knives) as weapons. I was barely five years older than they were. I had a lot of second thoughts afterwards, but the next day several of the teens told me that I'd done the right thing.

They agreed that when I punished everyone, it wasn't really fair—but life wasn't fair. More importantly, they said, no one got hurt. When teenagers tell you "you did the right thing," you remember. While this probably doesn't seem like a major incident, when you're 22 years old, things like this can have a big impact on you. It wasn't until I was writing this book that I looked back at this incident and really thought about why I reacted the way I did, and why they did what I asked. But I remember it was the beginning of a realization that I liked getting in the middle and settling conflicts.

Becoming a Mediator
By 1975, I had moved to San Diego and heard about mediation. I couldn't wait to become a mediator. In mediation, a neutral person helps two (or more) people in conflict to sit down and talk in a step-by-step way. The mediator helps them understand each other's point of view and helps them make agreements. The mediator doesn't make the decisions, but directs the discussion so the people in conflict can reach their own agreements. So I took a seminar on how to mediate, and became a volunteer mediator.

In my neighborhood, word got around that I liked settling conflicts. Neighbors dropped by and asked me to help them with their disputes with partners, neighbors, and co-workers. Of course, I did this all for free—and sometimes late at night. I thought about finding a career in mediation, but I didn't know whether there was such a thing as a professional mediator.

Becoming a Therapist
I decided to focus on families in conflict and individuals in distress. During the next 15 years I got a Masters of Social Work degree and became a psychotherapist, working in psychiatric hospitals and counseling clinics. I ran groups for schizophrenics and head injury patients. I counseled adolescents and their parents (an endless source of conflicts). And I worked with addicts and their families.

Some of our patients had more than one problem. For example, one man in our hospital substance abuse program was a severe cocaine addict—and an expert at starting conflicts. He had a personality disorder. When he stopped using drugs, he got worse instead of better. He started spreading rumors that the staff was using cocaine during lunch breaks.

He told patients they could ignore certain parts of the treatment program. He could sound very convincing, while blaming others for his own problems. Patients and staff got into big arguments over how to deal with him. He was a con artist and a drama junkie. We had to deal with him in a very united and tightly structured way.

Another patient had terrible mood swings. One day, while the patients were in group therapy, she ran across the room and physically attacked one of the large men, hitting him on the chest. Fortunately, he didn't react and we pulled her off. She had serious problems controlling her impulses and her mood swings. She also had a personality disorder.

When I was in training to be a psychotherapist in 1980, a manual came out with a new system of diagnosing mental health problems, including personality disorders. Our clinic had two experts come to teach us about it.

Learning how to deal with people with personality disorders became a routine part of our work. In many ways, they were people who got things backwards: they created conflicts that didn't exist because, in their own minds, other people were to blame for their problems. They felt constantly helpless and often depressed. Instead of solving their own problems, they were busy creating problems for others, without realizing how they were hurting themselves too! They always felt like victims.

These patients were the hardest to treat, because they took everything personally and blamed the people who were trying to help them. However, their problems weren't obvious at first to the unsuspecting, so many naïve staff and new patients would believe what they said—until they got to know them better.

Becoming an Attorney
While I enjoyed being a therapist, I still wanted to resolve ordinary conflicts between ordinary people. So, I became a volunteer mediator with the San Diego Mediation Center (now called the National Conflict Resolution Center). I took mediation training, I gave mediation training, and I handled many disputes referred by the police, the courts, and people in conflict themselves.

I decided if I really wanted to be a mediator, I should go to law school, since lawyers were starting to make mediation a popular alternative to going to court–and they were getting paid as mediators. When I opened my Law and Mediation Office in 1993, my goal was to build a practice as a family mediator, but I also decided to take family court cases as an attorney to get a couple of years of experience in court.

As I was splitting my time between mediations in my office and hearings in family court, it dawned on me that my angry court cases were dealing with the same issues as my cooperative mediation cases. The difference wasn't the issues, it was the personalities! In fact, in many of the "high-conflict" cases I recognized some of the same personality disorders that I'd worked with in psychiatric hospitals and clinics.

I was so familiar with personality disorders that I thought they were obvious to everyone. I was wrong. Attorneys and judges had no idea what I was talking about, and court-related counselors (who had no hospital or clinical training) thought personality disorders were unrelated or unimportant and shouldn't be considered in making divorce decisions.

Yet more and more high-conflict people were showing up in family courts— fighting for years and years over every issue, large and small. As I was learning, all it takes is one high-conflict person to make a high-conflict case.

So I wrote and self-published a book about high-conflict personalities in 2003 and started giving seminars to attorneys, judges, mediators, and therapists involved in legal disputes. I explained that much of this high-conflict behavior in court was a personality problem and not caused by the divorce. I used the term "high-conflict personalities," which later became High Conflict People. For short, I used the initials HCP for a High Conflict Person, meaning someone with a high-conflict personality.

In 2004, there was a sudden jump in interest in HCPs and how to handle them. I found two publishers, who each published a book of mine. I was asked to give seminars on HCPs to legal professionals in the United States, Canada, and Europe. In addition, I started getting requests for seminars from business organizations, schools, hospitals, and homeowners associations. It seemed HCPs were everywhere and causing a great deal of stress, disruption, and expense in all areas of our society.

Writing This Book

This book contains the most important 12 lessons I've learned about High Conflict People over the past 30 years—much of it by trial and error. I'm eager to give you this information, because I think it will make your life easier and because it will make all of our lives easier as more people learn how to manage HCPs.

In writing this book, I feel like I'm sharing some powerful secrets. Most people don't understand HCPs, but they have known several and realized that something was different about them. I've been explaining HCPs for several years to attorneys, judges, mediators, therapists, and people going through divorce. More recently, I've been explaining this to people in disputes with their neighbors, co-workers, and other family members.

They all have a similar response: "Now I see why my husband acts that way," "Now I understand why the woman next door couldn't resolve a simple dispute over our fence," "You must have met my boss—he does exactly what you described."

High Conflict People have predictable patterns of behavior and there are predictable ways to manage most of them once you understand their personalities. The mental health field has developed substantial knowledge about personality disorders over the last few decades, yet most of this knowledge hasn't been applied to the field of conflict resolution. Given this gap in knowledge, Janis Publications, a publisher of books on conflict resolution, asked me to write this book to share this information with the general public in a practical way.

The purpose of this book is to explain the basic HCP theory and key actions to consider in handling any type of HCP dispute. The focus is everyday disputes—neighborhood, workplace, family—but the ideas can be used with anyone in any type of conflict.

A Book of Opposites

In many ways, this is a book of opposites. My 12 tips are often the exact opposite of what you feel like doing. This is a normal response to this new information. I made many mistakes on the way to learning this approach. Don't be surprised if you regret some past actions you have taken in dealing with an HCP. I have experienced that on many occasions and still do sometimes. Yet, I have learned this is what works.

I've tried to make this book practical, so every Tip has a practice question and a Tip summary. Part I helps you understand the high-conflict personalities of HCPs and how to avoid responding in ways that make things worse. These are the seven "Don't do This" Tips. I like to get right to the point. Ideally, I would focus on the positive—what to do, rather than what not to do. However, these are very common and important mistakes that all of us make with HCPs, and it's the easiest way to explain them.

Part II focuses on "What to Do." It includes four key actions to consider in dealing with any HCP. I call it the C.A.R.S. Method™, and I've tried to make it easy to do. While the 12 tips I describe are important with HCPs, they can be used in any conflict situation, especially ones with high emotions and little cooperation from the other person.

To demonstrate the patterns of High Conflict People, I use many case examples. Some of these are taken from the news or court cases, and I cite the sources. Other stories are from my own experience as a mediator, attorney, or therapist. I've changed some details to protect people's confidentiality. Some examples are fictional stories inspired by real events to help demonstrate key points.

I've written this book in a conversational style, because that's how I am used to communicating with people under stress. But don't be fooled. The concepts in this book can be complicated. You may disagree with some of these concepts at first, and, as I said, the methods I provide may seem like the opposite of what you feel like doing in a high-conflict situation. But this is normal, so bear with me. Try these suggestions. I know they work. I had to learn the hard way, but you don't have to!

ACKNOWLEDGEMENTS

This book would not exist if it weren't for Janis Magnuson and Ray Sobol of Janis Publications. Four years ago, when major publishers had rejected my proposals, they picked up my first book and encouraged me to write this book for the general public. They were extremely patient while I kept pushing back my own writing deadlines—at least two years! They kept me focused on writing a very practical book, no matter how long it took. The book you have today is the result of their guidance, patience, and friendship.

I also owe so much to my wife, Alice, for her continued tolerance of my writing obsession. Not only has she given me the time and space (we share a study!) to write several books, but she has also been my most valued consultant on the mental health aspects of this subject—as a therapist herself and my toughest critic. Her wisdom has guided me repeatedly away from less helpful ideas and toward more clarity in my writing.

I want to thank Megan Hunter, who left her job with the Administrative Office of the Arizona Supreme Court primarily to promote and expand my seminars and writing. Now that we have co-founded the High Conflict Institute, LLC, her management skills have allowed me to focus on speaking and writing while requests for our services grow rapidly. Her feedback on this book and partnership in educating professionals about high-conflict personalities has been invaluable.

For over 20 years, my friends and colleagues at the National Conflict Resolution Center (formerly the San Diego Mediation Center) have sharpened my thinking about mediation and conflict resolution. Barbara Filner, Robin Seigle, Lisa Maxwell, and Trissan Maleskey in particular have given me pointers and encouragement in making this book relevant to anyone in a conflict. The dedication and skills of all of the staff and volunteers have been an inspiration to me.

Over the past 15 years, my family law and collaborative clients and professional colleagues have contributed greatly to my learning process and hope for helping people in conflict and in pain. You know who you are and I thank you greatly. Many others have given endlessly of their time in helping me refine my ideas and reading the text of this book, especially my long-term friends Dennis Doyle, Austin Manghan, and Norma Mark, who have given me detailed feedback that has made this a more useful book. I also want to thank Ellen Waldman for her critical feedback and suggesting the term "connecting" instead of bonding for this book, which helped lead to the four-step C.A.R.S. Method™.

Diane Buchman and Jenna Buchman continue to provide part-time office assistance to me, as well as very helpful feedback, including getting Tip #1 on track when I was struggling with the start of this book. Mariel Diaz has provided fresh energy to this work as a research assistant for the application of these ideas to family law professionals, as well as her suggestions on text revisions for this book.

My parents, Roland and Helen Eddy, have continued to be a source of inspiration well into their 90s. They don't hesitate to ask good questions that others don't ask, and continue to share their enthusiasm and knowledge about how people work and think. I thank them for being a source of comfort and inspiration for so many years, and for encouraging me to think that my work with people might be important.

Lastly, I want to thank Danielle LeClair Rakoz for her personal approach as my editor. She fit my style exactly, and developed an enthusiasm for this subject that went beyond her job. After attending one of my seminars, she asked me some of the most challenging questions about the HCP theory and she suggested whole new directions at key points in the writing of this book. I have agreed with almost all of her suggestions and I thank her for sharpening my writing—and thinking.

Part I: Understanding High Conflict People

Tip #1: Don't Take Their Personal Attacks Personally

CHAPTER

1

Tip #1
Don't Take Their Personal Attacks Personally

High Conflict People blame somebody else—almost anybody—when things don't go well for them. The person they blame could be a neighbor, a co-worker, a family member, or even a stranger. This "Target of Blame" could even be you. If you're not someone's Target of Blame yet, you could be soon. High Conflict People are increasing in our society.

I wrote this book to help people prepare themselves for this increase of blaming in our society. For the past 30 years I've been working to resolve conflicts as a mediator, therapist, and attorney. In every area of life I've seen an increase in "high-conflict" disputes, where one person takes no responsibility for being part of the problem or part of the solution. So the problem just gets worse. Take, for example, the neighbor from hell.

The Neighbor From Hell

"It's all your fault!" Alison screamed at her neighbor Pat.

Pat was shocked! Since Alison moved in next door three months ago, they'd gotten along just fine. But suddenly, Alison seemed to be another person, making loud noises at night and spreading rumors about Pat by day. Should Pat ignore her? Should Pat have an angry confrontation with Alison? She was tired and didn't know what to do.

The Arrogant Co-Worker

"It's all his fault!" Bob told the manager, pointing at his co-worker Jason.

Jason knew that Bob was arrogant and self-centered, but he never expected to be blamed in front of their boss—especially for something that Bob had done wrong. Should Jason tell the manager what's really going on? Should he ignore Bob? Or should he organize his co-workers to confront Bob or the manager? He didn't want to risk losing his job.

The Blaming Brother

"IT'S ALL YOUR FAULT THAT I LOST MY JOB AND MY APART-MENT!" Carlos wrote his sister, Maria, in an email. (He always wrote dramatically in bold and capital letters.)

Maria just sighed. He could never see all she had done for him. Carlos just kept blaming her for the problems he was constantly creating in his life. Should she continue to help him out? Should she cut off all communication and contact with him? Was she her "brother's keeper?" She was exhausted!

Alison, Bob, and Carlos are typical of High Conflict People. Their stories and many others in this book will help you understand the surprisingly predictable ways that HCPs think and act, and the surprisingly simple (I didn't say easy) methods for managing them.

The Increase In High Conflict People

Blaming others seems to be increasing. You've probably noticed. I've seen it working with disputes in families, schools, neighborhoods, businesses, hospitals, and the courts. It appears to be part of the increase in everyday conflict in our society. For example:

- In one study, over 80% of workers reported that at least one person in their workplace causes them serious stress (Cavaiola & Lavender, 2000).

- In 2006, for the first time, more workers reported "people problems" rather than workload as the number one stressor in the workplace (Hudson, 2006).

- In England, a poll in early 2006 showed that over the past several years most people reported an increase in petty crime and antisocial behavior in their neighborhoods (Rice-Oxley, 2006).

- In the United States, homeowners associations (HOAs) report that threats against board members are rising (Yi, 2006).

- The Wall Street Journal reported several studies that show an increase in high-conflict divorces over the past several years (Thernstrom, 2003).

While you've probably witnessed this increase in conflict and blaming (just watch the news), have you seen the *pattern* of this blaming behavior? Not everyone is constantly blaming others. But people with a certain personality pattern—perhaps 15% of our society and growing—seem preoccupied with blaming. I've been studying this high-conflict pattern for the past dozen years, and it's amazing. Though it's a growing problem, it's a *predictable* problem—and can be managed in most cases, *if* you understand it.

Targets Of Blame

High-conflict disputes have the same basic characteristics, regardless of whether they're about a friendship, a small amount of money, or even millions of dollars. There are at least two people involved:

1. **High Conflict Person (HCP):** This is someone who *constantly* gets into conflicts and often behaves badly. They *blame others* and *avoid* taking responsibility for their own problems or for changing their own behavior. Instead, they focus on the behavior of others. HCPs aren't just difficult people—they're the MOST difficult people, because they're preoccupied with confronting a Target of Blame, and the Target of Blame could be anyone—even you.

2. **Target of Blame (TOB):** When an HCP blames another person for problems that are more their own making, I call the wrongly blamed person a Target of Blame. The dispute is not really about the Target, *although it looks that way at first*. It's primarily about the person blaming the Target—the HCP.

HCPs *seek* Targets of Blame. Blaming others helps them feel better about themselves. This pattern of blaming is unconscious, meaning that they are totally unaware that it is a problem and that it is their *own* problem. HCPs are constantly in distress and blaming others. This helps them unconsciously feel safer and stronger. Yet they are *totally unaware* of the negative, self-defeating effects of this behavior. In a sense they're blind.

Since HCPs can't see the connections between their own behavior and their problems, their difficult behavior continues and their conflicts grow. That's why they're called "high-conflict" people.

High Conflict Personalities

High Conflict People have high-conflict personalities. Conflict is part of who they are. It's a life-long personality pattern of thinking, feeling, and acting. Time after time, they avoid taking responsibility for their problems. Time after time, they argue against feedback, regardless of how helpful or truthful it may be. And time after time, they try to persuade others to agree with their rigid points of view and to help them attack their Targets of Blame. The issues come and go, but their personality traits keep them in conflict. Their problems remain unresolved and the stress on those around them often increases.

From my own experience and the feedback of many people who take my seminars, the HCP personality pattern seems to be the same regardless of the kind of conflict or who else is involved.

High Conflict Personality Pattern

1. Rigid and uncompromising, repeating failed strategies

2. Unable to accept or heal from a loss

3. Negative emotions dominate their thinking

4. Unable to reflect on their own behavior

5. Difficulty empathizing with others

6. Preoccupied with blaming others

7. Avoid any responsibility for the problem or the solution

Perhaps you know someone with this pattern. Someone who insists that you, or someone you know, is entirely to blame for a large, small, or nonexistent problem. If so, he or she may be an HCP. However, before you rush to tell that person that he or she is an HCP, remember your commitment at the start of this book: **Don't openly label people and don't use this information as a weapon.** As you read further, you'll understand why this is so important.

Let me give you an example of this high-conflict personality pattern.

The Sleepless Father

When I was a therapist in the 1980s, I worked in a clinic for teenagers with drug problems. In one case, I counseled a 15-year-old boy who had experimented with marijuana and had once tried crystal methamphetamine with friends. His mother and father brought him to our outpatient clinic for individual therapy, hoping that he'd no longer use drugs, and because they believed he had an attitude problem. His grades at school hadn't been affected by his drug use, so I met with him to see if individual counseling was enough for him to stop and deal with his "attitude."

He seemed rather meek and had a history of being bullied and easily dominated by his friends. He said he didn't want to use drugs, but that his friends had pressured him into it. Of course, that's what many teenagers say, but in this case it appeared to be true.

We discussed ways he could say "No" when his peers wanted him to do things he didn't want to do. We talked about learning assertiveness skills so that he wouldn't be too passive or too aggressive with others. He seemed to feel good about our counseling session.

But when his father brought him back for his second counseling session, the father was furious, "Mr. Eddy, I woke up the other night at 2 a.m. and I was so upset about what my son had done to me by trying drugs that I couldn't get back to sleep. I realized that he was keeping me awake, so I went into his room, woke him up, and pulled him out of bed. It was his fault I couldn't sleep. Since he was keeping me awake, I told him he wasn't allowed to sleep either. Mr. Eddy, you'd better make him change his attitude. And quick. I don't want to lose any more sleep over this."

"I'll see what I can do," I told the father, surprised at his intense anger and concerned about his pressure on me to work miracles.

When I met with the boy we talked about the incident and he was very uncomfortable. He said his father was always angry, and to keep his father calm he had to agree with him. He told me that his mother had to agree with the father all the time too. We talked about ways he might cope with his father being upset, besides using drugs.

"Your father told you not to use drugs, didn't he? Weren't you afraid of getting into trouble with him about that?" I asked the boy.

"Yes, but he wasn't around and I didn't think I would get caught," he replied.

"Why do you think you used drugs?" I asked.

"I did it because I'm used to saying 'Yes' to everybody, including my father."

"So maybe we can help you decide when it's wise to say 'Yes,' and when it's wise to say 'No.' You always have a choice, you know. And you're responsible for your choices."

"I don't feel like I have a choice," the boy said.

"We'll have to work on that," I said.

I thought the session went well. I made notes to myself to talk more with his father, to help him see that intimidating his son might influence him to be easily intimidated by friends or bullies at school.

Unfortunately, just before the third session, the father called and cancelled his son's counseling—permanently. He said that his son wasn't progressing fast enough. The boy seemed to feel better about himself, and that irritated the father.

"After your last session with him, he's been full of himself. Thinks he has lots of choices in life. Boy, does he have that wrong!" the father said.

"Did he tell you that we discussed that he has to take responsibility for each of his choices?" I asked, hopefully.

"No, because I told him I didn't want to discuss it at all. I told him he better stop right now thinking that he has choices. **If you taught him that, Mr. Eddy, then this is your fault.** You haven't been helpful at all. I'm not bringing him back for any more counseling with you—or anyone else!"

And that was it. I felt like a total failure. At the time, I couldn't think of anything I might have done, or the boy could have done, to satisfy the father. The father's upset feelings weren't caused by his son's behavior—they came from inside of him.

Years later, I recognized that the father in this example was probably an HCP, and the son was his TOB. He blamed me intensely for a moment, but his son had been his Target of Blame for many years, and I imagine he continued to be for many more.

The father seemed to fit the pattern I described above:

1. **Rigid and uncompromising, repeating his failed strategies:** He endlessly repeated a very controlling strategy that didn't work and made things worse.

2. **Unable to accept or heal from a loss:** He appeared to take his son's drug experimentation as a personal insult to his own self-image as a successful parent, a loss of status he couldn't accept.

3. **Allows negative emotions to dominate his thinking:** He let his emotions control his thinking, especially fear of his son's problems and anger at his son's independence and his son's behavior that embarrassed him.

4. **Unable to reflect on his own behavior:** He didn't seem to be looking at anything about his own behavior, yet his own behavior seemed to be a huge part of the problem.

5. **Difficulty empathizing with others:** He didn't seem to have empathy for the boy, evidenced especially by pulling his son out of bed in the middle of the night to blame him some more.

6. **Preoccupied with blaming others:** He seemed clearly preoccupied with blaming his son—day and night. He even blamed me for teaching his son he had choices (and responsibilities).

7. **Avoids any responsibility for the problem or the solution:** He seemed to sincerely want to solve the problem of his son's drug use, but he didn't recognize that his own ongoing extreme behavior might be responsible for a part of the problem.

I started off with this example because I have a great deal of empathy for both the son and the father. The father wasn't a bad person; he just couldn't see the self-defeating effects of his own actions.

You might say, "Of course he knew that he shouldn't pull his son out of bed in the middle of the night. Everyone knows that!" I used to think that way too. It took me a long to time to realize this: **HCPs are truly unable to see the effects of their own behavior.** That's why they don't change their behavior and their conflicts get worse.

The "Issue" Is Not the Issue

I used to think that high-conflict disputes were over really big issues, like millions of dollars or complicated contracts. However, I've had cases involving millions of dollars and complicated contracts that settled quickly and quietly. And I've had cases of people fighting over just a few hundred dollars that ended up in bitter court battles. I realize now that, when an HCP is involved, the "issue" is not the issue. The high-conflict personality is the issue driving the case. Here's a rather disturbing neighbor example.

The Angry Homeowner

From time to time I speak at Homeowners' Associations and am asked to consult with Community Boards. These boards have volunteers of community members who address various issues for the benefit of the community. One of the issues is approving or denying the construction of fences, walls, room additions, and other changes to a home. As you can imagine, people can disagree on these highly personal matters, but most do so in a reasonable manner. However, I've recently heard of more incidents of harassment, lawsuits, and occasional violence. Here is one such case.

Lucy was a 78-year-old board member of her condominium association. For several months, one of her neighbors, Charles, was in a heated conflict with the board. He wanted help with a water damage problem, but the board wanted him to first resolve a non-approved addition he had made to his bedroom. When that was resolved, the board would deal with the water damage problem. Not an unusual problem for the board or for a homeowner.

However, one day he became particularly angry and forced his way into Lucy's home. He found her in her bedroom, grabbed her by the neck, and beat her head against the headboard of her bed. Because of her injuries, Lucy was barely able to speak after the attack. Charles was convicted of attempted murder and went to prison for seven years. Even though he'd clashed with the board for many months before Lucy had become a board member, he apparently focused all of his anger on her. He said he wanted her to die.

The attack reduced Lucy's ability to hear and her ability to see at night. She immediately left the board. (Yi, 2006)

I wasn't personally involved with this case, but it seems to me that Charles felt the "issue" of his condominium repairs was so important that Lucy deserved the full intensity of his wrath. Yet he refused to fix the problem that he first created (the addition without approval), which was the board's only requirement before addressing the problems he raised later. This is typical of HCPs. He was responsible for his part of the problem, but he couldn't make this connection. He appeared to believe it was all her fault. The "issue" was not the issue. She didn't deserve his violent behavior. The issue was his personality and his own actions.

Internal Upsets

Not only are they unable to see how they upset other people, but HCPs are unable to see that their own distress may be caused by feelings and thoughts within themselves. Many of their problems appear to be driven by their **own internal distress,** which they think is caused by the actions of others. They keep having spontaneous upsets that have nothing to do with what's going on around them or are triggered by minor or irrelevant events. Then they may act, or react, in a way that creates problems that didn't previously exist.

In other words, the problem may be entirely of the person's own making, but blamed entirely on someone else. When HCPs have a spontaneous upset, they think it was caused by their TOB. Therefore, throughout this book I refer to these crises as **Internal Upsets** or **IUs**: "**I** think it's **U** causing me to feel this way."

Close To Home

In August 2003, I read a letter to the editor in my local neighborhood newspaper by a father, Bill Hoffine, who was clearly preoccupied with his 14-year-old son's math performance at school. He explained how he spent about 200 hours during the previous year helping his son, Evan Nash, with math. He wrote that Evan was an honors algebra student and that Evan couldn't have done it without his help. He urged all parents to do the same and said he intended to continue his intensive math approach with his son for the next four years (Hoffine, 2003).

The letter stuck in my mind because it felt a little dictatorial and self-centered to me. It reminded me of the sleepless father of a few years earlier. I wondered what was going on behind the scenes.

What I didn't know was that the same week Bill Hoffine wrote his letter to the editor, a restraining order had been obtained by Evan's mother against him. Evan had reported to his therapist that his father had become suicidal and Evan was becoming fearful of his father. Mr. Hoffine had spent much of the past 14 years trying to get custody of Evan, trying to change his schools, and trying to limit his outside activities. There was a court file the size of a stack of phone books. Most court files are less than an inch thick. Apparently, Bill regularly threatened lawsuits against the psychologists and other professionals who became involved in his case.

By August 2003, Bill Hoffine had been unemployed for several months and had no visible prospects. He blamed Evan's mother for his debt of several thousand dollars, and he owed thousands in back child support. When the restraining order was served, it said he must stay 100 yards away from her and Evan. A friend reported that Evan was the only focus of his life.

On September 4, 2003, a few blocks from my home, Evan was running with his school's cross-country team on a city street when his father stepped out from behind a parked van and shot Evan several times. As Evan lay dying, his father left the scene and 10 hours later killed himself (Gross, Moran, & Hughes, 2003). These were tragic deaths that shocked the neighborhood and the family courts in San Diego. Local judges, attorneys, and mental health professionals held a meeting to try to understand what had happened and how to prevent such an incident in the future.

Yet this wasn't caused by a restraining order or a custody dispute. Hundreds of those happen every day without this type of outcome. Something was wrong inside Bill Hoffine. He was having Internal Upsets that no one else caused. From the reports, he appears to have had a high-conflict personality. He was certainly self-absorbed and preoccupied with controlling his son for his own needs. He certainly seems to fit the High Conflict Personality Pattern.

Was Evan his Target of Blame? Clearly his mother was a Target. Did he kill Evan because he blamed Evan for telling his therapist that he was in danger from his father, which led to the restraining order? Did he kill Evan to permanently take him away from his mother? Or did he not really think at all, and just associated Evan with his Internal Upset? Tragically, we'll never know.

Are There One Or Two HCPs?

In all of the high-conflict cases described above, it's clear that one person was responsible for escalating the case. Only one person appeared to be an HCP.

Yet many disputes look like they're caused by both people in the dispute—at least from the outside. In divorce disputes, some families are referred to as "high-conflict families" or "high-conflict couples." This generalization can be unfair. It creates a situation that treats both people in the dispute as equally at fault for the conflict, even if they're not. Many divorce professionals recognize that it is not always both parties driving the dispute (Friedman, 2004).

The assumption that both parties to a conflict are always at fault can occur in neighbor disputes, workplace disputes, and other settings. You commonly hear, "They just don't get along." "They're both at fault." "Why don't you both just stop fighting." "Just get over it." This does a great disservice to those who are caught up in dealing with HCPs through no fault of their own. They may get along fine with most people, but have become Targets of Blame for HCPs.

In many ways, HCPs are similar to addicts. We don't blame the addict's spouse for the addict's addiction. We don't blame the addict's arguments on "issues." The problem is the addiction. With high-conflict cases, the problem is *how* HCPs create and promote conflict because of their personalities, not *what* their conflicts are about.

However, in many cases there are two or more HCPs. I researched this question with a law school professor in early 2006. We distributed a survey to all the family lawyers in our county, with 131 attorneys responding. They said they believed 49% of high-conflict cases were driven by just one party (one HCP) and 49% by both parties (two HCPs); 2% were not explained. These lawyers averaged more than 15 years experience in their fields.

So you can't assume there are two high-conflict people fighting with each other, and you can't assume that it's always just one high-conflict person either. This means that you always need to keep an open mind.

In addition, this means that if you believe the other person in a dispute with you is acting badly and is an HCP, you may also be seen as an HCP by those around this conflict. I've seen HCPs who eagerly tell everyone that the other person in their dispute has a high-conflict personality, when in fact it is obvious that he or she has a high-conflict personality. They have it backwards. But sometimes it's not obvious on the surface. **You have to be very careful not to act like an HCP when you're around an HCP, or people might think that you're an HCP too.**

The following case suggests the possibility of two HCPs.

The "Hate Thy Neighbor" Case

Steve and Sharon owned neighboring houses in San Diego. According to news reports, Steve moved to the neighborhood first, and said that he got along with his neighbors. The first day Sharon moved in next door, she played her music too loud for Steve and he asked her to turn it down. The next night he thought it was too loud again, so he called the police. One day, after he complained to police several times, she put a stereo in her yard, turned up the music, and went shopping.

Steve also said Sharon put in a fence that prevented him from accessing part of his yard. He said her place smelled from her dog's excrement and her wind chimes were too loud. Sharon then bought more wind chimes. She said he was a busybody and had a weak personality. She said Steve rubbed everyone the wrong way.

Steve called the police dozens of times. He videotaped Sharon's activities after he accused her of trespassing on his property. Then Sharon put up a sign saying "a--hole." Steve said her actions against him were anti-gay, and they constituted a form of hate crime (Jones, 2003).

For six years they continued this battle, until they finally went to court in 2003. The newspaper said each was convinced he or she was absolutely in the right. During the trial the jury even went to the neighborhood to see their homes. At some point, Steve fired his attorney. In the end, the jury found in favor of Steve on a few of his claims, but did not award him any money for his alleged damages. He appealed, and in October 2005, the District Court of Appeal affirmed the jury's findings and rejected his claim for damages and his claim of discrimination (State Civil Litigation Notes, 2005).

Was Steve or Sharon an HCP? Were both HCPs? I never met them, so I can't say. However, from the news reports, each of them appears rigid and uncompromising, repeating the same failed strategies for six years! Neither seems to have taken responsibility for their part in the conflict, and each appears to have become the other's Target of Blame, for years, with an emotional intensity and endurance that's hard to blame on the "issues."

HCPs May Have Personality Disorders

Why do some people engage in such high-conflict behavior—bitterly attacking others verbally, legally, or violently—while most people don't act this way? From my training and experience as a therapist, I believe that the people who become HCPs have personality disorders—or some "traits" of a personality disorder.

When I worked as a therapist at psychiatric hospitals and clinics, I learned a lot about patients with personality disorders. Years later, when I became an attorney and mediator, I recognized that the people who were stuck in high-conflict behavior had the same characteristics as people with personality disorders.

A personality disorder is a long-term dysfunctional pattern of thinking, feeling, and behaving that affects many areas of a person's life. People with personality disorders are not crazy or stupid, and some are very intelligent. Instead, they have "blind spots"—especially regarding their behavior with the people close to them. They have daily personal problems that they keep repeating. Yet they don't recognize these problems and can't seem to stop themselves, even when their problems are obvious to everyone around them—and are harmful to themselves. They're stuck in self-defeating and self-destructive behavior.

Most are constantly overwhelmed by their own Internal Upsets and therefore lack compassion and understanding for the feelings and viewpoints of others. These traits lead them into conflicts with the people around them, but they're not aware of their own role in causing these conflicts.

People with personality disorders are psychologically unable to grasp the consequences of many of their actions. They don't have the psychological ability to reflect on their own behavior, and therefore they don't change their own behavior, even when it would help them. Instead, they *defend* their actions and personalities—and remain stuck repeating their self-defeating behavior.

Lack of Self-Awareness

People with personality disorders think, feel, and act in ways that are self-defeating and socially inappropriate. Yet they *lack self-awareness* of their self-defeating and socially inappropriate behavior. They truly don't realize this about themselves. They lack the ability to reflect on their own behavior and to change it to adapt to their environment.

Another word for this lack of self-awareness is *unconscious*, which I'll use throughout this book to mean lack of self-awareness. (Sometimes unconscious means asleep, or in a coma, but that's not the meaning in this book.) For example: Jane had no clue that her constant and extremely loud laughter was irritating to everyone around her. For her, it was *unconscious* behavior.

We all have some unconscious behavior. However, most of us regularly reflect on our own behavior and notice when we're having problems in our relationships. In fact, this is what most of us learned growing up. We continue to learn from the feedback we get—verbally and nonverbally—from those around us. However, people with personality disorders seem to lack this ability in many situations. In fact, they become extremely defensive if it is suggested that they have unconscious behaviors. They're unaware they might be unaware of anything!

For example: Sean avoids swimming. He almost drowned when he was 2 years old, but he doesn't remember that. For him, it's an *unconscious* fear. If he's told what happened, he might learn he's safe and work to overcome this fear. However, if Sean has a personality disorder, he'll become defensive, deny he has any *unconscious fears*, and tell us to mind our own business.

Lack of Adaptation

Since they lack self-awareness, those with personality disorders generally lack the ability to change their own behavior to fit changing social situations. In other words, they don't *adapt* to new situations to become more successful. For example, we put more clothes on when we're in a cold environment and take off clothes when it's warm. Likewise, we are constantly adapting to new social environments or social situations throughout our lives.

For example: Jeremy is used to yelling at people to get his way. The people around him seem to accept, or at least tolerate, this behavior. One day he was pulled over by a Highway Patrol Officer for speeding. Jeremy immediately started yelling at the Officer and ended up getting arrested. If Jeremy had *adapted* to the situation, he would have spoken respectfully to the Officer and not have gotten arrested—although he still may have gotten a speeding ticket.

Cluster B Personality Disorders

Most mental health professionals in the United States diagnose mental disorders using the Diagnostic and Statistical Manual (DSM-IV-TR) published by the American Psychiatric Association (APA, 2000), currently in its fourth edition, text revised. This manual identifies 10 specific personality disorders organized into 3 groups: Clusters A, B, and C. I believe that HCPs have Cluster B personality disorders—or less severe Cluster B traits. People with Cluster B personalities are commonly known as "high-drama" personalities that are highly emotional, highly energetic, and highly erratic. Their personality characteristics draw them into intense, ongoing conflicts on a regular basis—much more than occurs with the other clusters. People with these personalities often appear normal in many aspects of their lives until they're in a close relationship or in a conflict. Then they can be very dramatic and very difficult. They become surprisingly angry, emotional, extreme, and sometimes dangerous.

The four personality disorders in Cluster B are also known as the "severe" personality disorders (Bleiberg, 2001) because they engage in intense conflict and cause the most difficulties in society. The following four Cluster B personalities seem to drive most high-conflict disputes:

1. **Borderline**—People with Borderline Personality Disorder have extreme mood swings, fears of abandonment, clinging behavior, frequent and intense anger, and often use manipulative behavior.

    A Borderline's self-defeating cycle of behavior: Borderlines are driven by an unconscious *fear of abandonment,* but their behavior is so emotionally intense that people repeatedly abandon them. Because of their lack of self-awareness and lack of adaptation, they repeat the pattern of emotionally intense behavior and are repeatedly abandoned. This personality is described in more depth in Tip #3.

2. **Narcissistic**—People with Narcissistic Personality Disorder have an extreme preoccupation with themselves, contempt for others, and a preoccupation with being treated as superior.

    A Narcissist's self-defeating cycle of behavior: Narcissists are driven by an unconscious *fear of inferiority,* but their behavior is so offensive that those around them repeatedly react by trying to put them down and make them feel inferior. Because of their lack of self-awareness and lack of adaptation, they repeat the pattern of acting superior and are repeatedly put down. This personality is described in more depth in Tip #4.

3. **Histrionic**—People with Histrionic Personality Disorder are demanding of attention, emotionally intense—similar to Borderlines—but often with less anger and more drama, and they sometimes fabricate events.

    A Histrionic's self-defeating cycle of behavior: Histrionics are driven by an unconscious *fear of being ignored*, but their demands for attention are so irritating that people repeatedly try to get away from them or ignore them. Because of their lack of self-awareness and lack of adaptation, they repeat the pattern of demanding attention and are repeatedly ignored or avoided. This personality is described in more depth in Tip #5.

4. **Antisocial**—People with Antisocial Personality Disorder have extreme disregard for the rules of society, no remorse, and a willingness to hurt other people for personal gain.

   An Antisocial's self-defeating cycle of behavior: Antisocials are driven by an unconscious *fear of being dominated*, so instead they try to dominate others through deception or violence. This often leads to being fired or put in prison, where they're totally dominated by the authorities. Because of their lack of self-awareness and lack of adaptation, they repeat the pattern of trying to dominate others and are repeatedly dominated. This personality is described in more depth in Tip #6.

In many cases, a person with one of these disorders will have another personality disorder, or traits of another personality disorder. They're also more prone than the general population to addictions, suicide, and other high-risk behavior. People with one or more of these Cluster B personalities tend to have a great deal of anxious and aggressive energy, a drive to get attention, a tendency to be manipulative in relationships, and a willingness to repeatedly engage in conflict with others.

However, Cluster Bs can also be particularly charming, especially at the beginning of a relationship. Their "sugar-coated" personalities often seem too good to be true. These sugar-coated manners cover their undesirable and often abusive behaviors. They can be very appealing and seductive in relationships, business, and positions of power. They're driven to have power and control over others as an apparent way to cope with feeling helpless and out of control inside themselves—their frequent Internal Upsets. For these reasons, Cluster Bs are often High Conflict People.

However, not all Cluster Bs are HCPs. Some people with Cluster B personality disorders blame themselves rather than others and try to avoid conflicts. They're not all "high-conflict" people. Others are so general in their blame of the world, institutions, or "the system," that they don't focus on a specific Target of Blame, and it's unlikely that they'll ever become preoccupied with blaming someone else.

And some Cluster Bs do get counseling to overcome their disorders and may be "in recovery." However, this is rare, because a key characteristic of all people with personality disorders is that they don't think they have a disorder and don't need to change a thing about their own behavior.

Many HCPs Just Have "Traits"

Many HCPs have some "maladaptive personality traits," but not enough to meet the DSM criteria for a full personality disorder. While they're often stuck in their destructive patterns and are still difficult, they may be more able to change their behavior.

However, when people who just have traits are in high-conflict situations (court litigation, dysfunctional workplaces, intense neighbor or family disputes) they appear to have personality disorders. From my experience and training, I would say that about one-third of the HCPs I've observed would meet the criteria for a Cluster B personality disorder and about two-thirds have traits, but not enough for a personality disorder. Just having some traits may be enough to cause a person to have a high-conflict personality. But just having some traits is not considered a mental disorder.

Therefore, throughout this book, I don't distinguish between HCPs with personality disorders and HCPs with traits. What's important is to recognize the *pattern* of dysfunctional behavior so you'll know what to do, not whether they qualify for a mental health diagnosis.

Characteristics of High Conflict Personalities

	Personality Disorders (A mental health disorder)	**Maladaptive Personality Traits** (Not a mental health disorder)
Cluster B Personalities Borderline Narcissistic Histrionic Antisocial	Long-term extreme behavior, often self-destructive Same behavior problems in many different situations Extreme behavior noticeable since childhood or adolescence Chronic internal distress Emotions often overwhelming, especially anger Extreme lack of self-awareness Can't connect their own behavior to their many problems in life Strongly defends own behavior as normal and necessary	Some traits of a personality disorder, but not a full disorder Behavior problems stand out some of the time Sometimes noticeable problems since childhood or adolescence More internal distress and overwhelming emotions than the average person Often lacks self-awareness in relationships and under stress Sometimes very successful in some areas of life Sometimes has insights into own behavior problems
High Conflict Personalities A subgroup of Cluster Bs in the author's opinion, which only applies to those Cluster Bs with these additional characteristics	Preoccupied with blaming specific Targets of Blame See their Targets as all-bad, with no positive qualities at all Frequently misinterpret events and other people's intentions Get easily stuck in conflicts over minor or existent events Extreme emotional intensity about blaming their Targets Recruit others (Negative Advocates) to attack their Targets Frequent High Conflict Thinking (Explained in the next Tip)	

How Big Is This Problem Today?

In 2004, a study funded by the National Institutes of Health (N.I.H.) reported that 14.8% of the general population of the United States meets the criteria for the diagnosis of at least one personality disorder. Over 43,000 people were interviewed. The study covered only 7 of the 10 personality disorders. Since they didn't include Borderline, Narcissist, or Schizotypal, the percentage is likely to be higher. A follow-up study is planned that will include these three disorders (Grant, 2004).

This study was done because the lack of information on personality disorders was considered a "major gap" in the nation's health policies. The concern was that personality disorders seemed particularly associated with work problems, marital problems, and criminal activities. The results showed a slightly higher number of personality disorders among people living in urban areas and in younger age groups (18 to 29-year-olds had the most, then 30 to 44, then 45 to 64; 65 and older had the least). Since personality disorders generally don't change with age, this study reinforces the other indicators that personality disorders and traits are increasing in our society with each new generation.

Why Are HCPs Increasing?

People with personality disorders apparently exist in all countries and cultures, perhaps as part of the biological variety of the human race. However, I believe we're witnessing an increasing amount of high-conflict personalities in modern urban societies, for at least five possible reasons.

1. **Instability in early childhood:** Personalities develop primarily in early childhood, by age 5 or 6. Stable family relationships are an essential part of this process, so a child develops healthy coping strategies for being responsible and succeeding in future social relationships. The more stable and secure the first five or six years, the more secure and adaptable the person is as an adult. It's easy to see that young children over the last few decades have experienced an increasing amount of disruption to their important family relationships from substance abuse, divorce, child abuse, and so forth. Mental health researchers report that child abuse and neglect increase the risk of developing a personality disorder four times (Wekerle, 2006).

2. **Diminishing social glue:** Personality development depends on the "social glue" of many positive personal experiences throughout childhood. These include thousands of smiles, moments of empathy, hours of listening, friendly touches, praise, etc.—what I think of as "social glue bits." Over the last few decades, community ties have weakened, families have shrunk or broken up, and electronic devices have rapidly begun replacing personal contact. Children seem to be getting fewer and fewer of these personal social glue bits. They can't get them from television, movies, iPods, PDAs, or the Internet. Even cell phones and webcams leave out physical touch and other important in-person behavior. ATM machines, self-service gas pumps, subway turnstiles, and self-service store checkouts let us come and go without anyone giving us personal attention. Everyone experiences this, but we're witnessing the first generations to be raised with this diminished social glue as part of their personality development.

3. **Loss of personal behavior role models:** A powerful part of personality development is family and community storytelling about good and bad behavior. Yet, in today's world, print media and electronic media compete with family values and role models by providing ever-increasing drama and extreme behavior. Stories of conflict resolution that are self-centered, extreme, and/or violent make the evening news and popular shows, while normal problem-solving behavior occurs mostly out of sight. Children personally experience fewer examples and styles of resolving conflicts, and fewer opportunities to practice negotiation strategies in everyday life.

4. **A society of individuals:** In our urban cultures, we have created a Society of Individuals who can live and work on our own. We don't depend on others as much, so we don't have to compromise with them as much or even care about them. This reinforces self-centeredness and a drive for more control over our personal space and more desire for relationships with material goods. Ironically, the more socially isolated we are, the more fearful we seem to become in the world. Personality disorders and traits are significantly driven by chronic individual fears.

5. **Teaching self-centeredness:** Over the past 40 years our culture has placed a strong value on feeling good about ourselves. However, this self-esteem focus has inadvertently given people high expectations of receiving benefits for themselves, without learning as many skills to achieve or to give back to others. The effect is to teach narcissism as a cultural trait. Some researchers believe that *when* you are born is more significant than *to whom* you are born

in forming your personality (Twenge, 2006). For some people, but not all, these cultural traits may become stuck and exaggerated in their personalities.

6. **Openness to social complaints:** Part of the progress of our modern society is our belief in justice for all. This means our courts, workplaces, community organizations, and others have become much more fair and open to everyone. As a society, we're dedicated to helping victims of abuse and punishing perpetrators. This is a good thing, but it means we must learn to tell the difference between those who are true victims and those who just *feel* like victims and are complaining because of their personalities (although some people have personality problems *and* are true victims). Our procedures of fairness and openness unintentionally encourage complaints and prolonged disputes. We thoroughly and objectively examine limited "facts," without recognizing the significance of personality problems and how they can distort the "facts." This encourages those with personality disorders to seek validation and vindication for personal problems and upsets they can't handle inside themselves through the courts and other agencies. They know people will listen and take them seriously.

Of course, these social factors exist for all of us, yet we don't all develop high-conflict personalities. Even in families, there may be one or two members with a personality disorder or traits, and no one else—even though they experienced a similar family environment. It seems to be a combination of biology and social environment that causes some people to develop personality disorders and not others. We'll look at this with the main four high-conflict personalities addressed in the next few Tips.

Personal Attacks

High Conflict People are frequently in a state of distress because they have so many problems, but they lack the self-awareness and adaptation they need to resolve these problems. Simple or irrelevant events repeatedly trigger their Internal Upsets and they desperately want relief.

Since they think their Targets of Blame caused their problems, they attack them. They want to make their TOBs change their behavior or go away. The HCPs' distorted belief is that if their TOBs change or go away, they'll feel better. Their personal attacks often come in the form of Blamespeak.

Blamespeak is my term for the flow of negative feedback that High Conflict People often engage in, as they focus intense negative energy on their Targets of Blame. At first it may sound like they're giving intense criticism to a person who deserves it. However, after you become familiar with it, you'll realize that the person being criticized is usually an innocent Target of Blame, and the person giving the criticism is a High Conflict Person.

For example, a husband (although it could just as easily be a wife), going through a divorce, sends the following email:

> "Jane, I can't believe you're so stupid as to think that I'm going to let you take the children to your boss's birthday party during my parenting time. Have you no memory of the last six conflicts we've had about my parenting time? Or are you having an affair with him? I always knew you would do anything to get ahead! In fact, I remember coming to your office party, witnessing you making a total fool of yourself—including flirting with everyone from the CEO down to the mailroom kid! Are you high on something? Haven't you gotten your finances together enough to support yourself yet, without flinging yourself at every Tom, Dick, and Harry?"

Blamespeak

You can recognize Blamespeak by the following:

1. It's **emotionally intense** and out of proportion to the issues.

2. It's **very personal**: about your intelligence, sanity, memory, ethics, sex life, etc.

3. It's **all your fault**: the Blamespeaker feels no responsibility for the problem or the solution.

4. It's **out of context**: it ignores all of the good you've done and all of the bad the Blamespeaker has done.

5. It's often **shared with others** to emphasize how "blameworthy" you are and how "blameless" the speaker is. The Blamespeaker has no sense of shame, embarrassment, or boundaries. They'll speak this way about you in public. Unfortunately, Blamespeak often sounds believable to those who aren't informed about your situation.

High Conflict People live and breathe Blamespeak. HCPs use it as a method of unconsciously coping with conflict and avoiding responsibility for their own problems. It's all part of focusing on a Target of Blame.

Don't Take Their Personal Attacks Personally

For some people this is the hardest thing to do, and for others it's the greatest relief. In either case, it's the foundation of the rest of this book. Once you know that blaming behavior of High Conflict People is unconscious and comes primarily from their own personalities and Internal Upsets, you realize that you don't need to defend yourself, which is the normal human response to being blamed (although sometimes you need to protect yourself).

In today's modern world, our normal defensive reactions can be self-defeating. From my experience, I know that HCPs are more comfortable engaging in conflict when both people make it personal. Once you're hooked into this battle, it justifies their analysis that it is all your fault. After all, they think, "look at how unreasonable you're acting now." This makes it simple and manageable to them because it's personal.

This doesn't always mean there aren't real problems to solve and issues to address. It just means their personal attacks are based on their Internal Upsets rather than on a realistic search for solutions. **Personal attacks are about Internal Upsets, not about solving problems.**

This doesn't mean you have no responsibility for dealing with the problems they bring up. If you have a healthy personality, you'll be somewhat flexible, reflecting on your own behavior and looking for new ways to act in the future—you'll constantly change or "adapt." That's how human beings have made it this far. Even if it's not your "fault," you can still think: How could I solve this problem or act differently in the future to be more successful? I'm always asking myself how I can improve the way I deal with High Conflict People. **Fault is not the issue.** The issue is how to handle ourselves in all situations, even those with HCPs who primarily created the current problem.

You may have chosen to be in a relationship with the person. You may have chosen to stay in a difficult situation. We all share some responsibility for solving the problems in our lives, whatever the cause and however small our part may be. It's very important that you don't think, or say defensively, to the HCP: *"It's All Your Fault!"* Remember, personal attacks in either direction are not about solving problems.

How To Avoid Taking It Personally

1. **Recognize the signs of taking it personally.** You know you're taking it personally when . . .

    *   You feel you have to *defend* yourself.

    *   You feel *emotionally hooked* with fear or anger.

    *   You feel the natural *"fight, flight, or freeze"* responses.

    *   You start thinking *It's All Your Fault!* about the other person.

    *   You think there's only *one way* to deal with this problem and you have no choice.

    *   You feel you have to *prove* something to the other person or to other people.

    *   You feel the other person is *knowingly* taking advantage of you.

    *   You feel the other person is *knowingly* getting away with something.

With this list, I'm not saying the HCP's actions are okay and you should just ignore them. I'll discuss other methods of dealing with the HCP's misinformation and misbehavior. At this point, I'm just saying you'll become emotionally hooked and much less effective in dealing with an HCP if you get stuck thinking or feeling these things.

The goal is to solve the problem. HCPs avoid solving problems by becoming preoccupied with blame. If you take it personally and respond in a similar manner, you'll prolong the dispute, increase the frustration you experience, and possibly appear as though you're an HCP (or the only HCP) to other people who become involved in the case.

2. **Remind yourself that it's unconscious.** This high-conflict behavior isn't a conscious process for the HCP. He or she is not "knowingly" getting away with something or "knowingly" taking advantage of you. His or her actions are driven by *unconscious* personality patterns. This doesn't mean that everything they do is unconscious. Most HCPs I've handled have lied about something and knowingly engaged in behavior that's improper. But they're driven to do these "bad" things for unconscious reasons.

3. **There's always been a Target of Blame.** Before you and after you, the HCP will have treated somebody else the same way—because it's about the HCP's personality pattern of blame, not about you. This doesn't mean you shouldn't consider changing your own behavior, re-examining your own values, or making different decisions—you should always be considering ways to change and improve your life. It just means the cause of the *emotionally intense* and *negative feedback* from an HCP is his or her personality.

4. **Maintain your own mental and physical health.** You're much less likely to be triggered by an HCP when you're feeling good. You don't take on as much blame and it's easy to see that it's not all anyone's fault. On the other hand, when we get run down we're more likely to lash out at others and easily allow ourselves to get emotionally hooked. This part is our own responsibility—our part of the problem. And we must be continually aware of this. Getting exercise and enough sleep are good practices.

5. **Get support and consultation.** Checking out our responses with trusted friends or a therapist is essential when responding to a High Conflict Person. We often aren't conscious of when we're being defensive. Friends and therapists can be very helpful in seeing what you can't see. They can suggest positive responses you might not be able to think of under stress.

6. **Don't engage in a personal battle.** If you're already engaged in a personal battle, then disengage now. At any time, you can let go of taking it personally. Remember, HCPs are more comfortable making it simple and personal. It doesn't mean they're happy doing this; it's just that it's familiar to them. They feel safer being engaged in a conflict that's personal. So, you'll naturally feel like responding personally.

Once you realize you're about to respond personally, tell yourself: *Don't engage!* If you have already started responding in a personal, defensive manner, you can still tell yourself: *Disengage!*

This part is up to you. Remember: **Don't take it personally.** You don't have to defend yourself. **It's not about YOU!**

A Question

At the end of each Tip in this book, I'll ask a question to help you apply what we've discussed.

With what you've read so far, which of the following are good methods for changing an HCP's personally attacking behavior?

A.   Verbally confront the HCP about their aggressive behavior.

B.   Ignore the HCP's aggressive behavior.

C.   Give the HCP a letter explaining how their own behavior sabotages their relationships and personal goals.

D.   Belittle the HCP to draw their attention to their problems.

E.   None of the above.

While there are no absolutely right or wrong answers regarding each High Conflict Person, my recommendation is "E." Here's why: an HCP's difficult behavior is long-term, unconscious, and automatic. They truly feel their aggressive behavior is *normal and necessary*, so the common practices and reactions to HCPs rarely work and may make things worse.

A.   *Direct verbal confrontation* doesn't have an impact on changing their thinking. Their thinking is long-term and won't change with one person's confrontation, just as active alcoholics and addicts don't change their behavior when confronted by one person (which happens all the time throughout their drinking or using career).

B.   *Ignoring the behavior* will also not change it. HCP's thinking patterns are rigid and long-term. This won't change or improve by ignoring the behavior. Many people have wishful thinking that the bad behavior of others will change because they'll come to their senses over time. However, this isn't the case with HCPs. Their actions are unconscious and beyond the reach of their insights.

C.   *Long letters* also don't make an impact in explaining your actions or why the HCP's behavior is bad. HCPs will take it as a personal attack, even if it's not meant that way. Likewise, calm verbal feedback generally doesn't work because it's also taken as a personal criticism.

D. *Belittling HCPs* does not motivate them toward positive behavior change. For example, people will say things like, "You're stupid!" or "You're crazy!" or "You're evil!" or "You're immoral!" to them. These are personal attacks. They're not about an issue. They're personal and derogatory remarks, which don't work with anyone, especially with HCPs.

Generally, the temptation to confront, ignore, write long letters, or belittle HCPs comes from taking it personally. This is totally natural and we've all done it. I've been teaching this information for years and I still sometimes take what HCPs say personally! I just realize it sooner than I used to and tell myself to disengage more quickly. So you're not alone in facing this problem.

TIP #1 SUMMARY

Don't Take Their Personal Attacks Personally

1. High Conflict People (HCPs) have a long-term problem of blaming others.

2. HCPs appear to have Cluster B personality disorders or traits, with chronic unconscious Internal Upsets (IUs) that they mistakenly believe are caused by others—their Targets of Blame (TOBs).

3. HCPs truly want to feel better, so they attack their TOBs in misguided efforts to change or eliminate the danger they feel.

4. HCPs don't reflect on or change their own inappropriate behavior. Their problems and conflicts continue and often escalate into high-conflict disputes.

5. You know you're a Target of Blame when you are personally and repeatedly blamed or criticized in an intensely negative way by an HCP.

6. Remind yourself: It's not all your fault! The personal attack is not about you as a person!

7. Recognize when you feel defensive. See if you need to protect yourself physically or legally. Otherwise, you usually don't have to do anything—because it's not about you as a person.

8. Don't tell the HCP, "*It's All Your Fault!*" Avoid blaming the HCP as a person.

9. If you're engaged in an emotional battle with an HCP, you can disengage at any time. Remember, the HCP had a long-term pattern of blaming others before you and will blame others after you. It's not about you, so you don't have to defend yourself verbally to the HCP.

10. When dealing with an HCP, regularly get support from helpful friends and relatives and/or consultation from a therapist or other professional. You're not alone in facing this problem.

Tip #2: Don't Give Them Negative Feedback

CHAPTER

2

Tip #2
Don't Give Them Negative Feedback

One of the biggest mistakes you can make with High Conflict People is to give them negative feedback. Of course, this is what everyone does at first. But after you come to understand HCPs, you'll realize your life is much easier when you stop giving them negative feedback. Your HCP will be easier to handle and you'll sleep better at night. At least that's been my experience over the past several years, as I have come to understand their Cycle of High Conflict Thinking.

The Cycle of High Conflict Thinking

There are three steps in the Cycle of High Conflict Thinking.

Step 1: HCPs' Mistaken Assessment of Danger (M.A.D.)

This is unconscious and causes people with high-conflict personalities to believe and feel other people are a danger to them—a serious, even life-threatening danger. Even when problems are minor or nonexistent, they feel an intense internal distress. This may be triggered by a spontaneous Internal Upset or an external event that they misinterpret. They may feel another person has 'caused' this upset sensation. This doesn't mean HCPs are crazy, evil, or stupid, just that their perceptions are distorted. These distorted perceptions may be strong and HCPs believe them to be true, without any effort to check them out. In fact, there may be no logical danger at all.

Step 2: HCPs' Behavior that's Aggressively Defensive (B.A.D.)

HCPs' feel driven to defend themselves by going on the attack and taking aggressive action. These aren't just defensive behaviors, like walking away or trying to reduce the level of conflict. These behaviors are aggressively defensive and aimed at their Targets of Blame. They believe they must 'counter-attack.' In some cases, they actually try to physically harm or eliminate the Target they believe is causing their Internal Upset. This may be a loved one or person in position of power in their lives, but this drive to engage in B.A.D. is so strong it overrules any logical restraints.

Step 3: HCPs receive Negative Feedback (N.F.)

Their behavior usually triggers strong negative reactions in their Targets of Blame, who give them strong Negative Feedback in the form of sarcasm, put-downs, threats, blasts of anger, lawsuits, and sometimes even violence. Sometimes, however, the Negative Feedback may be "constructive feedback" from the Target of Blame or another person who is simply trying to help. Unfortunately, both kinds of feedback feel negative to HCPs because they feel all feedback is a personal criticism—that there's something wrong with them as a person (otherwise they wouldn't be getting feedback to change something). This, of course, triggers their *Mistaken Assessment of Danger* again. And the cycle repeats. It's not based on logical dangers, but it's the fundamental pattern of all high-conflict disputes. And you have an opportunity to stop the Cycle of High Conflict Thinking by not giving Negative Feedback. Instead, throughout the book I will give you several other things you can do.

The Cycle of High Conflict Thinking

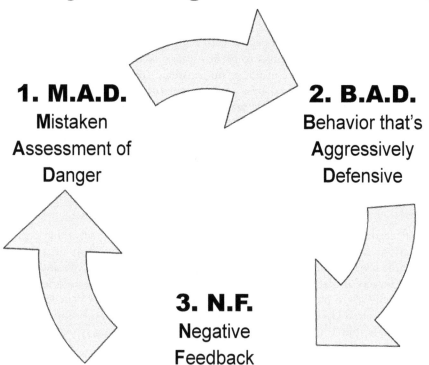

1. M.A.D.
Mistaken
Assessment of
Danger

2. B.A.D.
Behavior that's
Aggressively
Defensive

3. N.F.
Negative
Feedback

Mistaken Assessment of Danger—Why HCPs feel M.A.D.

Mistaken Assessment of Danger is where most HCPs' high-conflict thinking occurs. High-conflict thinking is highly defensive and highly distorted thinking that shuts down their more rational thinking. It's as though HCPs are in a life and death situation, so that they cannot think things through, but instead must be constantly on guard and ready for extreme action.

High-conflict thinking is based on the concepts of "cognitive distortions" and unconscious "defense mechanisms," which mental health researchers have studied for decades (Beck, Rush, Shaw, & Emery, 1979; Burns, 1980). While we all experience distortions and defense mechanisms some of the time, people with personality disorders experience them much of the time. Cognitive distortions are extreme thoughts that don't fit our present circumstances, but trigger intensely negative feelings. Unconscious defense mechanisms help us feel good about ourselves when things are really bad to help us survive. High-conflict thinking includes cognitive distortions and unconscious defense mechanisms that are particularly related to intense conflicts.

Common examples of high-conflict thinking for HCPs include the following:

1. **All-or-nothing thinking**—Seeing things in absolute terms, such as believing there is only one explanation for a problem and only one solution, when there may be several explanations and solutions.

2. **Jumping to conclusions**—Assuming the worst from very little information, especially regarding the future or other people's intentions. This starts a lot of unnecessary conflicts.

3. **Personalization**—Jumping to the conclusion that unrelated events were aimed at the HCP, such as taking it personally when a stranger cuts in front of the HCP in traffic.

4. **Emotional reasoning**—Assuming facts from feelings: *I feel in great danger, therefore I AM in great danger.* Or: *I feel upset around you, therefore YOU must have made me upset.*

5. **Mind reading**—The HCP believes he or she knows with certainty what another person is thinking, when that is not humanly possible.

6. **Wishful thinking**—The HCP may believe that he or she can attack or eliminate a Target of Blame, and his or her life will magically be completely better.

7. **Tunnel vision**—Being preoccupied with one narrow issue, while missing more important ones.

8. **Exaggerated fears**—Viewing safe or manageable situations as extremely dangerous for no objective reason.

9. **Projecting**—Seeing the HCP's own feelings and behaviors in another person, and not in himself or herself.

10. **Splitting**—Seeing some people as "all-bad," as if they can't do anything right and deserve bad treatment, and others as "all-good," as if they are perfect and can't do anything wrong.

We all have high-conflict thinking occasionally. These thoughts are automatic and highly defensive, to protect us in life or death situations. Yet there are very few life or death situations in everyday life anymore. So when HCPs have high-conflict thinking, they are over-reacting and actually creating high-conflict disputes. Their high-conflict thinking may have been accurate in past situations (such as an abusive childhood), but is generally not accurate in the present.

The distorted thoughts of high-conflict thinking often come from extreme comments we once heard from our parents, our friends, on the radio or TV, or in the movies. Anything we hear can pop into our heads as high-conflict thinking in a stressful situation. But high-conflict thinking when it is not a life or death situation can be unhelpful—and sometimes dangerous. So we have to examine our thoughts for potential high-conflict thinking before we take action so that we can avoid acting on thoughts that don't help. Otherwise, they can sabotage our relationships and derail our life goals.

Most people don't act on these inaccurate thoughts until they've had a chance to examine the full facts of the situation. In a sense, high-conflict thinking is like a computer.

Do you have a computer anti-virus program? I'll bet you do. It protects your computer from all the harmful information that comes over the Internet. Computer viruses are often disguised as neutral or good information, so you have to be careful. You're not responsible for the information that comes over the Internet, but you're responsible for protecting yourself from the harmful information.

Likewise, you're not responsible for all the thoughts that pop into your head all day long. You're just responsible for what you DO with these thoughts. What we think at any given moment comes from all of the information and misinformation we've heard and experienced over a lifetime. It's just like the Internet. You have to sort out what's helpful information for you and protect yourself from harmful ideas.

HCPs don't have a working anti-distortion program. They believe their distortions and unconscious defenses, and act on them as if they're true. They also have more distortions and unconscious defenses than most people, which is why they get into more difficult conflicts. They constantly jump to conclusions, take things personally, and project onto others.

Examples of High Conflict Thinking

Suppose you have a good friend named Chris at your job, in your neighborhood, or at your school. Suppose Chris is having a party and has invited all of your friends, neighbors, and co-workers, but not you. You might think, "Chris is a real jerk!" If you're like most people, though, you'd stop and think, "This seems unusual for Chris, I should check this out." You might go talk to Chris, who might say, "Oh, I thought you were busy that day or going to be out of town. Sure, come to the party." Or Chris might say, "You know I'm upset with you about something." Then you could talk it over and work it out. These are healthy, flexible ways of dealing with a problem.

On the other hand, an HCP might immediately jump to conclusions: "Chris hates me." Or all-or-nothing thinking: "I can never be Chris's friend again." Most of all, the HCP may stop there, and not check out these thoughts. Instead, the HCP might *act on* this intense high-conflict thinking: "I'm going to email everyone I know and tell them what a jerk Chris is." Then the situation grows into a big conflict that might not have previously existed.

1. **All-or-Nothing Thinking:** An HCP who was turned down for a job might think: "Everyone hates me – no one will ever hire me." Many people may think that way for a day or two, but then respond to it with realistic thoughts: "I'll get a job. It takes awhile. There are a lot of different jobs out there. It's just finding the right match. I might not have liked that job anyway. I'll get a better job."

Unfortunately, an HCP might give up for several months and believe that no one will ever hire him or her – while not considering a more realistic viewpoint and actually arguing *against* those who try to cheer him or her up.

HCPs frequently think in all-or-nothing terms. An event is all good, or all bad. The future is all ideal or all terrible. And so on and so on. This isn't true all of the time, but is much more frequent for those with high-conflict personalities.

One important aspect of HCPs' "all-or-nothing thinking" is the idea that a disagreement is "all one person's fault." Therefore, if someone says that HCPs have some responsibility for a disagreement or a conflict, it *feels* to HCPs as though they are being accused of it being "all their fault." They can't cope with that. Because they think in all-or-nothing terms, they feel compelled to defend themselves by making it all the other person's fault. "It's all your fault" is the way they cope with the chronic (and unconscious) fear that things really are all their fault. While this is clearly a cognitive distortion, it is not conscious to those who have a high-conflict personality. Therefore, when you confront them with the realities of grey areas and encourage them to share responsibility for problems, they will attack you in a rage and bitterly say, "No, it's all YOUR fault!"

2. **Jumping to Conclusions:** For example, an HCP might believe that he is about to be fired because a supervisor looked over with a frown at a meeting. It may have had nothing to do with the person or his job performance.

   A woman may jump to the conclusion that the next door neighbor allowed his dog to go on her lawn, when it was actually a stranger's dog. A man may jump to the conclusion that a family member stole his wallet, when in fact he misplaced it in a different drawer.

   On the other hand, a woman may jump to the conclusion that she will be hired for a job simply because she has satisfied all of the minimum qualifications. A man may think he's impressed a woman on his first date, when in fact she was quite turned off by him.

   Such false conclusions happen frequently in daily life. Most people check them out. HCPs believe in them – and act on them.

3. **Personalization:** HCPs take things personally that most people would consider routine parts of daily life that were not "intended" to be harmful.

For example, suppose someone suddenly pulls in front of you in traffic on the freeway, then drives slowly. You know you never met the person before. The problem is he's a lousy driver, and you take care to avoid hitting him. It's not about you.

An HCP may believe that the person cut him off "on purpose," and that now he has to "teach the other person a lesson." It becomes personal and the HCP feels that he has no choice but to act in an aggressive manner to "get back" at the other person. It can become all-consuming. I have seen far too many cases where one person takes personally the unrelated or unintentional behavior of others.

For example, an HCP may automatically assume that a neighbor is allowing his dog to bark loudly to purposefully bother her. She may call the city's Animal Control Department or complain to other neighbors, without even attempting to tell the neighbor that the dog was bothering her – because of her (cognitive distortion) that the neighbor did it on purpose.

Most people start by at least wondering whether it was unintentional and approaching the neighbor or ignoring it, but not by assuming it was "on purpose." This is what most people call "giving the benefit of the doubt." HCPs often do the opposite; they *assume* the worst and operate on that assumption without checking it out.

This HCP pattern drives many high-conflict disputes, especially between neighbors, co-workers, family members, and often strangers. This personalization is a tough way to live, and is highly distressing to HCPs. However, because this personalization is an unconscious cognitive distortion, they are not aware that they *don't* have to take other people's behavior personally.

4. **Emotional Reasoning:** Cognitive therapists have recognized "emotional reasoning" for decades in the treatment of depression and anxiety (Beck et al., 1979; Burns, 1980). Emotional reasoning means that the person "*feels* that it's true," so believes "it must be true."

For example, a person may do something that backfires and feel stupid for doing it. Most of us feel stupid some of the time. We wonder why we did something, and get angry with ourselves for this lapse in our behavior or understanding. But this feeling isn't a fact. Just because we *feel* stupid does not mean that we *are* stupid. All people make mistakes some of the time. Most people say to themselves, "That was a stupid thing to do – I'm going to try hard not to do that ever again."

The difference for HCPs is that they do not reflect on this, but instead lock onto their conclusion and then act upon it as though it were true. This includes being defensive and getting into fights with other people to "prove I'm not stupid."

It's not about intelligence. It's important to note here that intelligence is unrelated to personality. Some highly intelligent people are also high-conflict people. There are also high-conflict people who are less intelligent than average. The issue is not one of intelligence. The issue is these cognitive distortions over which the person has no knowledge and therefore no control. The solution, of course, is to become aware of our cognitive distortions and to check them out with valid, current information.

For example, an HCP may *feel afraid* that a relative is not going to invite her to a family gathering. Based on that feeling, she may start bad-mouthing that relative to others. "I feel left out, so it must be true: Aunt Mary hates me." Of course, it is possible that a relative would leave out an HCP because of past problems. But the HCP would interpret it as the host's fault, not her own: "I could never trust Aunt Mary – she was always out to get me." In real life, it could be that Aunt Mary has tried to cope for years with the HCP's emotional outbursts and has decided to protect the other family members at this year's event by not inviting the HCP.

5. **Mind Reading:** For example, an employee may think he *knows* that a co-worker is thinking about ways to get him fired. A woman may think she *knows* that her neighbor is going to dump trash in her yard while she is away. All of these things may be possible, but what is surprising about HCPs is how convinced they are that they know what another person is thinking. Another aspect of this is that HCPs often think that you know what *they* are thinking. They often start conversations in the middle of thoughts, as though you know all the thoughts they were having before they opened their mouths. They also think everyone else thinks the same way that they do. "Well, I would never do that, so she must have known it was wrong and did it anyway!" How do you know that she thinks what she did was wrong? "I just *know* how she thinks."

6. **Wishful Thinking:** Many HCPs wish so strongly for things that they think those things actually happened. For example: "You said you were going to sign the contract." Response: "No, I said I would look at the contract and get back to you."

"You said that I qualified for the discount on this product." Response: "No, I said that you did not qualify for the discount on this product."

"People will love me at my new job." Response: "That's possible, but it may take time."

"People will love my new line of products, despite what my staff tell me." Again, this may be true, but the certainty that HCPs have with their wishful thinking often substitutes for careful planning and considerations of alternate outcomes. Most people hope for the best, but are prepared for reality to be unpredictable.

The worst aspect of high-conflict thinking is that HCPs actually *believe* their wishful thinking that attacking their Target of Blame will solve their problems. They believe they will eliminate the source of their distress and sense of danger by attacking or eliminating their Target. There is no evidence for this; instead, it is their wishful thinking. If you were to ask HCPs specifically how their aggressive actions would lead to a better life, they can't give you the steps from here to there. It is another form of emotional reasoning that has no basis in reality. Yet they *feel* it so strongly and desperately that it becomes true in their minds.

7. **Tunnel Vision:** Often HCPs will focus on a fact that is actually true, but way out of proportion. For example, after a divorce, a father may have arrived late to the mother's house twice out of the last 30 times to exchange their child. The mother may become preoccupied with the two times he was late and continually remind him about those times, or ask for a change of the parenting plan at court because he's "always late."

8. **Exaggerated Fears:** See next section.

9. **Projection:** Just as a movie projector in a hidden booth throws a large image onto a screen, those with personality disorders frequently project their internal problems onto their environment. They then claim that another person has the problem that they in fact have.

For example, a spousal abuser will claim that it is the other spouse who is being abusive. Someone who is making false statements will claim the other is lying. One man who was diagnosed with Narcissistic Personality Disorder claimed it was really his wife who had this disorder—simply because she liked to shop! He was projecting his own disorder onto her.

We all do this a little bit. Say, for example, you are really angry at somebody you care about. Rather than your brain allowing you to acknowledge your anger at this person you depend on emotionally, your brain reroutes it so that you believe that the other person is the one who is angry. You can cope with that. But what happens is that you confront the other person with their anger; for example, "Why are you so angry with me today?" The other person may say: "I'm not angry with you at all."

Now you feel defensive and you insist that the other person is angry with you. But it is really you who is angry. If you are open-minded, you might say to yourself: "Wait a minute; if he's not really angry with me, am I really angry? Am I projecting my own anger onto him?" You may then examine your own behavior and thinking. With some reflection, you may realize that, yes, you were angry.

Unfortunately, HCPs do not reflect on their own behavior, feelings and thinking. Therefore, an employee may "project" her own behaviors (gossiping, loudly arguing on the phone, etc.) onto another worker, totally unaware that she is doing this. She might really believe that her co-worker is making things difficult for her. Thus, it becomes a high-conflict situation, with the HCP mistakenly thinking that she is a victim of the co-worker, and the co-worker mistakenly thinking the HCP is knowingly lying. While lying sometimes occurs, my experiences and observations indicate that HCPs usually honestly believe their projections!

10. **Splitting:** In splitting, HCPs truly feel and believe that another person or group is "all bad" and that they are "all good." This is a defense mechanism that unconsciously protects HCPs from feeling "all bad" (since to be partially responsible for a problem is equal to being totally to blame in the "all-or-nothing" thinking of an HCP). Therefore, HCPs *truly feel* and *truly believe* that the other party can do nothing good and is, in fact, an extreme "all-bad, evil monster." This helps HCPs feel okay again after there has been a problem. HCPs' emotions in splitting are so intense that they feel that lying is okay, hitting is okay, and even murder may be okay against the "all-bad, evil monster."

In high-conflict cases, some people say they wish the other person was dead. While this is usually a harmless statement, it is an example of "splitting." This type of thinking can lead to verbal, written, or legal attacks on the other person that most people would consider totally inappropriate. It is an all-or-nothing perspective that escalates otherwise solvable disputes.

I often see this in high-conflict divorce cases. In these cases, all ordinary forms of conflict resolution, such as mediation, negotiation, and collaborative efforts, don't seem to work. Publicly spreading rumors and other distortions against an "all-bad" person is a common example.

Splitting occurs in cases where you see domestic violence, child abuse, and false allegations of abuse. In domestic violence, HCPs *feel* and *believe* that they are justified in injuring or even killing the other party, because that party has done something so offensive that in their eyes it is socially acceptable to destroy that person. Combine this with the projections of a batterer (for example, he thinks she wants to have sex with her co-workers when he is having his own unacceptable thoughts about a female co-worker), and you have a highly dangerous situation – which operates totally unconsciously for HCPs.

HCPs believe that ordinary rules of decency, communication, and negotiation do not apply with "evil monsters." This "splitting" phenomenon makes it very difficult to resolve conflicts. HCPs truly believe that they "have to" treat a person this way. And they frequently tell others they should treat that person this way too. It is impossible to successfully argue with their thinking because their thinking is unconscious – and anything the other person does is seen as "all-bad!"

High Conflict Exaggerated Fears

People with high-conflict personalities have some specific high-conflict thinking that keeps dominating their lives. Each of the four personalities that are the focus of this book has a constant exaggerated fear, which appears to follow them wherever they go—in all social situations. These are unconscious relationship fears, and they're constantly being triggered by ordinary life events that they experience as crises because of their unconscious high-conflict thinking:

HCP Personality	Constant Fear
Borderline	Fear of Abandonment
Narcissist	Fear of Being Inferior
Histrionic	Fear of Being Ignored
Antisocial	Fear of Being Dominated

These fears *feel* life-threatening to the HCP, so you get a life-and-death survival response that truly doesn't fit most situations. HCPs feel they're already in high-conflict situations, fighting against numerous enemies. Their worst conflicts are usually with people close to them and people in positions of authority who they *feel* have harmed or disappointed them.

For example, HCPs with Borderline personalities are known for their mood swings and extreme emotions (Linehan, 1993). When they're in a conflict in a relationship, oddly enough, the conflict helps them feel emotionally connected and secure. This appears to be because they feel emotionally *empty* when things are calm and secure, which creates a sense of *insecurity* in the relationship (Lawson, 2004). They unconsciously sense danger when most people would say things are great. This is a common Internal Upset for Borderlines, leaving them in a chronic state of stress and doubt.

On the other hand, Antisocial personalities are known for getting into fights and hurting people for small or unimportant rewards. Research indicates that Antisocials may unconsciously mistake someone else's neutral facial expression as a hostile facial expression, and someone's fearful expression as a disgusted or neutral expression (Dadds, 2006). They may mistakenly sense danger when nothing is going on. They lack normal understanding and compassion for others. They feel anyone and everyone is a possible threat. This is a common Internal Upset for Antisocials, who often bring an attitude of mistrust and resentment into normal situations. Antisocials seem to have a chip on their shoulders.

Many people frequently have a Mistaken Assessment of Danger because of these cognitive distortions and constant fears, but this alone doesn't make them High Conflict People. HCPs are those with M.A.D. who *think* they need to act on these distortions and fears in an *aggressive* manner.

Behavior that's Aggressively Defensive—Why HCPs do B.A.D.

The second step in the Cycle of High Conflict Thinking is the belief that a dangerous situation *requires them to attack* and defend themselves from the person they believe caused the danger. Feeling M.A.D. and doing B.A.D. is what makes High Conflict People.

All of us experience the "fight or flight" response when we sense strong danger. It's wired into our brains to take action before we're even aware we're taking action. But most people prefer the flight approach to get themselves out of dangerous situations. It makes sense not to risk fighting in most situations. But HCPs automatically and unconsciously assume that an aggressive, fighting approach is the only option. They truly feel a sense of desperation, and it can be very motivating for them. To a high-conflict person it feels like a life-or-death situation, as the following example explains:

> Karen Ann, a borderline, explains what rages are like from the inside: "When I am angry, I am unable to rationally control myself. I am possessed by a whirlwind of emotions that cause me to act out viciously. The feelings overpower me, and I have to lash out to let them escape. It is an attempt to protect myself, knowing full well that what I am actually doing will drive a person away further."

> "When I rage at someone, they are no longer a real person with real feelings. They become the object of my hatred and the cause of my distress. They are the enemy. I get paranoid and believe they want to hurt me, and I am determined to strike out to prove a state of control over them." (Kreger & Gunn, 2007, p. 33, quoted with permission)

HCPs don't stop and think about the alternatives—they seem driven to engage in battle against the person they believe is dangerous: their Target of Blame. They're constantly energized by their M.A.D, and they use that energy for action—whether it's a verbal attack, a legal attack (a lawsuit for revenge or vindication), or a physical attack (anything from domestic violence to murder).

Many Targets of Blame report feeling like the HCP is on a campaign or on a mission to destroy them. It's this Behavior that's *Aggressively* Defensive. This isn't a mild or passive response to disagreement. It's a high-energy battle, whether it's fought with words or actions, and seems to take over the HCP, as Karen Ann described.

Take, for example, the Borderline who makes a Mistaken Assessment of Danger when things are calm. She may unconsciously start an argument to feel more alive—more emotionally connected and secure. This surprises and offends the Target, who commonly escalates emotionally as well: "What do you mean? You're the one who...!," etc. This increases the Borderline's defensiveness, when she just wanted to feel emotionally connected. She *lacked awareness* of how her own Internal Upset led to starting an argument and of how such aggressiveness could trigger upset feelings for the other person.

As described above, an Antisocial might have an unconscious Internal Upset and strike out at someone he senses could be a danger to him. He may say afterwards, "I had to do it because he was getting ready to hit me. I know it." This can all happen in a split second. People are frequently caught by surprise by these types of aggressive Antisocial behaviors. They seem to come out of nowhere, but they're really Behaviors that are *Aggressively* Defensive—they truly think they're necessary to defend themselves.

Negative Feedback—Why Targets Feed the Cycle of High Conflict Thinking

Targets of Blame and others commonly feed the Cycle of High Conflict Thinking without even realizing it. They *feel* attacked by the HCP and naturally feel the urge to retaliate—to attack back by giving Negative Feedback. "Can't you see how stupid you are?" "Look in the mirror when you say that!" "You're not making any sense!" "You must have a High Conflict Personality! Look at you!"

All of this Negative Feedback simply increases the HCP's Mistaken Assessment of Danger—and feeds the Cycle of High Conflict Thinking as the HCP then reacts with more Behavior that's Aggressively Defensive. Negative Feedback is about logic, not about the HCP's fears, so it misses the point regardless of how well-intentioned it may have been. "I want to help you and I suggest that you change such-and-such behavior." Even that feels like Negative Feedback to an HCP. Any feedback about their past behavior is received as Negative Feedback. They take it very personally and believe you're criticizing them as a person. This is an example of their all-or-nothing thinking.

By understanding this Cycle of High Conflict Thinking, you may be able to escape being a Target of Blame. Here's an example to demonstrate how understanding can influence the outcome of a workplace conflict.

George and Tony

George and Tony were two salesmen who worked with the company for 15 years and who both wanted a promotion. Instead of promoting George or Tony, their manager, Anne, decided to promote someone from outside their department instead. George and Tony had completely different reactions.

Tony was furious. He absolutely believed he deserved the promotion. His sales record was higher than George's, and he knew the field better than any newcomer. He emailed Anne to tell her that she'd made a terrible mistake and wondered how she could be so stupid. Then he emailed her division manager and complained that she'd made an impulsive decision, was lax in disciplining her sales force, and wasn't competent for her position.

Tony became depressed and missed a couple of days of work without calling in. He later told Anne that he'd been too sick to call in, but his claim sounded flimsy to her. He was reaching the middle of his career and was concerned that he'd reached a dead end with the company because of Anne. He felt he had to make her see the error of her ways. He asked for an appointment with her and planned to use the appointment to persuade her to give him the promotion.

Like Tony, George also realized he was getting older for the job and wondered if he'd reached a dead end. He put his energy into researching other job options. He also asked to meet with Anne, but rather than wanting to use the meeting to convince her she'd made a mistake, George planned to use his appointment to ask for feedback on his job performance, including his strengths and weaknesses, her suggestions on how to move up in the company, and whether she thought that was likely.

Anne met with George first and encouraged him to take a management course to prepare himself for future opportunities with the company. She also shared with him how difficult her decision had been to promote someone else. She knew he was well liked and respected by the other people in the sales department, and his sales record was strong.

Tony's Meeting with Anne

Before the meeting, we know that Tony had been wrapped up in some high-conflict thinking.

From M.A.D.: Tony felt that being passed over for promotion was entirely Anne's fault. He took it personally, but knew nothing about how her decision was made. He felt his entire future was in her hands and that she was a threat to his personal existence.

To B.A.D.: He thought he could persuade her to change her mind by 'showing her the error of her ways,' even though the decision had already been made. During his meeting with Anne, Tony tried to point out how frustrated he was, that he was getting older, and felt like he was at a dead end. He told her she wasn't really qualified to make this decision, since he'd been with the company longer than she had. He tried to persuade Anne that her decision was flawed and he should be given the promotion.

Anne told Tony his behavior in raising this issue and dumping his personal and emotional frustrations on her was inappropriate. She said the decision was final and if she'd realized this was the purpose of his meeting with her, she wouldn't have met with him. She denied his request to give him the promotion. Tony felt so angry he stormed out of her office without saying goodbye.

From M.A.D.: Tony misjudged Anne as the cause of all his problems—getting older, dead end job, etc.—so she became his Target of Blame.

To B.A.D.: He aggressively tried to change her mind with his emotional intensity about his own frustrations, and he made it personal by saying she wasn't qualified to make this decision. His actions were self-defeating, but he didn't realize it.

Let's look at how Anne handled Tony. Anne let herself become obviously angry with Tony for challenging her decision. She told him he was being inappropriate and that had she known his purpose in meeting, she wouldn't have met with him. Did this influence Tony? Certainly. He became so much more emotionally upset that he impulsively stormed out of her office. Could she have influenced him in a more positive manner? Probably.

If Anne hadn't given Tony feedback on his behavior (even though his behavior was inappropriate), but instead empathized with his frustrations and spent a few more minutes with him, he would probably have calmed down and felt his concerns were heard. This would likely have reduced his assessment of danger, which would have *reduced* his drive to aggressively defend himself.

Influencing an HCP's Behavior

Influencing an HCP's behavior often starts with you. It helps to recognize that the HCP's thinking is based on a Mistaken Assessment of Danger. Then you realize that almost any feedback you give an HCP about inappropriate behavior, no matter how well intentioned, will reinforce that you're a threat. You simply can't give useful feedback to HCPs while they are upset—and in most cases you can't give feedback to HCPs at any time. Instead, I've learned it's much more productive to use the four methods described in the second part of this book. The first method is to give the HCP some empathy, some attention, and/or some respect, if possible and appropriate.

Empathy, attention, and respect, or E.A.R., reduce the HCP's assessment of danger. These basic human needs are what HCPs (and everyone else) always want and need. It's just that HCPs don't know how to get these needs met. Instead, they act aggressively, which makes it much less likely that they'll get any empathy, attention, or respect. In fact, one of the most natural feelings to have in response to an HCP's aggressive behavior is to *withhold* empathy, attention, and respect. It takes a while to reverse this natural urge.

Tony's Escalation

After his meeting with Anne, Tony felt even more upset and in danger, so he escalated his aggressively defensive behavior. To protect himself from what he perceived as Anne's error, Tony started sending emails to people on the sales force, pointing out problems the company had and his belief that Anne was incompetent. Word got back to Anne, and to Diane, her division manager. Diane decided to meet with Tony and Anne.

Diane told Tony she could empathize with his frustrations and that years ago she'd been turned down for a promotion as well. She told Tony she respected his good sales record and that he'd been a valued employee. She suggested that Tony had options and to take a few days off to consider them. One option was to continue to work at the company, in which case he'd have to stop any public criticism of company employees, including Anne, which included email. She put the responsibility for Tony's decisions back on Tony. If Tony had any questions or feedback, the manager said he should feel free to call her and she gave Tony her office phone number.

Amazingly, Tony quickly calmed down and thanked the manager. He also apologized to Anne for being so frustrated with her. He decided to take the rest of the week off to think about his options.

Tony's Cycle of High Conflict Thinking

Let's analyze Tony's high-conflict thinking. To do so, it helps to picture the Cycle of High Conflict Thinking that occurs in all high-conflict cases.

The Cycle of High Conflict Thinking

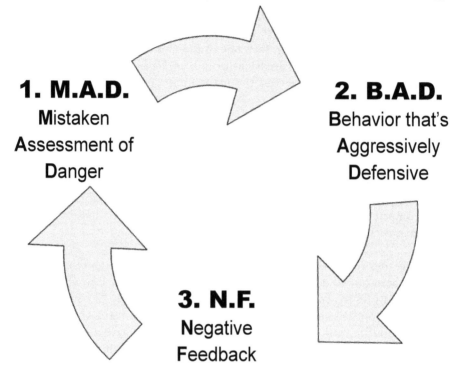

1. M.A.D.
Mistaken
Assessment of
Danger

2. B.A.D.
Behavior that's
Aggressively
Defensive

3. N.F.
Negative
Feedback

1. **M.A.D.** Tony feels distressed and has a spontaneous *sense* of danger — he mistakenly assesses Anne as the all-powerful cause of his problems. While his life, future, and career are complicated issues, he senses that everything is caused by this one person.

2. **B.A.D.** Tony attacks Anne, whom he blames for all of his distress — she becomes his Target of Blame. This attack is verbal, intense, and self-defeating. It's highly aggressive behavior, but he feels he's defending himself and that this is normal and necessary behavior.

3. **N.F.** Anne, as Tony's Target of Blame, naturally feels like responding to the attack by criticizing Tony directly and emotionally. For Tony, this increases his feeling of distress and Mistaken Assessment of Danger. His cycle escalates into more Behavior that's Aggressively Defensive—sending criticizing emails to the other salespeople. And the Cycle goes on and on.

Anne's Negative Feedback

You can see that Anne's feedback was negative; she allowed herself to become obviously angry with Tony. She told him she wouldn't have met with him if she'd known he wanted to challenge her decision. She told him he was being inappropriate. This is pretty mild feedback. From Anne's point of view, this response was totally natural and appropriate. In fact, if Tony hadn't been an HCP, such an approach might have worked fine. But with an HCP, any feedback about the HCP's inappropriate behavior, no matter how mild, constructive, or well intentioned, is usually interpreted as negative feedback.

Tony came to her in a high state of distress. He'd already assessed her as an extreme danger, so from Tony's point of view Anne's feedback reinforced this sense of danger. None of this was conscious to him at the time, and he may never become conscious of it. As Karen Ann described earlier, she becomes aware of what she's doing at some point, but has difficulty controlling it. Many HCPs never become self-aware.

Tony just reacted with aggressive behavior; he stormed out of her office. This obviously hurt Tony's position with Anne. But it also made Anne's life more difficult because Tony started sending scathing emails to others about her, and her boss became involved.

The Division Manager's Response (Part I)

Diane, the Division Manager, took a different approach with Tony. She told Tony she could empathize with his frustrations and that she'd also been turned down for a promotion years ago. She told Tony she respected his good sales record and that he'd been a valued employee. She let Tony know she would pay attention to his concerns by giving him her office phone number. By responding to him this way, Tony was immediately calmed. He felt the manager cared about him and gave him credit for his hard work. Tony felt the manager was on his side rather than against him. Tony's Mistaken Assessment of Danger was quickly and significantly reduced.

Of course, this rapidly reduced sense of danger is temporary with an HCP, as his personality didn't change with this one interaction. However, his relationship with Diane may be positive in the future, because he'll associate her with empathy and respect. Tony will think of her as an ally rather than an enemy. Anne may forever be associated with his fear and anger, and may forever be seen as his enemy. With HCPs, even a brief interaction with negative feedback can establish a negative relationship that's hard to overcome.

If we look at Tony's Cycle of High Conflict Thinking, we can see that Diane has broken the cycle. By not responding with Negative Feedback, but instead giving Tony her Empathy, Attention, and Respect (E.A.R.), she hasn't reinforced Tony's Mistaken Assessment of Danger, but instead has reduced it.

Unlocking
The Cycle of High Conflict Thinking

1. M.A.D.
Mistaken
Assessment of
Danger

2. B.A.D.
Behavior that's
Aggressively
Defensive

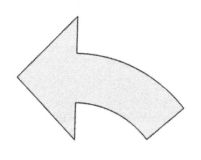

3. E.A.R.
Empathy
Attention &
Respect

1. **M.A.D.** Tony felt distressed and had a spontaneous *sense* of danger.

2. **B.A.D.** Tony attacked Anne, whom he blamed for all of his problems—Anne became his Target of Blame.

3. **E.A.R.** The Division Manager, Diane, showed *Empathy, Attention, and Respect* for Tony. This reduced his sense of danger and stopped his Behavior that was Aggressively Defensive because it didn't feel necessary to him any more.

   The Division Manager unlocked the Cycle.

Empathy, Attention, and Respect (E.A.R.)

Honestly showing your empathy, attention, and respect may be the opposite of what you feel like doing at the time, so it takes practice. Lots of practice. In fact, it's so hard to wrap your head around this idea that we'll talk about it in depth in Tip #8. In the meantime, here are a few brief comments.

- It doesn't have to take much time— sometimes it only takes a minute.

- It doesn't mean that you agree with the person.

- It has to be honestly felt, or the HCP's Cycle of High Conflict Thinking will continue.

- It is the reverse of the usual fight or flight response that B.A.D. usually triggers.

- It takes lots of practice to give your E.A.R. when you're being blasted with someone's Behavior that's Aggressively Defensive.

- Once you know someone is an HCP, it helps to use your E.A.R. from the start.

The Division Manager's Response (Part II)

Sometimes you need to do more than show empathy, attention, and respect. Often you have to set limits on the HCP's Behavior that's Aggressively Defensive. This is a very important part of handling HCPs.

Diane, the division manager, suggested that Tony had options and may want to take a few days off to consider them. One option was to continue to work at the company, but that required him to immediately stop any public criticism, even through email, of any company employee, including Anne. She put the responsibility for Tony's decisions back on Tony. She was setting limits on Tony by saying that continued employment depended on stopping his negative emails.

Of course, she could have threatened him with consequences for any future negative emails, regardless of his future with the company. But she didn't emphasize the negative. She just presented stopping the negative emails as an option, which was less threatening to Tony at the moment. This way, she continued to show empathy and respect for Tony throughout the conversation, and in this case it worked—he immediately calmed down.

But suppose he continued the negative emails. At any time she could try to impose consequences. But if she did it without using Empathy, Attention, and Respect, he could escalate his Behavior that's Aggressively Defensive anyway, even if it hurt him. That's the trouble with just focusing on consequences with HCPs; if you escalate HCPs emotionally, they often don't care if their Behavior thats Aggressively Defensive (B.A.D.) hurts them in the future.

Looking at the Cycle of High Conflict Thinking, you can see that Diane broke the Cycle by Setting Limits. Of course, this might include more formal disciplinary procedures, but the basic principle is learning to balance Setting Limits with giving your Empathy, Attention, and Respect (E.A.R.).

Blocking
The Cycle of High Conflict Thinking

1. M.A.D.
Mistaken
Assessment of
Danger

2. B.A.D.
Behavior that's
Aggressively
Defensive

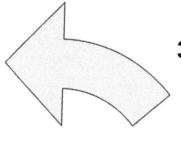

3. E.A.R.
Empathy
Attention &
Respect
<u>AND</u>
Setting Limits

1. **M.A.D.**   Tony felt distressed and had a spontaneous *sense* of danger.

2. **B.A.D.**   Tony attacked Anne, whom he blamed for all of his problems— Anne became his Target of Blame.

3. **E.A.R. and S.L.**   By showing *Empathy, Attention, and Respect* and *Setting Limits* for Tony, Diane used the power she had to indicate that certain behavior would have consequences. This was not done in a dramatic or threatening manner, but in a matter-of-fact manner that was less likely to trigger more M.A.D.

         Diane blocked the Cycle.

Setting Limits

Setting limits is not a simple subject when an HCP is involved. It's like walking a tight rope or walking on eggshells. Yet it's often necessary. If you avoid setting limits with an HCP, you risk an escalation of conflict in your life—no matter how empathetic and respectful you might be. *This is because HCPs generally can't stop themselves.*

Remember, their behavior is driven by their own spontaneous Internal Upsets— their feelings of distress and danger. While you can calm down an HCP with your E.A.R., this won't change his or her personality. Sometimes it changes their behavior toward you as the Target of Blame, and sometimes it has only a very brief impact. We'll talk about setting limits in depth in Tip #11. In the meantime, here are a few brief points.

- Setting Limits is not aggressive. The goal is not to harm or destroy the other person, or to threaten the person unnecessarily.

- Setting Limits is not passive. The goal is not to ignore Behavior that's Aggressively Defensive, which HCPs can quickly escalate if they feel there are no realistic limits.

- Setting Limits is assertive. The goal is to protect yourself by putting limits on the HCP's behavior—stopping the behavior without attacking the HCP. Tip #11 addresses many ways to do this.

- Often, setting limits doesn't require saying anything, just acting *differently.*

- Setting limits is best done in a matter-of-fact manner, with empathy and respect.

Simple and Easy?

This may all appear very basic and easy. But the reason I have developed the Cycle of High Conflict Thinking is to help you think under pressure, especially when you're dealing directly, on the spot, with an HCP. If you can remember the Cycle and how to avoid responding with Negative Feedback, you may be able to stop the Cycle. If you think about Setting Limits, you may be able to respond realistically and assertively rather than giving in to the natural urges to retaliate or avoid dealing with the HCP.

A Question

Suppose George and Tony get into an argument at the office. George has been wondering if Tony has a High Conflict Personality and how to respond to him. He wonders if Tony is exaggerating or even lying about his success with some important clients. George feels like he wants to set Tony straight and challenge his statements so Tony won't think he's superior to the other people in the sales department. Which response would be best?

A.   "Tony, you're full of hot air and you know it!"

B.   "Tony, you're full of hot air, but you don't know it!"

C.   "You're right. You're the most incredible salesperson here!"

D.   "So what are your plans for this weekend? Anything fun?"

E.   "I'd like to believe you, but what you're saying doesn't make sense."

My favorite answer is "D." It completely changes the subject to something neutral that Tony usually enjoys—talking about his weekends. It avoids any direct or indirect challenge to his likely unconscious and distorted thinking about himself.

There is nothing to be gained by arguing with his logic or giving him negative feedback, so change the subject. My experience with HCPs is that they'll change the subject along with you most of the time. In many ways, it seems you're helping the HCP shift out of their own negative emotions and into positive emotions. This shift from negative defensive emotions to positive emotions helps them feel better too. Generally they won't fight you on changing the subject because it's a relief for them too.

A.   *Tony, you're full of hot air and you know it.* This kind of statement will escalate Tony's defenses and Cycle of High Conflict Thinking. Besides, he believes what he's saying, or at least the need to say it. So he won't admit that he's lying or exaggerating even if he knows that he is.

B.   *Tony, you're full of hot air, but you don't know it.* This kind of statement won't help. If he's having cognitive distortions, he's unconsciously making false statements and not aware of it. He'll just become more defensive and attack back.

C.   *You're right. You're the most incredible salesperson here.* This kind of statement is sarcastic, which triggers his defensiveness and more cognitive distortion. It might feel good to George for a minute, but the harm done will take a while to repair.

E.   *I'd like to believe you, but what you're saying doesn't make sense.* This kind of statement is the second best choice, but it will still trigger Tony's feelings of defensiveness, because he's being challenged on his absence of logic, which is a criticism of his thinking. If he's an HCP, he'll be used to getting defensive when people challenge his logic. This is still Negative Feedback about him.

Don't Give Them Negative Feedback

Despite everything I've said, you'll still be tempted to argue with an HCP's logic and give negative feedback. This is natural. But don't. Let me briefly repeat the reasons so they'll pop into your mind when you're confronted with this temptation.

You may feel irritated and want to point out how wrong their statements are. You may become sarcastic or just plain angry. This is the stuff that makes great television, but *can ruin your life for months or years* when you're dealing with an HCP.

You may feel sympathetic with the HCP and want to point out the errors in their thinking in a gentle way. However, even that will often backfire. Personal feedback just *triggers their hypersensitive survival feelings.*

Remember, expecting HCPs to take a little bit of responsibility for causing the problem or for fixing the problem *will trigger their all-or-nothing thinking* and they'll try to intensely prove they bear absolutely no responsibility for the problem. Otherwise, they'll feel it's all their fault, and that's psychologically unbearable—even though it may be mostly true.

Simple Do's and Don'ts with Upset HCPs (or Any Upset Person)

DON'T	DO
Don't directly criticize them.	Do empathize with their frustrations.
Don't make threats.	Do reassure them when you can.
Don't point out inconsistencies.	Do pay attention and listen.
Don't make suggestions.	Do respect them for their good qualities.
Don't attempt to give constructive feedback.	Do try to lower their need for defensiveness.

In the next four Tips, I'll describe the four most common High Conflict Personalities. Notice the Cycle of High Conflict Thinking and the high-conflict thinking that goes with each personality. Also notice what works and what doesn't work in dealing with them.

Don't worry; I'm not saying you have to accept how an HCP treats you, or even stay in a bad situation. Instead, the methods I propose are generally more effective, save energy, and reduce the conflict. In Tips #8 through #11 I'll give you four methods to consider instead of giving Negative Feedback. If you're in a difficult situation right now, you can skip ahead to those Tips.

TIP #2 SUMMARY

Don't Give Them Negative Feedback

1. The Cycle of High Conflict Thinking maintains and escalates conflict with three steps:

   Step 1: The HCP's Mistaken Assessment of Danger (M.A.D.)
   Step 2: The HCP's Behavior that's Aggressively Defensive (B.A.D.)
   Step 3: Your Negative Feedback (N.F.)

2. HCPs' Mistaken Assessment of Danger is based on their frequent high-conflict thinking, which everyone has occasionally. But HCPs believe these thoughts are true and act on them without checking for accuracy, including:

   - All-or-Nothing Thinking
   - Jumping to Conclusions
   - Personalization
   - Emotional Reasoning
   - Mind Reading
   - Wishful Thinking
   - Tunnel Vision
   - Exaggerated Fears
   - Projecting
   - Splitting

3. High Conflict People with Cluster B Personality Disorders or Traits appear to have the following chronic Exaggerated Fears, which are the cause of many of their Internal Upsets because they are repeatedly triggered by ordinary events:

   Borderlines...............................Fear of Being Abandoned
   Narcissists..................................Fear of Being Inferior
   Histrionics.................................Fear of Being Ignored
   Antisocials................................Fear of Being Dominated

4. In an effort to relieve their Internal Upsets, HCPs attack their Targets of Blame, who they mistakenly believe "caused" their feelings of being abandoned, inferior, ignored, or dominated. This is why they engage in so many Behaviors that are Aggressively Defensive. Their logic is dominated by these cognitive distortions, which drive the Cycle of High Conflict Thinking.

5. Angry Negative Feedback or even well-meaning Negative Feedback about HCP behavior is perceived as a threat, which increases their Mistaken Assessment of Danger, which then increases their Behavior that's Aggressively Defensive.

6. Instead of giving Negative Feedback, the Cycle of High Conflict Thinking can be stopped by:

    •   Connecting with Empathy, Attention, and Respect (E.A.R.)

    •   Setting Limits on Misbehavior (S.L.)

Tip #3: Don't Bend Boundaries With Borderlines

CHAPTER

3

"I have a problem with boundaries."

Tip #3
Don't Bend Boundaries With Borderlines

"It's All Your Fault!" Alison screamed at her neighbor Pat.

Pat had owned her condo for three years before Alison moved in next door. They were both 28 years old and liked each other right away.

"I'm so excited to be moving in next door to you," Alison said after they first met and had spoken for a few minutes. Pat thought Alison was great. She was full of energy and natural charm, and would be more fun than the former neighbor, who just seemed to work all day and night. Pat invited Alison over a few times for a glass of wine. Soon Alison said, "You could easily become my best friend. We have so much in common."

But within weeks, Alison was screaming at Pat, "My boyfriend never would have split up with me if it wasn't for you! It's all your fault!"

At some point in your life you've probably met someone with this "Love-You, Hate-You" type of personality. They can really surprise you with their sudden anger that comes out of the blue, or a sudden shift from friendliness to intense rage. Later on, they may be friendly again, as though nothing wrong ever happened.

The patterns of people with this type of high-conflict personality are characterized by:

- A fear of being abandoned, which results in clinging behaviors and manipulation

- Seeking revenge and vindication when they feel abandoned

- Dramatic mood swings, with extreme positive then negative views of people

- Sudden and intense anger, even at minor incidents

- Impulsive, risk-taking, and self-destructive behaviors

The more extreme form of this personality is Borderline Personality Disorder. Those who meet the criteria for Borderline Personality Disorder (BPD) represent about 2% of the general population, which means about 6 million people in the United States. Not everyone with BPD is a High Conflict Person. Some Borderlines don't focus on a Target of Blame, but rather blame themselves or constantly shift their focus of blame. But there are many HCPs with Borderline Personality Disorders because the above traits repeatedly get them into conflicts with anyone near them.

BPD is one of the most common forms of high-conflict personalities—perhaps the most common form. For our purposes in understanding high-conflict personalities, the above pattern of behavior is what matters. It doesn't matter if they have a Borderline Personality Disorder, or just maladaptive traits of this disorder. What matters is the pattern of behavior and how to handle this pattern in conflict situations. If you understand their problems, you may be more effective at containing and managing them.

Many of their problems come from being abused or traumatized in their early years. Research indicates that approximately 75% of Borderlines experienced some form of abuse in childhood: physical abuse, sexual abuse, emotional abuse, or serious neglect. From these experiences, they may repeatedly feel traumatized in adulthood by ordinary events that trigger their unresolved traumas. They may have also learned impulsive and manipulative behaviors as a method of coping with these traumatic or abusive situations. (Linehan, 1993).

In the past it was believed that approximately three-quarters of those diagnosed with BPD were women, but it appears that men are increasingly having this disorder. The cyclical pattern of domestic violence is commonly associated with men who have this disorder, so BPD is a significant problem for both men and women in our society. Some Borderline men tend to demonstrate this pattern of impulsive anger and violence in the home rather than in public (Dutton, 1998). Some Borderline women often express their anger toward their children with physical and emotional abuse (Lawson, 2002, 2004).

From my experience in family courts, it appears that women are increasingly involved in violence against men. Even though overall youth violence has actually decreased over the past 15 years, girls are becoming equally as violent as boys. False allegations in court and in everyday life also seem to be increasing and are often made by both Borderline men and women.

A Confusing Term

The term Borderline is really left over from almost a century ago when mental health professionals first developed terms for different mental health problems. People labeled with this disorder were considered on the border between neurotic (having problems in daily living) and psychotic (out of touch with reality, such as having delusions). The term was a catch-all category, but in 1980 the American Psychiatric Association used it for this specific type of personality disorder. For practical everyday purposes, you might think of people with Borderline Personality Disorder as people on the border between love and hate, constantly swinging back and forth, with little control over their emotions.

Referring to someone as a Borderline describes some common characteristics of the person, but not the whole person. It can be similar to referring to someone as an alcoholic or a diabetic, a Californian or a Canadian. When I refer to Borderlines (and other HCPs) in this book, I don't mean to imply that this is all they are. Borderlines are often successful in many aspects of their lives. However, because of their patterns of behavior, they often sabotage their good qualities and skills with inappropriate anger, mood swings, and relationship chaos.

High Conflict Dynamics

In my experience, Borderlines, with either the disorder or just maladaptive traits, drive most high-conflict disputes. This is because they're preoccupied with issues of abandonment, even in common everyday events. To prevent feeling abandoned they react with efforts to control and manipulate others, or they rage against those they believe have abandoned them. People generally don't like to be treated this way, and minor events quickly escalate into high-conflict disputes for many Borderlines.

Borderlines quickly switch back and forth from extremely positive feelings to anger and hate—mostly at the same people they loved or liked. When the feeling of being abandoned is strong, they may file lawsuits against those they cared for, in an effort to punish them or to feel in control.

On the other hand, because of their tendency to act impulsively, they may be brought to court as defendants after they lose control and hurt others—for everything from minor offenses such as shoplifting to major offenses such as murder.

One of the most important lessons I learned as a therapist was that Borderlines tend to put people into two extreme categories: extremely wonderful or extremely terrible. As a helping professional, I had to watch out for a Borderline's tendency to idealize me as a therapist and put me up on a pedestal because I knew they would eventually feel disappointed, and I'd be blasted with anger for being a terrible therapist.

Potential Targets of Blame must be watchful for this dynamic with possible HCPs who are extremely nice to them. For example, if you accept praise about how wonderful you are from a Borderline, you'll risk getting an equally intense blast of anger when (in their eyes) you fail. And you will fail in their eyes, because their expectations are unrealistic, and real life always sets in. However, if you can keep a good balance, you can handle them.

Preoccupation with Fear of Abandonment

The underlying Mistaken Assessment of Danger for Borderlines is fear of abandonment. This is the driving force for their clinging behavior in relationships, including multiple phone calls for reassurance, an uncomfortably high level of relationship intensity, and demands for loyalty to help them feel secure. They can never get enough attention, and they can never let go.

A possible example of this constant drive for attention is the story of David and Annette. After several incidents of violence against her, Annette finally got a restraining order against David and separated from him. He continued to try to contact her in very dramatic ways, as described in the court papers for their divorce. Two examples are the following.

> On May 7, 1996, David showed up at Annette's place of employment. He barged into her office, called her several names, and blamed her for his inability to have surgery on his arm. She didn't know why he was blaming her. As far as she knew, he was working with a program that was going to pay the costs of the surgery.

> On December 22, 1996, sometime after 10 p.m., two men noticed a fire across the street from where they were. They ran over to investigate and found a burning car smashed into the building. They contacted David, who was the only person nearby, and asked if he knew what had happened. He said he did, as it was his car. They asked him if he'd lost control of the car. He said no, he was making a statement to his "girlfriend" (really his wife, Annette) who worked in the building. He left before the firefighters arrived on the scene. (Borrelli v. Borelli, 2000) (Minor edits for ease of reading)

Let's look at David's possible Cycle of High Conflict Thinking:

Step #1: Annette's restraining order and unwillingness to talk to David may have felt like an extreme danger—a Mistaken Assessment of Danger (M.A.D.).

Step #2: Therefore, he appeared to feel that he had to engage in Behavior that was Aggressively Defensive to get her attention (B.A.D.). This was the pattern of their relationship.

Step #3: Early in their relationship, we could imagine that Annette may have given him Negative Feedback (N.F.) about his erratic behavior. But by the time they separated, she Set Limits on his behavior by obtaining a restraining order and moving to an unknown location. It wouldn't have been appropriate for her to provide Empathy, Attention, and Respect with him, because she needed to have no contact with David to be safe.

News reports are filled with examples of this dramatic type of Borderline relationship behavior. Yet this occurs all the time in less dramatic forms, so people don't realize that this behavior arises out of the Borderline's Internal Upsets—their unconscious Fear of Abandonment.

Instead, victims are often asked, "What did you do to make him so angry?" Since Borderlines get the cause of their emotions and behavior backwards (**I** think **U** caused my Internal Upset), the people around them often get it backwards too. They don't know that some people are stuck in their cognitive distortions and that Borderlines have a lifetime preoccupation with this fear of abandonment.

Alison and Pat

When Alison accused Pat of causing her boyfriend to split up with her, Pat was shocked at Alison's sudden, intense anger. She'd met Alison's boyfriend only briefly on two occasions. Soon after she moved in, Alison confided in Pat that her boyfriend was a jerk who never wanted to visit her at her new condominium. She asked Pat for advice. Pat was uncomfortable getting involved in Alison's personal affairs, but she finally suggested that Alison could assert herself with her boyfriend and tell him how important it was that he visit and spend time at her place.

Later, Alison dropped by and said that she and her boyfriend had a terrible fight after she followed Pat's suggestion and "asserted herself." When Pat heard the description of their fight, she wondered if Alison had confused being assertive with being highly aggressive.

A few days later, Pat heard loud banging and yelling coming from next door. It was about 11:00 at night, and Pat was in bed. She heard Alison screaming at someone and a few subdued comments from a man. Then it got quiet.

A few days later, again late at night, Pat heard more banging and yelling from Alison's condo. Then there was a knock on Pat's door. When she opened it, she was greeted by a man holding his bloody nose with his bare hand.

"Could I come in and clean up my nose?" Alison's boyfriend asked.

"Are you okay? Is it broken?" Pat said, waving him in and steering him to her bathroom sink.

"It'll be okay," he said. "But after what Alison just did to me, I'm not sure this will last much longer. I tried to get her some help, because I really do care about her. But she's so unpredictable. I thought she loved me, but I can't take it if this keeps up."

After he cleaned himself up, he left and Pat never saw him again. However, Alison came over the next day and angrily confronted Pat. "I understand that you made friends with my boyfriend last night! I want you to know that I don't appreciate you interfering in my relationship with him. I thought you were my friend! I don't trust you anymore!"

Pat was dumbstruck and didn't know what to say. After all, she'd tried to help Alison succeed in her relationship with her boyfriend, and this was the "thanks" she got?

"Do you want me to explain what happened?" Pat asked Alison.

"Hell, no!" Alison said, and stormed off back to her condominium.

The Noises

When Pat went to bed that night, she heard Alison banging around her condominium making noises she'd never heard before. It seemed as if she was throwing pots and pans around her kitchen. Then Alison pounded on Pat's wall and played her music loud. It seemed to Pat that Alison was saying "I'll punish you!" But why? For simply helping Alison's boyfriend clean up his bloody nose?

Pat put on her robe and went next door. She pounded on Alison's door. Alison answered.

"Can you please keep it down, Alison?" Pat demanded.

"Why should I, after what you've done to me? I can't sleep because of thinking about what you and he did to me. So why should you be able to sleep, if it's your fault?"

"That's absurd. That's crazy!" Pat exclaimed. "I didn't do anything with your boyfriend. I helped him for five minutes—to clean up the bloody nose you gave him. Then he left."

"I don't believe you! You're lying!" Alison exclaimed. "He split up with me today, because of you. I know exactly what you're thinking and what you're planning. You're not my friend anymore. Go away." Alison shoved Pat away from her door and slammed it shut.

Pat didn't know what to do, so she just went back to bed. To her surprise, the noises stopped. "What a relief," she thought to herself.

The next morning, Pat found a sign taped to her door: "This is the whore next door." Pat immediately took down the sign. But she was shocked and didn't know what to do. She had an important meeting to go to, so she decided to leave Alison alone for the time being. That night, about an hour after Pat went to bed, Alison again put on loud music, stomped on the floor, and banged pots and pans in the kitchen—waking Pat up. Pat was really tired and decided to try to ignore her. The next morning there was nothing on her door, and the next night was quiet. But Pat still worried about running into Alison.

She felt like she was walking on eggshells, not knowing when Alison would have another outburst of rage. She had no idea how to respond to Alison and her anger. She'd never met someone who created so much conflict in her life and seemed oblivious to it. She thought about writing a long letter to Alison, explaining exactly what happened with the boyfriend. She wanted to tell Alison to grow up and be more realistic.

Pat also thought about confronting Alison about her inappropriate behavior by knocking on her door and telling her what's what. Then she thought she would simply ignore Alison, in hopes that Alison would calm down, come to her senses, and stop behaving in this manner. Finally, she decided to go visit her sister for a couple of days and to think about what to do next.

When Pat returned to her condo, there were no signs on her door and Alison was quiet at night. Pat felt relieved that she had calmed down.

The next night there was a knock on her door, and it was Alison. Pat hesitated about opening the door, but decided she'd better see what was going on.

When she opened the door, Alison was really friendly and asked, "Can I borrow your corkscrew? I can't find mine. I have a new boyfriend and we're celebrating our first week together with a bottle of wine. Actually, I'd like you to come over and meet him. Then you can tell me what you think of him after he leaves."

Pat was amazed. It was as if Alison had lost her memory. How could she possibly expect Pat to be friendly after all that had happened the previous week? Should she lend her a corkscrew? Should she meet the new boyfriend?

What is Alison's Problem?

To understand how Pat might respond we need to understand what might be going on in Alison's mind.

Is Alison having an Internal Upset? It sure appears that she is. She truly blames Pat for her boyfriend splitting up with her. This is obviously her own responsibility because she punched him in the nose—and whatever else she might have done. This is typical of how HCPs lack awareness of their own behavior and of the effects of their behavior on others. When something goes wrong or someone leaves them, "Someone else must have caused it."

It turned out that Alison was used to being in these kinds of conflict scenarios. All her life she had easily gotten into arguments with people and sometimes physically assaulted them. She had never suffered any real consequences for her actions.

Her parents tolerated it because they felt they didn't spend enough time with her as a child. Alison said it was their fault that she behaved this way, and they believed her. They also figured she would outgrow it as she became an adult. Sudden mood swings had been a part of her life for as long ago as they could remember. But she didn't outgrow these behaviors. They became part of her personality.

Alison's friends thought she was exciting and spontaneous. They encouraged her dramatic behavior and laughed about her occasional physical confrontations. These events seemed justified by the other person's "stupid" behavior. Also, Alison's romantic relationships were always very intense. She just figured, "This is life!" If her boyfriends offended her she felt it was her job to set them straight. If it took a little push or shove or slap from her, they always "had it coming," she told herself. She thought of herself as a strong, independent woman.

Alison saw nothing wrong with her behavior and perceived it as normal. It was part of the pattern of her life. It felt normal and necessary to her.

Understanding Alison's Personality

Does Alison have Borderline Personality Disorder (or traits)? If you're not a trained and experienced mental health professional, you wouldn't be able to make a diagnosis. But as a Target of Blame, it could help you to privately recognize (and keep to yourself) the possibility of a "Love-You-Hate-You" type of HCP. If she has this type of personality, then she has a relatively predictable pattern of problems, which can often be handled with some specific responses.

Let's look at what we know about her pattern of behavior, based on the list on the first page of this Tip.

Fear of abandonment? Alison viewed Pat as totally loyal because they'd been friendly and shared a glass of wine from time to time. Somehow, in Alison's way of thinking, Pat abandoned this high level of loyalty by helping her boyfriend clean up his bloody nose.

Remember, Alison said, "I understand that you made friends with my boyfriend last night! I want you to know that I don't appreciate you interfering in my relationship with him. I thought you were my friend! I don't trust you anymore!"

How does being a friend prevent Pat from helping someone with a bloody nose? If you understand the logic of Alison's Love-You-Hate-You thinking, it makes sense that anything positive you do for her Target of Blame will feel like a betrayal—anything! Her thinking is all-or-nothing. You're "all-good," or you're "all-bad." When (not if) a Love-You-Hate-You person feels abandoned by you, their positive attitude toward you can change in a second.

Dramatic Mood Swings? Alison was particularly charming at the start of her neighborly relationship with Pat. Remember, early on she said, "You could easily become my best friend. We have so much in common." Just a few weeks later, she was screaming at Pat, "My boyfriend never would have split up with me if it wasn't for you! It's all your fault!" A few days later she was asking Pat to lend her a corkscrew, as if nothing had ever happened between them.

Does that sound like mood swings to you? It's actually the nature of Love-You-Hate-You personalities. Their moods swing in both directions. Just because they've become extremely angry with you doesn't mean they won't be extremely friendly again in the future. It may feel like a split personality. Each mood is often disconnected from the prior mood, so they jump back and forth with these mood swings and often don't realize it themselves.

Sudden and intense anger? Remember how angry Alison was? She wasn't even interested in what Pat had to say to explain what really happened. She said, "Hell, no!" in response to Pat's offer to explain the reality of the situation. Does this remind you of Karen Ann's statement in Tip #2?

> "When I rage at someone, they are no longer a real person with real feelings. They become the object of my hatred and the cause of my distress. They are the enemy. I get paranoid and believe they want to hurt me, and I am determined to strike out to prove a state of control over them." (Kreger & Gunn, 2007, p. 33, quoted with permission)

Karen Ann has reached a level of self-awareness that Alison isn't even considering. Karen Ann recognizes that her rage may actually hurt her. "It is an attempt to protect myself, knowing full well that what I am actually doing will drive a person away further" (Kreger & Gunn, 2007). This fits the Cycle of High Conflict Thinking, as Karen Ann is striking out in an effort to protect herself based on a Mistaken Assessment of Danger. Karen Ann has begun to become self-aware, which will be an important part of her recovery as a Borderline. For Alison, there is no sign of self-awareness.

Seeks revenge and vindication? Do you think Alison was seeking revenge by making noise to purposefully bother Pat? Was she seeking vindication by posting the notice "the whore next door!" so that others might think poorly of Pat and feel bad for Alison? Does she seem to fit this Love-You-Hate-You pattern?

Impulsive and self-destructive behaviors? Sure. She hit her boyfriend impulsively without really thinking. She shoved Pat. She's destroyed both close relationships, probably permanently.

These behaviors are common for those with Borderline Personality Disorder or traits. Can this disorder be treated or changed? Indications are growing that there can be successful treatment for this disorder.

Causes and Treatment

The development of personality disorders may arise from one or more causes. For anyone with this disorder, the contributing factors may be a different combination of the following:

1. Biological factors, such as genetic tendencies or temperament at birth.

2. Childhood factors, including child abuse and neglect, a severe trauma, or serious disruption to the child's early attachment to his or her parents.

3. Social learning factors, including role models with personality disorders, more reinforcement for negative behavior than for positive behavior, or negative values in the larger community, such as encouraging self-centeredness and tolerating uncontrollable moods.

Treatment may involve learning certain skills or having corrective emotional and behavioral experiences with the help of a highly skilled therapist specifically trained in treating BPD. Some people have overcome the disorder and only have occasional BPD traits. In a sense, they're in recovery just as an alcoholic may be in recovery. They'll still have to be careful throughout their lives not to relapse back into thinking, feeling, and behaving the way they did with the disorder.

Over the past several decades, the most frequently used treatment has been long-term individual psychotherapy, sometime five years or more. However, more recently, new therapies have used cognitive and behavioral approaches in short-term individual therapy and in groups. Cognitive therapy of personality disorders uses techniques initially used for depression and anxiety (Beck & Freeman, 1990). These approaches are highly compatible with the analysis of this book, as my own training and understanding of High Conflict People is based on my training as a cognitive and behavioral therapist.

The Dialectical Behavioral Treatment (DBT) approach developed by Marsha Linehan in Seattle has been well researched as particularly effective in treating BPD. It includes training to help Borderline patients self-regulate their emotions and behavior, and teaches self-acceptance and tolerance for the co-existence of opposites, such as being angry at someone and still loving the person, or making mistakes and still being a competent person. The DBT approach has grown rapidly over the past 10 years and shows a lot of promise for the future.

Medications have been largely ineffective at treating personality disorders, although many Borderlines have other related problems, such as depression and anxiety, that are helped with medications. Surprisingly, many therapists have observed that one of the most helpful treatments for some Borderlines is Alcoholics Anonymous (AA) and similar 12-step groups. Apparently, the structure and ready availability of these group meetings can help Borderlines handle fears of abandonment and regulate their emotions on a regular basis.

Alison's Big Crisis

Alison's new boyfriend didn't tolerate her mood swings and anger. While celebrating their first week together, she slapped him and he ran out of her condo, yelling "I'm getting out of here. You're crazy!" He quickly got in his car and drove off.

Alison had drunk several glasses of wine. But this didn't stop her from running after him. When she saw him drive off, she got in her car and chased after him. She quickly found him stopped at a stop sign, and she rear-ended his car. Someone called the police, and two people restrained her as she was pounding on his driver's door window. He had whiplash and a bloody nose.

Alison was arrested and the new boyfriend quickly got a restraining order against her. After three days in jail, she was given the alternatives of an inpatient alcohol treatment program or staying in jail. She chose the treatment program.

In her treatment program, she was required to attend AA meetings. She also had a therapist who told her she had a "dual diagnosis." She was an alcoholic and she had an emotion regulation problem. He wouldn't give her a label for the emotion regulation problem, though he did tell her there was a lot of hope for her—but only if she took responsibility for the emotion regulation problem.

"I'll do anything at this point," Alison said. "I know I screwed up. I know it will happen again. I just don't know what to do." And she started crying loudly.

Her counselor handed her a box of tissues. "I guess this proves my point about emotions, don't you think? Now, can you try crying a little softer right now? There are lots of other folks here, and I don't have enough tissues to go around."

She broke into a little laugh through her tears. "Okay. What do I have to do?"

A Year Later

A year after she was arrested, Alison arranged to meet Pat. Alison's father had sold the condominium soon after the incident, and Pat was quite relieved. She wasn't sure what to expect from Alison, but she'd sounded more mature than ever before. They didn't get together over a glass of wine. Instead, they arranged to have coffee at a local coffee shop.

Alison started by saying, "Thanks for agreeing to meet with me. I want to tell you how sorry I am for all the trouble I caused you, and for blaming you and for putting that sign on your door. I don't need to talk about it, I just want you to know how sorry I am to have treated you so badly."

Pat was pleased to hear all of this. She wasn't sure whether to ask questions or discuss things or what.

"I'm going to a lot of AA meetings, and I am working on my AA twelve steps. Right now I am making amends with people I treated badly, and you were one of them. I've also learned that I have to look at my part in my problems and not just blame other people. I know I tend to make a lot of assumptions, and I have a hard time controlling my emotions."

"You don't have to say anything, if you don't want to. I just wanted you to know that I am taking responsibility for my life now—and for my emotions. I have to consciously work at it every day. One day at a time."

Pat didn't know what to say. She finally said, "I'm pretty amazed that you're telling me this. I have to admit that I was afraid of you and pretty angry with you. But I understand how hard it must be to tell me all of this. So, thank you."

When Pat told Alison that she'd been angry and afraid, she saw a flash of irritation cross Alison's face, but Alison sat still.

When Pat was done responding, Alison stood up and said, "I better not stay too long. I don't want to impose on you. Thanks for getting together with me. I was glad to have you as a neighbor, even if I didn't always act that way."

After she left, Pat thought that Alison still had some rough edges to her personality, but she seemed to be making conscious efforts to improve herself.

"One day at a time," she thought and smiled.

This was an ideal outcome and I've seen it happen. But it doesn't occur often enough. Ironically, people with a substance abuse problem in addition to a personality disorder have more resources available for treatment, since personality disorders have been ignored so much in the past. Some of the same lessons that need to be learned and practiced for recovery from alcoholism can be applied to Borderlines and to all HCPs: looking for "their part" in the problem, living a balanced lifestyle, taking responsibility for regulating their emotions, and being sensitive to their effect on others. These can all be learned with a lot of practice in a structured program of change.

It's not clear whether Alison was told she had a Borderline Personality Disorder. Until recently, mental health professionals did not tell their Borderline clients that they had this disorder. The fear was that it would trigger too much resistance to learning new skills and stigmatize the client. More recently, some therapists have begun telling their clients they have this disorder and treating it as a positive awareness, because there is treatment, and their own patterns begin to make sense to them as part of a common disorder. Someday, perhaps, a "recovering Borderline" will be as common as a recovering alcoholic or addict.

While it's very exciting to see people in recovery from substance abuse problems and from personality problems, unfortunately it often takes a serious crisis and severe consequences before they enter a program of change. Someday, perhaps, our society will become better at recognizing personality problems and pressuring people into treatment programs, as many employers do now with getting employees into treatment programs for alcoholism and other addictions.

News Flash

A recent newspaper article described an angry young woman. She was driving her Cadillac on a normal city street on a Sunday evening when she drove into the car in front of her. The man felt his car being pushed, even though he was putting on the brakes, almost 60 miles per hour. He would have crashed into another car at an intersection, but he pulled his car into the curb, where it ground to a halt. The young woman backed up her Cadillac and slammed into the man's car again.

Ms. Cadillac then drove into the intersection and crashed into a car driven by a woman whose 12-year-old daughter was also in the car, pushing it almost 200 feet.

Then Ms. Cadillac aimed her car into a pickup truck waiting for the light to turn at the next intersection. She hit the pickup hard, causing it to roll over and its passengers to hang upside down by their seat belts. This crash left Ms. Cadillac unconscious in her collapsed car.

What was going on? Apparently, Ms. Cadillac, a 23-year-old, had just had a fight with her boyfriend, who wanted to break up. After a few beers, combined with her anti-nausea medication (she was pregnant), she claimed to have gone for a drive to clear her mind.

Does any of this fit our Love-You-Hate-You personalities? Fear of abandonment? Mood swings? Impulsive anger? A drive for revenge against any Target she could find? Since I haven't formally interviewed Ms. Cadillac, I can't diagnose her. But this pattern of anger and blame against anyone handy seems awfully familiar. Was it because of the alcohol? I've heard of many drunk driving accidents, but never a story like this with such a focus of rage and willingness to purposefully attack anyone nearby with a car on a city street. For a few minutes, three different drivers seem to have become her Targets of Blame (Braun, 2007).

In The Office

An example of a three-year workplace dispute with a possible Borderline is described in the following court case. Two doctors involved in her case said she "may have a borderline personality disorder." See what you think.

Ms. W was hired to work as a researcher at Georgetown University in 1990. Within a few months, she informed her employer that she had a disability and requested special accommodations. The department tried to accommodate her requests, but she said they were "not always adequate." (In the following quotes I have made very minor edits for smoother reading.)

> Beginning in 1992, Ms. W received both written and verbal warnings about her behavior and interactions with co-workers and supervisors, informing her that if she didn't change her behavior, further disciplinary action would be taken.

In November 1992, after making an oral complaint that the University's accommodations were inadequate, Ms. W filed an internal complaint with the University's Office of Affirmative Action Programs ("AAO"), requesting that the AAO devise a plan to provide her with 'suitable working conditions.'

The AAO conducted an investigation of Ms. W's complaint, during which time Ms. W took paid administrative leave. The AAO concluded that there was 'no evidence to support Ms. W's complaint of discrimination based on disability, harassment, and retaliation.' In late January, after the AAO issued its determination, Ms. W received a departmental memorandum regarding her inappropriate behavior. Ms. W returned to work in February 1993. She also received an annual performance evaluation stating that she hadn't met the University's standards for affirmative action because of her previous racially and ethnically insensitive remarks directed at African Americans.

After the AAO inquiry, departmental memorandum, and performance evaluation, additional incidents between Ms. W and her co-workers and supervisors ensued. For example, one employee expressed concern that Ms. W might try to physically harm a co-worker. On April 30, 1993, after receiving reports of such incidents, the University informed Ms. W of her termination. (Weigert v. Georgetown University, 2000, 2-3)

Ms. W then sued the University for violating the Americans with Disabilities Act (ADA) by discharging her from her position and retaliating against her for lodging complaints. To qualify under the ADA, she had to show that she was in fact disabled. She claimed she had four disabling conditions: "an unspecified neurological condition; hypothyroidism; impairment from her medications; and claustrophobia."

However, the court examined each of her claims of disability, and decided that she did not have disabling impairments.

These were her claims:

1. She claimed she was disabled from hypothyroidism, but provided no evidence at all while she was employed.

2. She claimed "that she could not tolerate fluorescent lighting or glare from other light," but her neurologist during her time of employment said that "every study conducted on Ms. W was normal and nothing clinically about her indicated definite neurological disease."

3. She claimed she had to take medications because of "narcolepsy [an illness of suddenly falling asleep during the day time], although she repeatedly declined to be tested for this condition...." But she also claimed that her "medication itself caused an impairment." The court disagreed.

4. She said "that she suffered from claustrophobia during her employment as a result of the installation of dividers in her office...." However, the doctor's note she submitted didn't show any finding from that doctor. The court decided that even if she had claustrophobia, it didn't impair her general functioning at work or outside of work.

While she claimed to be disabled, the court also noted that she had an active life without being limited in her major life activities, which is part of the definition of disability. The court noted:

> Ms. W worked a 40-hour work week throughout her employment, commuted 45 minutes in each direction, cared for her children, took graduate courses at Georgetown University, studied karate, and vacationed at the beach....

> She was able to commute to work and did not, for example, use alternative transportation to protect herself or others from her reaction to sunlight or glare. Moreover, she took vacations at the beach where the sun and glare from the water could have exacerbated her condition. Ms. W contends that her illness jeopardized the completion of her studies, yet she does not say how. For example, she did not attempt to ameliorate the lighting conditions in her classrooms. Indeed, she testified that she would "just step out as needed" if the fluorescent lights in the classroom affected her.

> Finally, Ms. W's husband's testimony that his wife could not work for pro-longed periods does not suffice to establish a substantial limitation in a major life activity. Rather, the record discloses that she maintained a full-time work schedule, cared for four children with the help of her husband, and pursued a graduate course load during the relevant time. In view of the record, the court determines that the plaintiff was not substantially limited in the performance of major life activities. (Weigert v. Georgetown University, 2000, 25)

The court case goes on to describe her typical behavior on the job:

> Ms. W also contends that the University denied her the secretarial support of Ms. Gearhart. Dr. Green acknowledges that she complained to her about this situation. However, Dr. Green explains that Ms. Gearhart provided secretarial support to the whole division and Ms. W often demanded immediate atten-

tion to her projects without regard to Ms. Gearhart's other duties.... From the record, it appears that Ms. W's demand for immediate attention without regard to the needs of others was a consistent problem both in her work environment and in her clinical relationships. She failed to demonstrate that she was treated differently than the other employees in regard to secretarial support.

Ms. W's doctors also observed her behavioral problems. Dr. Behlmer testified that the manner in which Ms. W interacted with the staff and her lack of sensitivity to other patients—especially her demands that Dr. Behlmer leave scheduled appointments immediately to confer with the unscheduled arrival of Ms. W—were not conducive to the patient/doctor relationship. For example, Dr. Behlmer testified that Ms. W used pressure tactics to force the doctor to refill her medications. According to Dr. Behlmer, Ms. W was "manipulative," demanded immediate attention, and "requested things associated with threats." Eventually, Ms. W's behavior caused a rupture in their relationship.

Dr. Dale, who treated Ms. W after Dr. Behlmer, stated that "one day she might say to you you're an angel, you're wonderful. I couldn't ask for a better doctor. Then the next day you're the worst doctor in the world, you're trying to kill me." These reports suggest a consistent behavioral problem and lend credence to the University's assertions that its actions did not relate to disability discrimination or retaliation. (Weigert v. Georgetown University, 2000, 18-19)

Do you see any familiar issues of a Love-You-Hate-You personality in this case?

Mood swings? Extreme positive, then negative statements about people? Remember what Dr. Dale, who treated Ms. W after Dr. Behlmer, said, "one day she might say to you you're an angel, you're wonderful. I couldn't ask for a better doctor. Then the next day you're the worst doctor in the world, you're trying to kill me."

Sudden and intense anger? Dr. Green reported receiving "reports about problems with her interaction with other employees and her 'rude and abrasive' interactions with colleagues" Id. at 56. One employee expressed concern that Ms. W might try to physically harm a co-worker.

Impulsive and risk-taking behavior? Ms. W impulsively demanded attention in all settings. According to Dr. Behlmer, Ms. W was "manipulative," demanded immediate attention and "requested things associated with threats." With the secretarial staff, "Ms. W often demanded immediate attention to her projects without regard to Ms. Gearhart's other duties...." And with her peers, "Ms. W's demand for immediate attention without regard to the needs of others was a consistent problem both in her work environment and in her clinical relationships."

The point here is to recognize a *pattern* of high-conflict behavior that might help you decide to use certain methods for dealing with an HCP, which I will describe below.

Empathy and Setting Limits

It helps to realize how long these problem behaviors went on in this workplace and how many other people became involved in trying to manage this possible High Conflict Person. If you're dealing with a similar situation, this is a good example of why you need to deal with it sooner rather than later. This is how high-conflict disputes often grow, because HCP behavior is aggressive, intimidating, and hard to deal with. You can see how Ms. W threatened secretaries, colleagues, and superiors. This type of personality problem can affect numerous people as Targets of Blame.

However, I also want to point out how HCPs lack awareness of their own behavior. I wouldn't be surprised if Ms. W honestly believed she was acting appropriately in each situation. Since she may have sensed that she was in danger (Mistaken Assessment of Danger), her actions may appear necessary and normal to her in order to defend herself. If she had a difficult past, you can understand how she might have gotten stuck in this high-conflict thinking. Unfortunately for her, it did not work in this job.

Since HCPs honestly don't realize their behavior is causing their problems, it may be easier to develop some empathy for what such a person may be going through. It also helps to understand that you need to set limits as soon as possible because such people can't stop their own misbehavior.

Don't Bend Your Boundaries with Borderlines

The following are several specific suggestions for handling or avoiding conflicts with Love-You-Hate-You personalities. You can use these with anyone, but they're particularly relevant to Borderlines with High Conflict Personalities.

Borderlines are preoccupied with a fear of abandonment, so they push normal social boundaries to feel more secure, until people push back and seem to reject them, which they often do. Then the Borderlines go into a rage and try to get the person back into their lives or punish them for leaving. The best protection against both ends of these mood swings (closeness, then rage) is to establish boundaries from the start by creating realistic expectations.

More than any other High Conflict Personality, Borderlines develop extreme expectations of their relationships with others. If you reinforce a Borderline's extreme fantasies of you, you'll eventually be blasted with anger for disappointing him or her. It's best to avoid reinforcing any expectations and to instead minimize your positive qualities and present yourself as an average person who shouldn't be treated as an ideal. Here are some suggestions:

1. **Don't act too big.** Make yourself average in their eyes. If a Borderline (or anyone) wants to gush over how wonderful you are, thank him or her, but suggest that you're really fairly average and ordinary. Then you're less likely to be blamed for disappointing him or her later on.

2. **Don't reinforce unrealistic expectations of intimacy**. Whether you're in a romantic relationship, a professional relationship, or a business relationship, be careful not to raise expectations of closeness. Everyone needs space in a relationship, and that's normal. Borderlines expect an unusual amount of intimacy in order to feel secure. They can be excessively charming, quick to form close friendships, and desirous of many favors to show secure commitment. When this eventually gets uncomfortable, as it always does, they create a crisis to push you away, or they feel rejected when you simply seek ordinary relationship space.

3. **Create clear expectations in your relationship.** Whether with neighbors, co-workers, family members, or strangers, set clear expectations for who will do what and when, and stick with them. If you say you're going to repair a fence by the end of the month, then do so. If you don't want to get together outside of work, then make that clear and simple from the start. Borderlines will push you to do more tasks and favors than you want to. Avoid the temptation to give in if you prefer not to do something; otherwise, it'll set a bad precedent.

4. **Pay attention to your gut feelings of discomfort.** Often, your gut feelings will be the first to tell you that a Borderline has entered your life. You might really like someone, and find him or her charming, attractive, intelligent, and persuasive. Yet you also may feel a gnawing sensation of being pushed or imposed upon. As a nice person, you might ignore that gut feeling, and think that you'd be rude or irresponsible to set limits on this nice person or poor victim

of circumstance. Pay attention to that feeling and see if there are any signs of a Borderline personality. If there are, move cautiously and realistically in the relationship as soon as you realize this.

5. **Remind yourself that you have the right to be assertive.** You have the right to be assertive in all relationships, even around people who are particularly vulnerable or report having been victimized by others. If you feel like you don't have the right to speak up, to object, to say "No" for fear of hurting someone's feelings, you may be in the presence of a Borderline (or other HCP). This is all the more reason to assert yourself and set limits. When in doubt, consult with friends or professionals to see if you're being reasonable in setting limits with someone. Borderlines generally trigger a desire in others to "walk on eggshells." If you feel this way, it'll be important to become assertive as soon as possible in the relationship. The important differences between assertive and aggressive will be discussed later in the book.

6. **Take boundary violations seriously, including violence, threats of violence, and verbal attacks.** Borderlines are known for impulsive behavior that violates normal relationship boundaries. It's not normal or healthy for someone to verbally abuse another person, or to hit her or him. It's not a sign of caring or commitment. It's a sign of a *pattern* of behavior that's likely to continue and to escalate—not a mistake that'll go away. When Borderlines violate normal social boundaries, it's a routine part of their relationship pattern. If you don't set limits on this behavior at the start, the behavior will probably grow. If you're not sure what to do, consult with a counselor, a mediator, or an attorney who is familiar with these types of neighbor, co-worker, or other disputes.

7. **Don't try to fix their problems or get them into treatment by yourself.** Many people react to Borderlines by trying to help them with their many problems. You can easily become their "rescuer," their "enabler," their "co-dependent," who tries to fix everything for them. They'll love you for this—at first. Inevitably, they'll become enraged with you for doing something "wrong," probably something you thought was a good thing. It's also rare to get a Borderline into treatment by yourself. It usually takes a crisis, a group, or an employer to push someone effectively into a treatment program. This is commonly called an "Intervention." Speak with a counselor if you think an Intervention would be a good idea, before you do anything else.

8. **Be patient.** Borderlines can be successful workers, caring relationship partners, and a joy to be around much of the time. They can often adapt to changes if they have time and support. They don't respond well to "hammering out issues or agreements," but they often do respond positively to changes that come in small steps. Then they can adjust emotionally to each step. They also resist pressure, so you're better off showing patience rather than impatience with them. Remember to give them your Empathy, Attention, and Respect, even when Setting Limits with them.

A Question

Let's return to Pat's dilemma when Alison knocked on her door. Remember, just a few days after raging, making noise, and posting a hateful sign on Pat's door, Alison cheerfully asked her for a corkscrew and to meet her new boyfriend. As you learned above, this is typical of the mood swings of Borderlines who are HCPs. They'll be friendly, then blame you, then be friendly again.

Which of the following would you recommend to Pat?

A. Angrily tell Alison that she will get nothing from you after the way that she treated you the week before.

B. Give her the corkscrew and go with her to meet her new boyfriend. Tell her afterward what you think of him.

C. Give her the corkscrew, but tell her you'd rather not meet her boyfriend. Tell her that's her personal business and you'd rather not intrude.

D. Don't give her the corkscrew and tell her you'd rather not meet her boyfriend, but that you appreciate her asking you.

E. Tell her that you're in a rush and have to leave immediately.

While there is no absolute best answer when it comes to High Conflict People, I think "C" and "D" are both equally good answers, for the following reasons.

C. Give her the corkscrew, but tell her you'd rather not meet her boyfriend. Tell her that's her personal business and you'd rather not intrude. By saying "No" to meeting Alison's new boyfriend, Pat will set a limit on the closeness of a relationship with Alison. Especially given the noise and note on the door, Pat needs to keep strong boundaries with Alison. Remember that Pat had earlier allowed herself to comment on how Alison could handle her relationship with her previous boyfriend. Ordinarily, this is something that a friend would do. However, once you know you're dealing with a Love-You-Hate-You personality, it's especially important to avoid getting involved in the HCP's relationship issues with others. That's an important social boundary to set limits on with Borderline HCPs, and they often want to involve you in their other relationship issues. Don't! Regarding the corkscrew, see the next answer under "D."

D. Don't give her the corkscrew and tell her you'd rather not meet her boyfriend, but that you appreciate her asking you. By saying "No" to meeting Alison's boyfriend and to her request for a corkscrew, Pat risks a confrontation with Alison because lending a corkscrew is a normal social behavior. However, if Pat says "Yes," by doing Alison a favor she's ignoring how inappropriate Alison has been recently. It would certainly be appropriate to say "No," but to be honest, I would personally say "Yes." The corkscrew is normal social behavior and I would want to be as ordinary and routine as possible, to avoid creating further issues with Alison.

However, I would certainly consider saying "No" and would respect anyone who did. You just might suffer another night of noise until you found another solution to having an HCP neighbor. The key issue here is Choosing Your Battles (see Tip #12). This is a personal choice based on the circumstances and your priorities at the time.

If you said "No" to the corkscrew request because you don't want to encourage Alison's drinking, keep in mind that it probably wouldn't make any difference. Unless Alison is involved in a treatment program, she'll find a way to drink regardless of what you do.

E. Tell her that you're in a rush and have to leave immediately. This answer dodges the issues of engaging with Alison, as well as dealing with the corkscrew issue and meeting the new boyfriend. This is sometimes the best approach in the short term. You avoid dealing with Alison and there is nothing that requires you to deal with her directly. She may just ignore being brushed off by Pat, or she may take it very personally and seek revenge again, as she has in the past. This is a personal judgment call, but is one of the realistic options. It would be my third best answer.

A. Angrily tell Alison that she will get nothing from you after the way she treated you the week before. While this answer is tempting, it would simply engage Pat in a very personal battle that Pat can't win. It won't bring insight for Alison. Instead, this direct and angry confrontation will merely escalate Alison's Mistaken Assessment of Danger, and she'll engage in Behaviors that are Aggressively Defensive—such as banging pots and pans, and posting signs about Pat, as she did before.

B. Give her the corkscrew and go with her to meet her new boyfriend. Tell her afterward what you think of him. While this answer is also tempting, it does not set limits on the personal relationship that Pat has with Alison and would create closer expectations. Then, after Pat gave her opinion of the new boyfriend, Alison would be upset about something—and blame it on Pat. Pat is better off not getting involved at all with Alison's boyfriends. This is a normal social boundary that's even more important with someone with a Love-You-Hate-You personality.

TIP #3 SUMMARY

Don't Bend Boundaries With Borderlines

Characteristics

1. Borderlines are known for their sudden mood swings and intense anger.

2. Borderlines are preoccupied with fear of abandonment.

3. Borderlines often start relationships with charm and sudden urges for intimacy.

4. Borderlines idealize people they like, but then attack those same people for disappointing them.

5. Borderlines have often experienced early childhood abuse, trauma, or parenting disruptions.

Managing Borderline HCPs

1. Have clear boundaries for your amount of contact and level of closeness.

2. Discourage an idealized picture of your talents or personal qualities.

3. Respond matter-of-factly to requests for reassurance.

4. Take threats of violence or spreading rumors seriously.

5. Avoid taking responsibility for fixing his or her problems.

Tip #4: Don't Diss The Narcissists

CHAPTER

4

Tip #4
Don't Diss the Narcissists

"Bob is so arrogant. Someone needs to bring him down to earth," thought Jason.

Jason and Bob had just finished a trip doing research and interviews for an article for their big-city newspaper. Bob's last name came later in the alphabet, but he insisted, "Since I did most of the work for this article, my name should be first under the headline."

Jason thought to himself, "Does he think I'm an idiot? He did about 10% of the work on this project, and was totally manipulative in getting me to do the work that he's now claiming credit for."

Jason made all the hotel arrangements in the town where they did the interviews for the articles. He contacted the local newspaper, local police, and local community leaders to set up interviews and gather information. Jason was the one who kept in touch with the home office, while Bob saw all the sights of the city and put most of his energy into picking up attractive women to give him the tours.

"I can't wait 'til we get back so I can get away from this guy," Jason thought.

People with Narcissistic personalities think and act like they're better than everyone around them. They constantly get into conflicts. Who wants to be around someone who thinks, "I'm Very Superior" to you? We are constantly tempted to "diss" (show disdain or disrespect) for those with this type of personality. But don't, for the reasons explained below.

The pattern of those with Narcissistic "I'm Very Superior" personalities is characterized by:

• Has a very superior self-image

• Is absorbed in themselves

• Feels "entitled" to special treatment and attention

• Lacks empathy for the feelings and needs of others

• Takes advantage of relationships to serve their own desires

Those with extreme characteristics of this personality have Narcissistic Personality Disorder. Estimates in 1994 were that nearly 1% of the general population has Narcissistic Personality Disorder (APA, 2000), which equals nearly 3 million people in the United States.

However, over the past 30 years, parents and teachers have been told to put a big emphasis on building children's high self-esteem. Research has shown that this emphasis has actually taught today's young adults to be more narcissistic, anxious, and depressed than ever before. The results have shown that programs to build self-esteem overemphasized *feeling good* rather than *doing good*. So children haven't learned as many skills for success, but think they deserve success and are frustrated (Twenge, 2006). Therefore, I expect that the percentage of people with Narcissistic Personality Disorder is now higher than 1%.

Some signs of this trend are contained in comparisons between the decades. In the 1950s, when teenagers between 14 and 16 were asked if they agreed with the statement that they were an "important person," 12% said yes. Thirty years later, 80% of teenagers agreed with that statement. College students in 2006 were higher on indicators of narcissism than college students in 1987 (Twenge, 2006).

So the trend toward increased narcissism has been increasing for the past 50 years. However, while each generation may be showing more narcissistic traits, not everyone has a Narcissistic Personality Disorder.

For purposes of understanding High Conflict Personalities, the above characteristics are easy to recognize in everyday life. You probably know someone who fits the "I'm Very Superior" description.

They seem to invite disrespect and criticism at every turn. Their superior attitude is usually out of proportion with their accomplishments. Many successful people have a dose of this attitude, but having a Narcissistic Personality Disorder or some of its maladaptive traits means the person is dysfunctional. Even if they are successful now, it's likely their success will be ruined in the future because they eventually alienate everyone.

A small dose of superiority is present in many professions, business, and politics. It can help people keep going when others would give up. Narcissists believe in themselves against all odds, and sometimes that can be helpful in a competitive world. However, too much narcissism is dysfunctional and can be a highly destructive force in any social environment. When a person has Narcissistic Personality Disorder (NPD), he or she has significant impairment in social relationships and/or significant internal distress.

High Conflict Dynamics

From my experience, people with Narcissistic Personalities (NPs are those with the disorder or some maladaptive traits) are present in a large number of high-conflict cases. In fact, NPs seem to become involved in business disputes and lawsuits between professionals more often than other high-conflict personalities.

For one reason or another, NPs have developed a coping mechanism of believing that they'll achieve incredible success and have incredible personal qualities. Such people can be very charismatic, as they believe in their own fantasies in a compelling way and inspire others to believe in them. This doesn't always last, and those who have invested in them, emotionally and/or financially often become very angry with them.

NPs often become involved in high-conflict disputes because they're high risk-takers, disdainful of others, and generally oblivious to the consequences of their own actions. They often feel like victims, when in fact their own behavior usually causes the events that upset them. With these characteristics, compromise and respect for others are difficult or nonexistent.

Narcissistic Personality Disorder is identified primarily in men, but many women also have this disorder or traits (perhaps 25% of NPs are women from my observations). NPs generally don't pursue mental health treatment, except for help with a separate problem, such as anxiety or depression. They can't see themselves as contributing to their problems. If you confront them with their own behavior, they'll become extremely defensive and will often go on the offensive by verbally attacking you.

Narcissists are harder to work with than Borderlines because they don't care as much about relationships and they don't perceive themselves as needing to change anything. While conflicts with Borderlines often occur because they get too close, conflicts with Narcissists often occur because they're too emotionally aloof. They truly think they have high self-esteem, but they're easily triggered by anything that threatens their confident self-image.

Contrary to the traditional view that Narcissists have low self-esteem, recent research shows that they have high self-esteem. It's true they are particularly sensitive to *challenges* to this high self-image and will attack those who challenge their superiority. The results show that Narcissists are no more aggressive than the average person when nothing is going wrong. However, they'll aggressively attack someone when they experience a "narcissistic injury" (Baumeister, 2006).

Narcissistic Injuries

We all have narcissistic injuries from time to time. This is the extreme sense of hurt any person has when things feel personal—that there is something wrong with oneself as a person. For example, a person applies for a job for which he's well qualified. However, a hundred other well-qualified people also apply, and he doesn't get the job. He feels devastated, even though other people would see that he was unlikely to get it because his chances were one in a hundred. Yet, the jobseeker may take it very personally, because he sees himself as superior—even superior to the odds. This is a narcissistic injury. We all experience them occasionally, but this doesn't mean we have Narcissistic Personality Disorder.

In contrast, NPs constantly feel narcissistic injuries from life events, even routine events. In reality there's no one to blame, but NPs find someone to blame because it "must be somebody else's fault," it can't be theirs. They find a Target of Blame to attack. This approach can lead to legal disputes from breach of contract obligations, to domestic violence, and even to murder.

Demands for special treatment and admiration often earn the resentment of others around NPs, who often characterize them as obnoxious, self-centered, and rude. While many people in daily life have these qualities occasionally, those who qualify for a diagnosis of Narcissistic Personality Disorder don't succeed in important areas of their lives because of these qualities. In employment settings, disputes may arise because the Narcissistic person can't accept feedback or being treated as an ordinary person. NPs may be sued for harassment in employment because they are oblivious to the impact of their insensitive remarks and demands towards employees.

In business relationships, NPs may be sued for breach of contract because they don't interpret their actions as negative or harmful when everyone else does. In criminal relationships, NPs may injure others because they don't feel they are being treated like the special people they are. On the other hand, others may seem to "injure" NPs because they can no longer stand NPs' attitudes and behavior.

Bob and Jason

"You know, it's not true when you say you did the most work," Jason finally said to Bob as they were driving back.

"That's a lie and you know it!" Bob replied angrily. "You're the one who's lying! If it wasn't for me doing all the important work, we wouldn't have an article to take back to the paper."

"Well, we'll see when we get back!" Jason said, without any idea of what would be seen when they returned. He just knew he was extremely frustrated from spending a week on the road with Bob.

"Oh yeah! We WILL SEE when we get back!" Bob responded, much louder than Jason.

Jason was completely frustrated, but not willing to keep fighting with Bob. "Okay, let's just change the subject," suggested Jason.

"I'm done talking with you about ANY subject," Bob retorted.

The day after they got back to the office, the managing editor, Mr. Johnson, called Jason and told him he wanted to see him. Bob's cubicle was right next to Jason's, so Jason asked, "Hey, Bob, do you know anything about a meeting with Mr. Johnson?"

"No, I don't have a clue. What's up?" Bob replied.

"He wants to have a meeting with me. I guess you're not included then."

"Don't know anything about it," Bob replied, and turned back to his work.

Even before their trip, Jason had been growing increasingly frustrated with Bob's attitude in the next cubicle. Bob would take phone calls for personal matters, speak loudly and argue with people on the phone, and distract Jason from his work. And each Monday morning, Bob had to tell Jason how great a night he had with his latest conquest in the romance department. Jason doubted much of this was true. He wondered whether to bring up any of these problems in his opportunity to meet with Mr. Johnson.

"So, you and Bob got a great story in that small town. I hope you're proud of the work you did under his guidance," said Mr. Johnson.

"Yeah, it was a great story. I really enjoyed setting up the interviews, meeting with everybody, and having the chance to really develop this story for the paper." Jason decided not to say anything about Bob until he'd heard what Mr. Johnson had to say.

"You know, Jason, I've been pretty happy with your work at this paper. And what I'm going to say now doesn't mean anything about my belief that you do good work. But Bob did have some concerns that make me troubled about you and your relationships with your co-workers. In short, I'm wondering whether you should continue with this division of the paper."

"What could he say bad about me?" Jason asked. He was shocked to hear that Bob was complaining about him. But then he remembered their conversation in the car, and how Bob said, "We'll see!" when Jason hinted he might complain back at the office. Of course, Jason didn't have any serious plans to complain. He just wanted Bob to know he shouldn't keep trying to lie about this stuff. Now he realized he should have just kept his mouth shut instead of pushing Bob's buttons.

"Bob says he and the other workers have been having problems with you for quite some time, but he didn't want to bring it up and appear to be complaining. He reluctantly told me that you're really on the phone a lot with personal matters in the office, and that you really talk loudly and get into arguments, distracting him from his work. Then, on the road trip last week, he explained he had to do all the work setting up the interviews and getting background information."

"What?" Jason exclaimed.

"Now, I don't think of you as a slouch. In fact, I've been impressed with your hard work. But if you're rubbing Bob and the other reporters the wrong way, I'm not sure you should keep working in this department. I'm thinking it might be better if you were to go work in the circulation department. What do you think about all this?"

Jason was really frustrated at this point. Obviously Bob was lying. "He is describing his own behavior and claiming it's mine," he thought. Should he tell Mr. Johnson that Bob was lying? Should he take this opportunity to get away from Bob? "It's not fair," he thought to himself, "that I should be punished for something that's Bob's problem, not mine."

"Let me think about it," Jason finally said, deciding not to respond out of anger. "Thanks for letting me know your concerns."

What should Jason do? What should Jason say to Mr. Johnson? Let's try to understand Bob first.

Bob's Emotional Facts

Bob jumped to the conclusion that Jason was a dangerous threat to him—his automatic Mistaken Assessment of Danger. Therefore, he felt he "had to" go to the managing editor and intensely complain about Jason, to protect himself from Jason's threat. Bob's intense complaining about his fellow worker was Bob's Behavior that's Aggressively Defensive.

Remember, Jason said, "We'll see" about returning to the office and exposing how much work they each actually did. While Jason didn't really mean to do anything at the office, and didn't have a history of complaining, he merely said it to Bob to try to slow down Bob's grandiose thinking about himself. Bob, on the other hand, took it as Negative Feedback. Bob then escalated it, by blowing it out of proportion and seeing it as an all-or-nothing situation. He truly believed he "had to" go to the managing editor.

Then Bob's brain started to generate false information about Jason. You'll notice that Bob's emotional facts were really projections from Bob's own behavior. But he can't see that. They're the first "facts" that popped into his mind, when he thought about Jason. He'll become very attached to them, especially if he's confronted with them and told he's lying.

Understanding emotional facts makes conflict resolution much simpler. When I'm in a mediation with two parties who are arguing over the facts, I don't get stuck focusing on the reality of the facts. I tell each party it's possible they are correct, but that I'll never know. Instead, I privately understand that this comes from their anxiety and may be their high-conflict thinking. So, I focus on the future and what each party can do in the future to solve the problems at hand.

Jason's Response

Jason wondered what was going on and how he could handle it—especially Bob's hateful behavior toward him. He decided to try to analyze Bob's point of view, recognizing that Bob might have some high-conflict thinking.

Jason took out a pad of paper and wrote (because, after all, he was a reporter):

Does Bob have signs of high-conflict thinking?

"Bob seems to want me fired or transferred. I wonder what he might be worried about? I've noticed others in the department try to avoid him, but I can't because we work together so often. Is it just because I'm closest to him? Does he see me as a threat? As a danger?"

Personalization? "Yes, Bob took it really personally that I said I might talk about his behavior back at the office. I guess he took this as Negative Feedback. I think I'll avoid threatening him in the future with statements like that. He seems to take every little thing as a threat to his existence. Maybe that's his All-or-Nothing Thinking. I have to empathize with how stressful and draining life must be like living inside his head."

Projection? "Yes, big time! He said I was bothering him by talking to him frequently, when in fact it's Bob who does this all the time. I guess I'll just be aware of this for the future. If he tells others that I'm at fault, I'll decide then whether to explain what's really happening. Maybe I'll get a witness to show how Bob interacts with me."

Splitting? "Yes, big time! He's presenting himself as 'all-good' to management and me (and other reporters) as 'all-bad.' It'll be important to handle this perception so that no one believes it. So far, Mr. Johnson seems to partially believe I'm at fault, but not completely. I think I need to give him a more accurate picture of what's really going on."

Emotional Reasoning? "Yes, the 'facts' he told Mr. Johnson about me were a complete projection on his part. Does he realize it? I don't know. It could be unconscious. I won't confront Bob with this projection yet, in case it's completely unconscious. He would just get extremely defensive and not do anything positive because of my feedback."

Do I have possible high-conflict thinking about this?

All-or-nothing thinking? "I guess this issue isn't the end of the world—so it's not all-or-nothing survival for me. Bob's a jerk, but it's obvious that he feels inadequate and doesn't have friends. I guess I don't have to hate him or try to be his best friend. In terms of this job, it's not my goal to stay here more than another year. I just want to build up some experience and put this paper's good name on my resume. So this issue won't determine my whole career. But I do need to improve my relationship with Mr. Johnson. I won't assume he's entirely against me. I guess I almost slipped into all-or-nothing thinking, but I think I can be more realistic and less extreme."

Personalization? "At first I was taking Bob's behavior toward me really personally, especially on our trip. I thought I had to, and could, set him straight. But now I'm starting to see that Bob has a serious problem that isn't about me, it's about everyone he deals with at work (and probably everywhere else in his life). Other reporters are irritated with him, and we've started talking about ways to avoid believing the rumors about each other that he spreads. 'Oh, that's just Bob' has become the expression around here. It sure helps to not personalize things by knowing I'm not alone in handling this."

Projecting? "I can't tell if I'm projecting anything onto Bob yet. I'll keep thinking about it."

Splitting? "I'm really tempted to say 'It's all your fault, Bob!' While I believe our department's problems are primarily because of his projections, rumors, and splitting, I also know that the company and we reporters share some responsibility for fixing this. I also recognize that Bob has a lot of good reporting skills. I just don't want to work near him much longer. I can avoid 'blaming' Bob in a negative, emotional manner, but I do believe we need to take some kind of action, or the department is going to lose some good people. I guess I'm having thoughts that aren't splitting, but healthy problem-solving. I think I'll talk to the other reporters about ideas for talking to Mr. Johnson."

Emotional Reasoning? "Just as I was writing all this down, I felt a lot less emotionally upset. I think I can work on these issues as workplace issues and not just as a personal conflict with Bob."

Jason finally decided to talk to another reporter about the problems he was seeing and to ask for his input and perspective. They agreed they didn't want to just blame Bob, but that they needed to do something soon or the office was going to lose a lot of good people. They agreed to talk together to Mr. Johnson in the near future.

The New Reporter

A new reporter joined the staff and Bob was threatened by her assertive energy and good looks. He thought it obvious that she would go far in her career. Bob suddenly found all kinds of misbehavior on her part. He complained to Mr. Johnson.

Bob: "Patty is making me uncomfortable with her sexual advances toward me. She's dressing in a very provocative way, which is making it hard for me to get my work done. I think she's having a negative influence on the other reporters. Can't you do something about this?"

Mr. Johnson: "I wasn't aware of any of these problems. I'll talk with her and see what's up."

Mr. Johnson met with Patty and found nothing out of the ordinary in her appearance or behavior. She said, "I really enjoy working here, but Bob seems kind of difficult. He's quite self-centered and preoccupied with telling me how to do my job. He seems to think he knows everything there is to know in this business. He's making me really uptight. I wouldn't be telling you this, but several other people in the department have told me he's a problem. I just thought you should know. At some point his weird sense of humor is going to go too far and someone is going to sue for sexual harassment."

Mr. Johnson had started to see some signs of these problems himself. He really wanted to avoid having to deal directly with this, since it would involve a major upheaval when his department was on the verge of financial cutbacks.

He had agreed to move Jason's cubicle away from Bob's, and he thought that would solve the problem. But now Patty was the new person next to Bob, and she had the same complaints, except she was younger and seemed to be more assertive about saying how difficult Bob was.

"Or maybe she's the problem," Mr. Johnson thought. But then her description fit what Jason had been saying. It was starting to seem more and more that Bob was a High Conflict Person, and that the situation was getting worse, not better (as HCP situations often do).

What should Mr. Johnson do? Does Bob have an "I'm Very Superior" Personality? If Mr. Johnson thinks he does, will it help him in deciding how to deal with him?

Does Bob have an "I'm Very Superior" Personality?

Does Bob have a superior self-image? From all reports, he does. This might suggest he also fears having his superior self-image challenged.

Is Bob self-absorbed? Does he demand excessive admiration? From Jason's reports, and now Patty's, he seems to have a pattern of these attitudes and behaviors. Bob posted Letters to the Editor about his great articles on the office bulletin board, which seemed to be blatant bragging. While most reporters received both positive and negative letters, Bob seemed to think his were a big deal compared to those of everyone else.

Does Bob feel entitled to special treatment? Would he feel especially hurt and enraged if he were to be seen in a negative light by Mr. Johnson? He acts as though he has a special relationship with Mr. Johnson. Mr. Johnson has a gut feeling that Bob would be really upset with *any* negative action on his part and that he would take it *very* personally.

"If this is true, any disciplinary action I take against him may trigger intense anger on Bob's part, and he may bring a lawsuit against the company in retaliation," thought Mr. Johnson.

What should he do? He's not ready to fire Bob, but he's not willing to let his behavior disrupt his department more than it already has. He decides to take action.

Conflict Resolution Training

Mr. Johnson decides to have an outside facilitator provide an all-day training on conflict resolution skills for the whole department. This would help everyone, and he thought Bob might realize there are better ways to handle his concerns. This would help avoid Bob personalizing office problems, which could help him focus on his work—which has been very good in the past.

Outcome

The reporters had a day of conflict resolution training, which actually was a great team-building experience. Everyone talked about working together more closely and giving each other more patient and respectful feedback. The only person who got nothing out of it was Bob. He complained it was meaningless and that he already "knew all that." He was superior to learning communication and conflict resolution techniques. They were a "waste of his time."

Unfortunately, another characteristic of Bob's "I'm Very Superior" personality was his tendency to exaggerate. Soon after the conflict resolution training, two other staff members noticed a serious contradiction in an article that Bob had written. It had several statements they knew had to be false. They did a little homework on their own and then brought the information to Mr. Johnson.

Setting Limits

When Mr. Johnson saw the proof of Bob's false statements, which the paper had unwittingly published, he and a security guard told Bob he was fired and escorted him and his belongings out of the building that very day. Mr. Johnson arranged to meet with him at a secure and safe location (since fired narcissists can be potentially violent) to discuss his termination and possible severance pay. He told Bob that if he agreed to sign a waiver of all claims against the company he would receive a severance package. Mr. Johnson also told him that he had a lot of writing skills and he might want to try writing some fiction. He told Bob if he wanted to stay in touch, he should feel free to call him. Bob signed the waiver and accepted the severance package. He never called Mr. Johnson.

Handling a Narcissist

Several important issues in handling Narcissists are demonstrated in this. Ironically, "I'm Very Superior" personalities can be the most sensitive of the four High Conflict Personalities. Narcissists can't handle direct criticism.

Jason avoided directly criticizing Bob. He changed the subject and always had a reason he needed to get away from him. Mr. Johnson treated Bob with respect at all times, even after he decided he needed to terminate him. He identified his strengths and complimented him, without false compliments or exaggerations. He was respectful in taking his time and giving Bob some chances to learn new skills, such as with the conflict resolution training. He went through proper procedures, and he was ready to act when a new problem, the false information, was brought to light.

With all HCPs, you never know when they'll cross the line that forces setting limits with them. In time, NPs in particular get themselves into trouble, because they're generally oblivious to the likely consequences of their risk-taking behavior. They often can't stop themselves. It helps to prepare for quick action, because sooner or later they may inadvertently expose their patterns in a very dramatic way. Alison's inability to stop herself from her own impulsive actions is another good example of this characteristic of all HCPs.

The Band

Ten years ago, Barnacle Rot was a popular young band in the seaside city where three of its members grew up together. Their careers as musicians took off when they added Rick as their lead guitar player. Rick could play, and he knew how to write songs that would sell. They became moderately successful, traveling the country and playing their very danceable music in medium-sized clubs. But troubles were brewing in the band almost from the start.

Rick saw himself as the star of the group. The others saw everyone as equal. "Here's how I want it to be…" he would start off many sentences when they were rehearsing or planning a tour. This sounds innocent enough, but it had to be his way! When the others disagreed with him, he would raise his voice until everyone else shut up. They tolerated this behavior because he was good at sensing what audiences liked. They figured this was the price of working with a very creative person.

At shows, he started to insist on playing louder than the rest of the group, and they sometimes fought over the controls of the sound. Then one day, as they were playing one of his songs, someone in the audience yelled out, "This song sucks!" Rick got angry over this. He threw down his guitar and jumped off the stage, pushing his way through the crowd to the heckler. When some people around him held him back from punching the heckler, he punched them instead. A fight broke out and the band was told to leave.

Barnacle Rot started to get a reputation as a "difficult band," and it got harder to get gigs. Finally, the three original members told Rick he had to get counseling, "You were great, man, but now you're screwing it all up. No one wants to hire us—they say that with our reputation the insurance costs too much. Get some help."

"No way! What do you mean?' he yelled. "You're the ones who are idiots. They don't want us because we sound lousy. If you had any talent, like I do, and if you would spend as much time playing as I do, then we'd be great. You're the ones who are blowing it. I have a future. If you'd only do what I tell you to do, you'd have a future too!" And he walked out.

Finally, the original three decided to fire Rick from the band. They found a new lead guitar player and set up a schedule of shows. But Rick sued the band and got a court order against them performing as Barnacle Rot while the case was pending. "I made this name. You were nothing until I came along. Just a bunch of incompetent teenagers."

When they performed, they would explain, "Someone won't let us use the name we've had for the past 10 years. Can you believe that! Someone who made our lives a living hell." While they didn't say Rick's name, everyone knew who they were talking about it. It was in the news, and both sides of the conflict were interviewed a few times about "who was to blame." The news media loved it. Rick said he had never been so humiliated in his life, and that he was going to fight hard in court to prove he was right all along.

Legally, the court decided that they were all equal partners in the business. After two years of court battles, the original three were awarded the business and the name Barnacle Rot. However, the court found that they had wrongfully terminated Rick from the band, and Rick was awarded one-quarter of the business value, which was $800,000, based on their best years—which were several years ago by that point. Finally, with their legal fees and loss of income, the other three members couldn't pay. They each declared bankruptcy and had to sell their homes.

When he was asked if he felt bad about what happened to the others, he said, "Why should I feel bad for them after what they did to me? I'm the victim here. Why should I care? Bye, bye, Barnacle Rot."

Does Rick have an "I'm Very Superior" personality pattern? Let's look for a pattern.

Does he have a very superior self-image? He wanted to play louder than the others. He said he had a future and they didn't. He was seriously offended by the heckler who seemed to suggest his music was inferior. "This song sucks!" Maybe the heckler was a real fan who liked his other songs, but not this one. It doesn't matter, because with this personality pattern, even the smallest criticism is a "narcissistic injury," as described with Jason and Bob.

Was he absorbed in himself? Remember that he often started discussions with how he wanted it to be. This is not a problem on its own, but then he wouldn't listen to the others, and insisted on doing it his way.

Did he feel entitled to special treatment and attention? He felt entitled to play louder than the others. He felt entitled to the name of the band, even though the others owned it before he joined. He felt entitled to be listened to. He felt entitled to large sums of money because of "what they did to me."

Did he lack empathy for the feelings and needs of others? His insults in calling the rest of the band "idiots" and "incompetent teenagers" showed a lack of empathy. He never apologized. He insisted they do things his way, without concern for their feelings or needs. When his former band members declared bankruptcy and lost their homes, he showed no regrets, even though he didn't have to declare bankruptcy or sell his home.

Did he take advantage of his relationships to serve his own desires? It's not clear whether he took advantage of his relationships with the others. He may have just used them to promote his own career, but they also benefited from their relationship with him.

In looking at a personality pattern, some characteristics may stand out and others might not fit. All you need to do is see if an HCP might fit one of these personality patterns. This points you toward some of the methods you might want to try in handling that particular HCP.

Mistakes Were Made

When you compare how Mr. Johnson dealt with Bob with how the band members dealt with Rick, you can see some of the mistakes the band made.

Negative Feedback vs. E.A.R.: Mr. Johnson, and eventually Jason, were careful not to give negative feedback to Bob. When Mr. Johnson fired Bob, he did it while showing Empathy, Attention, and Respect. In contrast, the band members jointly confronted Rick and told him he needed counseling. They also talked about him publicly in a very negative way.

Telling Rick he needed counseling could have been an important step, if done in a very careful way. Perhaps if the band had sought professional advice, they might have set up an Intervention, which might have gotten Rick successfully into counseling.

Then the band members publicly complained about Rick in a way that he was sure to hear about. They were venting their frustration, and hoping what they said might motivate him to get help. However, this Negative Feedback increased Rick's Mistaken Assessment of Danger and he increased his efforts to win in court—which he did! The band would've been much better off not to comment publicly. Or, if they had to say anything about Rick, tried to say something positive. They didn't realize they were dealing with a Narcissist.

Setting Limits: When Mr. Johnson set limits on Bob by firing him, he escorted him out of the building with a security guard and left no room for Bob to object. He also offered Bob the hope of severance pay. When the band fired Rick, they simply reacted. They didn't consider the possibility that they could owe him one-quarter of the value of the band. They should have consulted an attorney or business advisor before doing anything rash.

They also should have offered him some hope if he cooperated with them, like a monetary payment. Instead, they set limits, but without thinking about how powerless they were to get him out of their band and their lives. Often, with any High Conflict Personality, your efforts to get them out of your life actually creates conflict that brings them in closer. HCPs don't let go easily. Their conflicts are all about relationships. Setting limits must be done carefully and with enough power that the HCP doesn't come back to haunt you. That power comes with understanding how HCPs think, so read on!

News Flash (A Family Matter)

Isaac Stern was a world-famous violin player. He died in 2001. He had been married three times and during the probate of his estate there were family conflicts. After several years of litigation, the court punished the executor of Isaac's estate for improper actions. Here's the final outcome from the news on May 6, 2005:

> A probate court judge in New Milford, Conn., has ordered the former executor of Isaac Stern's estate to pay Stern's children hundreds of thousands of dollars, The Associated Press reported yesterday. The three adult children, from Stern's second marriage, had sued the former executor, William Moorhead III, for more than $2 million, contending that he had improperly valued the estate and transferred assets to the third wife of the violinist. Judge Martin Landgrebe also criticized Mr. Moorhead for paying himself $313,000, calling it "outrageous, improper and unjustified." He ordered that the money be repaid, along with $250,000 spent on a Central Park West apartment used by Mr. Moorhead as an office from which to manage the estate. The judge also said that selling items like violins that had been bequeathed to the children caused them to suffer "incalculable personal loss."
>
> From The New York Times on the Web © The New York Times Company. Reprinted with Permission.

Analysis

Does the executor have any "I'm Very Superior" personality patterns? I'll let you decide.

Does he have a very superior self-image, driven by a Fear of Being Inferior? It's hard to know from this short article.

Was he absorbed in himself? This is also hard to know.

Did he feel entitled to special treatment and attention? Did he treat himself to other people's money and assets (like use of the expensive Central Park West apartment)?

Did he lack empathy for the feelings and needs of others? Did he seem concerned about how the children might feel having their father's irreplaceable items, like prized violins, sold instead of given to them?

Did he take advantage of his relationships to serve his own desires? Do you see any evidence that he used his position as executor to serve his own interests?

Remember, if people have some of these characteristics, you might want to handle them as if they have this type of HCP pattern and deal with them accordingly. In this case, did his children focus on giving the executor Empathy, Attention, and Respect? By the time of this lawsuit, it's unlikely, although they may have tried E.A.R. In this case, it appears they focused on Setting Limits, which is often necessarily done by the courts, because the executor seemed unable to stop himself.

The Doctor

As I said at the beginning of this Tip, many professionals have some traits of narcissism, which may help them succeed in their careers—as long as those traits don't become maladaptive. One profession that is examining itself a lot these days is the medical profession, especially regarding doctor behavior.

In his best-selling book, Blink, Malcolm Gladwell described a study of which doctors get sued and which ones don't. If you agree with my HCP theory that high-conflict cases are not driven by issues, but by high-conflict personalities, you won't be surprised by the results of the study. The study found that the biggest factor in whether a doctor got sued was his or her *relationship* with the patient, not whether mistakes were made.

The doctors who didn't get sued spoke respectfully to their patients, listened, and paid attention to patients for at least three more minutes per visit than the doctors who got sued. The essence of the research study showed that tone of voice was the biggest factor—it didn't even matter what the doctor said! What mattered was the way the doctor said it. If the doctor's *tone of voice* was less "dominant" and "more concerned," the doctor was much less likely to get sued (Gladwell, 2005).

Doctors who don't get sued sound like they have empathy for their patients and are the opposite of someone with Narcissistic Personality Disorder. But what happens, or should happen, to a doctor who has NPD? Is there treatment? Is anyone Setting Limits?

In the case of Kirbens v. Wyoming State Board of Medicine (1999), the doctor was a surgeon who was eventually diagnosed with a Narcissistic Personality Disorder. The following description comes from his appeal to the Wyoming State Supreme Court. I have made some very minor edits to the court opinion to make it easier to read.

> The Board concluded that Dr. Kirbens had violated several provisions of the Medical Act by performing inappropriate or unnecessary surgeries upon several patients. Dr. Kirbens' physician, Dr. Irons, testified that, in his opinion, Dr. Kirbens can't practice medicine with reasonable skill and safety and poses a significant risk to the health and safety of others by virtue of his disability. From hospital records of adverse actions against Dr. Kirbens, the Board concluded two hospitals suspended his privileges because of either possible incompetence or misconduct. (Kirbens v. Wyoming State Board of Medicine, 1999)

Dr. Kirbens also had a bipolar disorder, which generally includes a few months of depression followed by a few weeks of somewhat manic (inappropriately exaggerated high energy) behavior. Bipolar disorders can generally be treated with medications, so these disorders don't necessarily interfere with a person's ability to work. However, Narcissistic Personality Disorder doesn't have a medication treatment at this time. So when people have both of these problems, the personality disorder usually remains the biggest problem.

In this case, in 1997, one of the hospitals suspended Dr. Kirbens for an indefinite period. Then another hospital reported that he'd violated state medical practice law and a patient died. "In July of 1997, Kirbens agreed to temporary restrictions on his practice, including a prohibition from surgical or invasive procedures" (Kirbens v. Wyoming State Board of Medicine, 1999).

After that, more patients were listed as being harmed by Dr. Kirbens. What should be done? Here are the steps Dr. Kirbens went through:

> In early November, 1997, Dr. Kirbens attended a Professional Assessment Program for alcohol and drug screening. Those results proved negative [apparently he didn't have an alcohol or drug problem], and the program recommended that Dr. Kirbens enter a Physicians in Crisis Program. He did so on December 15, 1997. In a letter dated December 31, 1997, Dr. Richard R. Irons stated that he had diagnosed Dr. Kirbens with bipolar affective disorder Type II and **narcissistic personality disorder** and was treating him for these conditions. (Kirbens v. Wyoming State Board of Medicine, 1999, 1058) (Emphasis added)

So Kirbens' problem was recognized and he was receiving treatment. Do you think he should be allowed to go back to work as a surgeon? If not now, when? Do you think he should ever work as a surgeon again? As a doctor of any kind? These are important questions regarding the future employment of anyone with a diagnosis of a personality disorder. Certainly if they don't submit to treatment, their long-term personality pattern of difficulties will continue and may get worse. But what if they've been clearly diagnosed with NPD and are receiving treatment for it?

A Survey Of What To Do

In a 2004 survey, medical center executives were asked how they handle "problem" doctors. Seventy percent of the executives said it was the same doctors over and over again who had behavior problems. These problems included:

- Disrespecting others
- Refusing to do tasks
- Yelling
- Insulting others

Does any of this fit the characteristics of the "I'm Very Superior" personality pattern described at the beginning of this Tip? Disrespecting and insulting others is extremely common in high-conflict disputes with "I'm Very Superior" personalities. And regularly showing arrogant behaviors and attitudes are a specific symptom of Narcissistic Personality Disorder.

This survey indicated that most doctors behave appropriately throughout their careers. However, they recognized that some doctors repeatedly violated the rules and standards for ordinary social behavior. These are known as "disruptive physicians." Many or most of these disruptive physicians were considered to have personality disorders. Medical center executives are recognizing this problem and are beginning to get more training in dealing with personality disorders. They said the people most often on the receiving end of problem behaviors aren't patients, but people just below the physician in the chain of command, such as nurses and support staff—these people become Targets of Blame.

In handling these problem doctors, two-thirds were given written warnings and roughly half were required to get counseling. Some were suspended, given probation, limited in their practices, reported to state boards, and/or given financial penalties. Most of the executives reported that these interventions were successful, at least part of the time, but about one-third of the HCP doctors were fired. Finally, some medical center executives admitted they did nothing and tried to avoid the problem (Weber, 2004).

Setting Limits

How did Dr. Kirbens' case turn out?

> On January 6, 1998, Dr. Kirbens claimed that the applicable Wyoming statute authorized voluntary relinquishment and requested the Board to allow him to relinquish his license, or alternatively, to agree to a temporary suspension.... He asserted that he was an impaired physician because he could not practice medicine with reasonable skill and safety due to mental illness or physical illness.... At the hearing, he admitted wrongful acts that he claimed were not intentional or willful and requested the Board's help with his physical and mental impairment....

> His own doctor recommended that Dr. Kirbens not practice medicine in any form **at this time....**

> However, the Board revoked Dr. Kirbens' medical license and ordered he pay a civil penalty of $5,000.00. (Kirbens v. Wyoming State Board of Medicine, 1999, 1058-59)

The Wyoming Supreme Court upheld the Board's decision to revoke Dr. Kirbens' medical license. You might wonder why the Board and the Supreme Court would object to him voluntarily relinquishing his license. It appears they wanted to take it away. If Dr. Kirbens voluntarily gave up his license, it might leave the door open for him to get it back and practice medicine again in any form in the future. In this case, they found "that Dr. Kirbens' actions were not accidental, and were, therefore, willful actions in violation of the statute." They also determined that his actions were not caused by a disability and therefore were not protected under the Americans with Disabilities Act.

The result was that Kirbens could not practice any form of medicine again. This answered the question about whether he could return to work as a surgeon or any other type of doctor. But this outcome isn't always the case for problem doctors. In response to the 2004 Medical Executives' Survey, one physician executive described his own experience. He stated that two supervisory colleagues confronted him in a sensitive manner and established boundaries for his performance while he learned about himself and corrected his past poor behavior. He acknowledged that he'd become a better leader in dealing with other problem doctors. He emphasized the importance of treating them sensitively and professionally, while not tolerating improper behavior.

Conclusion

In most of the cases so far in this book, the relationship with the HCP has been terminated. In workplace examples, the HCP has been fired. However, as a Target of Blame you may not have the power to do that, or it may not always need to be the case. In some cases, requiring the HCP to get counseling has worked, including Alison in Tip #3 and some of the doctors described in the survey in this Tip. However, this is a power that an employer or the legal system may have, but a power that most Targets of Blame don't have. Yet you may have personal power to set limits on your own relationship with the HCP. Sometimes that power lets you encourage the HCP to get counseling—"to deal with the stress that you're under." Sometimes, little things can make a big difference, as described below.

A Question

Suppose you work at a job with several cubicles next to each other. Suppose that the person in the next cubicle, Chris, argues loudly on the phone on a regular basis, disturbing your work. If you've already determined that Chris has an I'm Very Superior personality, which approach might be most successful?

A. Tell Chris to SHUT UP!

B. Humorously wave to Chris with both hands to lower his voice when it happens.

C. Ask to have your desk moved farther away from Chris.

D. Talk to your supervisor about telling Chris to lower his voice.

E. Talk to several co-workers and jointly tell Chris to quiet down.

As always, there's no absolutely correct answer when it comes to HCPs. In general, I would start with "*B*," because it doesn't escalate Chris, is humorous, and doesn't involve other people in the department. Depending on how severely Chris is an HCP, he may be able to change his own behavior a little and the problem will be solved. However, if you have already determined that he has an "I'm Very Superior" personality, then he may not change his behavior and you might try another approach.

Try *D. Talk to your supervisor about telling Chris to lower his voice.* Do this if you think you can convince your supervisor that Chris's behavior is a problem. You don't want to hide the realities of Chris's difficult behavior from your employer, and you may not be the only one reporting a problem. A stronger action may be taken by your supervisor if the behavior keeps up.

Try *C. Ask to have your desk moved farther away from Chris.* But do this only if you think your employer will not blame *you* for being difficult. Setting personal limits on your physical contact by moving might be the most realistic approach to solving this problem.

A. Tell Chris to SHUT UP! Of course, this rarely works with HCPs. While this might work with the average person, Narcissists take criticism extremely personally and he's likely to escalate it into a major battle that you'll regret.

E. Talk to several co-workers and jointly tell Chris to quiet down. This is likely to escalate Chris rather than change his behavior. When a peer group confronts an HCP, it triggers a greater Mistaken Assessment of Danger, because it appears more threatening than when an individual approaches him. One or two people in authority are usually much more effective in getting behavior to change. This was what worked for the last doctor described above.

Don't Diss the Narcissists

Narcissists seem driven to invite criticism. They're insulting, demanding, arrogant, self-absorbed, and lack empathy. It's natural to feel like "putting them down" as strongly as you can. However, this Negative Feedback doesn't work. Instead, it triggers their Mistaken Assessment of Danger and escalates them into higher and higher conflict behavior.

While it isn't obvious from their behavior, they're actually extremely vulnerable. This is one of the greatest misunderstandings about Narcissists. They may appear strong, but they become very defensive if their superiority is challenged. The "I'm Very Superior" personality is a thin shell for a potentially very defensive and vulnerable person. But this is so far removed from their conscious thinking and tough-sounding behavior that they (and, perhaps, you) may never believe it.

Particularly avoid Negative Feedback with Narcissists. They rapidly increase their Behavior that's Aggressively Defensive with surprising intensity, because they believe they are supposed to be treated as superior and beyond criticism.

Handling Narcissistic HCPs

If you're a Target of Blame and not in a position of power over a Narcissist, there are still things that you can do with the power you have.

1. **Find their strengths and regularly compliment them.** It doesn't cost you anything to give a Narcissist a compliment, even though it may feel like the last thing you want to do. Compliments are like food to Narcissists, and they're always starved for them. Make sure not to exaggerate or make false compliments. This will only set you up for future conflicts when the Narcissist starts telling others of your compliment.

2. **Remind yourself to resist the urge to "put them down."** It's human nature to put down those who act superior without deserving it. In our democratic culture—whether in your neighborhood or in your workplace—no one likes people who put themselves above everyone else. Even highly successful people respect others and avoid seeking too much praise. Narcissists stand out in this culture, and they make easy targets. Resist the urge, or the Narcissist may come back to bite you.

3. **Don't withhold your empathy, attention, and respect.** We're tempted to punish Narcissists by withholding our Empathy, Attention, and Respect. They may be the ones who need it the most and who are hammering you with obnoxious, self-defeating behavior just to get it from you. Surprise them and just give them your E.A.R. It will save you time—and from being hammered.

4. **Keep an arm's length relationship.** As with the other High Conflict Personalities, make sure to keep a comfortable distance. Don't be too impressed at the start of your relationship, or Narcissists will come to depend on you to give them endless flattering attention. Also, avoid being too rejecting of Narcissists.

They'll take it as a personal insult and "narcissistic injury." Just find a reasonable middle ground that can help you contain the Narcissist while going about your business.

5. **Don't feel like you have to listen too long.** Narcissists are eager for your attention and often won't let go of it. Practice setting limits on your conversations by having another activity that you need to do. Listen attentively for a few minutes, then let them know you have to go. Then, with confidence, get to your next activity. If you waver, they'll keep you in their grip. The exception to this rule is if you're an official of some kind and you're only going to have one meeting with a Narcissist. In this case, it often helps to make the meeting as long as possible so they can get everything off their chest and not feel rushed or cut off. With this openness, they usually relax a bit and don't need as much time.

6. **Use indirect reasons for changing behavior.** If you must try to get a Narcissist to act differently, focus on a reason for doing it that is outside of your relationship. "The homeowners association has a policy that requires you to do XYZ." "Our company won't allow us to do ABC." "You'll really impress everyone in the neighborhood if you install this type of fence" (without saying: "instead of the one you're considering"). This helps the Narcissist save face. Just focus on the new, good behavior, without pointing out that the prior behavior was bad.

7. **Explain the possible negative consequences of certain behavior.** Narcissists are often preoccupied with the moment and their perceived status and respect. They often overlook the consequences of their immediate actions. Sometimes educating a Narcissist about the possible consequences is a surprise. "I hadn't thought about that," he or she might say. Pointing out positive consequences of planning may be helpful. Of course, much of this may have no impact. If Narcissists feel that you're sincerely trying to help them, they might listen. Otherwise, don't bother lecturing or talking down to a Narcissist—they can't handle it and they'll just attack you back.

TIP #4 SUMMARY

Don't Diss The Narcissists

Characteristics

1. Narcissists have an unconscious fear of being seen as inferior.

2. Narcissists are very self-centered and self-absorbed.

3. Narcissists expect special, superior treatment.

4. Narcissists react extremely negatively to any Negative Feedback.

5. Narcissists exhibit frequent disrespect and disdain for others.

Managing Narcissistic HCPs

1. Recognize real strengths and accomplishments.

2. Listen with empathy.

3. Keep an arm's length relationship.

4. Use indirect, positive reasons for changing behavior.

5. Explain the consequences of various courses of action.

6. If possible, take action to get the person into some form of treatment to change behavior.

7. Set limits on the relationship, or carefully terminate it if appropriate.

Tip #5: Don't Get Hooked by Histrionics

CHAPTER

5

TIP #5
Don't Get Hooked By Histrionics

"Either you're with me or you're against me!" Carlos, age 38, screamed into the telephone at his sister, Maria, age 42. "People listen to you," he said. "It's all your fault I lost my job! You should have talked to my boss and helped clear up his false impressions of me, like I asked you to."

"Carlos, you're responsible for your own life. I can't fix every problem you get yourself into. It's not my fault. It's your fault. It's your life and your responsibility," Maria replied.

"See how you talk to me!" Carlos replied angrily. "It's true you never cared about me or what happened to me. You never wanted a younger brother."

"That's not true, and you know it!" Maria responded in exasperation.

Carlos continued, "So, since I'm losing my job, I'm also losing my house. You have to let me stay with you, again. If you'd helped me keep my job, this wouldn't be your problem. But now it is your problem, and you have to fix it. So starting on the first of the month, I'll be moving in again."

"Don't try to blame me for this, Carlos." she replied. "Remember the time I helped you out by going to the Homeowners' Association meeting?"

"Yeah.... Don't remind me of the worst period of my life," he replied.

"And one of mine too. I was so embarrassed when I got the full story after defending you at that public meeting. Remember? You told me your neighbors were making noises in the middle of the night, keeping bright lights on that poured into your bedroom, and making harassing phone calls to you. Boy, was I embarrassed when I found out that those neighbors hadn't been home for weeks, and were away on vacation the whole month you complained about. And a dozen neighbors wrote letters to prove it. I'm not going through that again. And you're not moving back in with me either."

"You know they were all lying! They were just out to get me. You should never have believed them. It was a conspiracy to get me out of the community. Now, you've got to let me live with you again! You have to! It's all your fault this is happening to me. If it wasn't always you were the good kid and I was the bad kid when we were growing up, this never would have happened to me. You owe it to me."

At that point, Maria felt a pang of guilt. It was true that their mother favored her. Their mother always seemed to pick on Carlos and give Maria all the breaks. That's when this all started, she thought to herself. Maybe I should help him out one more time.

"I'll think about it, Carlos," Maria replied reluctantly. "I'll have to think about it."

Histrionic "Always Dramatic" personalities can be extremely irritating with their high-intensity emotions and constant claims of crises. However, these histrionic emotions change rapidly. They're all on the surface, with no real substance to justify them. Listening to them, you tend to feel wound up, with no place to go.

In extreme cases, these "Always Dramatic" personalities have Histrionic Personality Disorder (HPD). In 1994, the American Psychiatric Association estimated that approximately 2 to 3% of the general population of the United States has HPD, with the majority being women (APA, 2000). However, while the 2004 NIH study confirmed that those with HPD are about 2% of the population, it indicated that those with HPD are equally men and women. Perhaps this difference is because of the study itself, or perhaps men have caught up to women in being histrionic in the past 10 years.

The pattern of Histrionic personalities includes:

• A drive to be the center of attention, because of intense Fear of Being Ignored.

• Being dramatic and theatrical, with intense shifting emotions, but few facts and little focus.

• Exaggerating and sometimes fabricating events.

• Difficulty focusing on tasks or making decisions.

Histrionics are hard to miss. They're always trying to get your attention. At times you may feel like you're witnessing a performance rather than an authentic interaction with the person. If you feel a lack of empathy for the dramatic display of distress by someone, it may be an indicator of Histrionic Personality Disorder (Beck & Freeman, 1990). If the person seems proud of or excited by a description of traumatic experiences, this may be a further indication of HPD.

Superficial Relationships

Histrionics operate so much on the emotional surface that relationships with them are difficult and superficial. Those close to a Histrionic usually maintain an emotional distance while dealing with them and the problems they cause. Those who remain in their lives often become resigned to letting someone else's crises be the focus of their lives.

Histrionics can be fascinating and exciting. Friendships and romantic relationships with Histrionics usually start intensely, but end up as disasters. They may be stormy for years, then have dramatic endings. Temper tantrums, manipulations, and angry outbursts can be common.

A Histrionic may use emotions to get your attention, to make countless demands on you, and to try to persuade you of something. However, these emotions are generally more superficial and unfocused than the intense emotions of someone with Borderline Personality Disorder.

Histrionics may seek out authority figures to help them solve problems, then become easily disappointed. They're very suggestible and may incorporate recent news events into their own stories of harrowing experiences. In legal disputes, they may allege that they are victims of the latest abuse trend in the news.

Fabrication, or making things up, is common and appears in a range of behaviors, from simple exaggeration to the complete description of nonexistent events. Researchers describe many Histrionics as unconcerned about truthful details if distortion does a better job (Ford, 1996).

While noted for their skills at lying, Histrionics are generally not considered to have the same hostile motivations as those with Antisocial personalities. However, some researchers have found a close similarity with antisocial behavior for some Histrionics. Apparently some prisoners, when deprived of the ability to engage in antisocial behaviors like lying and cheating, will shift to Histrionic crying and whining behaviors instead (Ford, 1996).

Generally, this deceitfulness is intended to get people to pay attention to them or to like them. However, since most of their emotions are simply on the surface, their deception and shallowness eventually anger or irritate most people—who then try to escape being around them. True intimacy is unlikely for Histrionics. They deceive themselves as much as anyone.

High Conflict Dynamics

Neighborhood and workplace disputes may give the Histrionic a great opportunity to get attention for no real reason. Their complaints may draw attention, but then turn out to lack any real substance. Histrionics can alienate people around them quicker than most HCPs. Their constant emotional alarm-sounding pushes most people away, fast.

Those with HPD may attempt to shock or surprise family, friends, neighbors, co-workers, and professionals with provocative behavior or with reports of provocative behavior by others. Disputes are often marked by frequent crises, emergency phone calls, or sudden appearances by the HP and dramatic reports of someone else's misbehavior. However, the Histrionic's emotions and provocations are usually the source of the problem—the other people's behavior often doesn't fit the dramatic complaints.

Carlos's Email

Carlos sent Maria a not-very-subtle email:

"MARIA, YOU JUST DON'T GET IT! YOU HAVE TO HELP ME OUT. IT'S YOUR RESPONSIBILITY AS MY SISTER, AND YOU KNOW IT. FAMILIES HELP EACH OTHER OUT IN TIMES OF NEED. AND I'M DESPERATE NOW. REALLY, REALLY DESPERATE. I DON'T SEE HOW YOU CAN FACE YOURSELF IN THE MORNING, KNOWING THAT I'M GOING TO BE LIVING ON THE STREETS WHILE YOU HAVE YOUR COMFORTABLE HOME. HOW DO YOU THINK IT MAKES ME FEEL, THAT YOU SPENT MONEY ON REMODELING YOUR BATHROOMS, BUT YOU WON'T EVEN LET ME—YOUR OWN LITTLE BROTHER—USE THEM! HOW CAN YOU SAY I DON'T MATTER TO YOU? THAT I'M JUST A SPECK IN YOUR UNIVERSE? YOU'RE SO SELF-CENTERED, MARIA, I'M ASHAMED TO HAVE YOU FOR MY SISTER. IF YOU HAD ANY SENSE IN YOUR SWELLED HEAD, YOU'D REALIZE THAT THERE'S ONLY ONE RIGHT THING TO DO. YOU HAVE TO LET ME LIVE WITH YOU! IT'LL JUST BE FOR A LITTLE WHILE, UNTIL I GET ON MY FEET AGAIN. DON'T BE STUPID ABOUT IT. JUST GET OVER IT AND TELL ME WHEN I CAN MOVE MY STUFF INTO YOUR GARAGE."

A little upset, would you say? Do you think he wrote the email capitalized, bolded, and underlined because he was upset about his present situation? No, he always writes this way—to get people's attention, he hopes. While some people emphasize a word or two with bold or underlines from time to time (I know I'm guilty of that), he always writes his way. If you ask him how upset he is on a scale of 0 to 100, he'll tell you 1,000!

He's a bit dramatic, and it has little to do with what's happening in his life right now. This is his life-long high-conflict thinking. In response to his unconscious Mistaken Assessment of Danger, his Behavior that's Aggressively Defensive is dramatic verbal (and email) attacks. He's constantly—and superficially—emotional.

Ironically, after receiving what she calls his "wall of anger" on a regular basis, Maria has tuned out most of this intensity. In fact, she now takes off the all-caps, bold and underline before she reads his letters—one of the benefits of computers. But don't tell him that.

Did you notice the words he used? He said she didn't "get it," that she should "get over it," that she was avoiding "your responsibility." Ironically, HCPs frequently speak in these blaming terms that more realistically apply to themselves. Remember, they get it backwards. They truly think this way because they're projecting what they can't see in themselves onto the people around them.

While this can be especially irritating, it also gives you some clues as to what their hidden issues may be. It's presented in such a superficial flurry of phrases that it doesn't mean anything, but it sounds like it does. To the unaware bystander, it could sound very convincing and other people could think that it sounds like Maria is the one with the problem.

So, how should Maria respond? She's really feeling defensive. She didn't say he was a "speck in her universe." Her bathrooms were badly in need of repair. And after taking so much care of her mother and her brother her whole life, the accusation that she was self-centered really bugged her. She doesn't realize this is his projection onto her, so she feels she has to defend herself.

> "I think he needs to be set straight. He can't treat me this way. I'm going to tell him who's self-centered," she thought to herself. She started writing her own angry email, but then stopped and thought, "What do I really want out of this? I guess I really want him to focus on what to do next, since there's no way I'm letting him live here." Then she composed a different email.

Maria's Response

"Hi Carlos. I got your email. I was thinking you should get a newspaper and make a list of the rentals in your area. Do you think you would rather live with a roommate during this transition, or get a smaller place on your own? If you want to show me the list, I can help you make some phone calls."

And that was it. That was all she wrote. I'll bet this isn't the email you expected her to send. Short and to the point! She didn't engage with him in a negative exchange—despite how hard he tried to engage her. She set limits on the emotional discussion by focusing on "What's the Next Task?" She didn't defend herself because she didn't take it personally. At 42, she's slowly becoming aware that she doesn't need to defend herself. She's not going to change Carlos with an angry reply. She also didn't emphasize that she didn't want him living with her. She sidestepped the issue. It was unnecessary to rub it in and trigger his negative emotions again.

She gave him a very specific suggestion (to make a list of possible rentals), which he may or may not reject. I've seen many cases in which HCPs did use the suggestion because they didn't know what else to do. Many HCPs can't focus themselves, and so they take suggestions, but only when presented without negative comments. On the other hand, some HCPs will react negatively to any suggestions. It doesn't hurt to try in most cases. She also let him know that she would help, so it became a task for both of them. This isn't necessary, but in this case Maria thought it might ease things a bit. We'll see.

Persuasive Blamers

All HCPs can be Persuasive Blamers, but Histrionics can be especially persuasive because of their steady flow of high-intensity emotions. Our brains, especially our right brains, are highly sensitive to the emotions of others—especially alarm-sounding emotions. When combined with information that someone (a Target) has harmed the emotional person (a Histrionic), these emotions can unconsciously persuade you that it's true.

The following pattern has the familiar dynamics I've observed in many high-conflict disputes:

1. Histrionic personalities are driven by their strong emotions, and the intensity of their emotions can make them look, act, and sound like victims.

2. People today are especially concerned about helping victims and punishing perpetrators, so they're especially vulnerable to the dramatic stories of Histrionics.

3. Histrionic personalities are constantly bending or fabricating emotional facts. They often don't know where the line is between true and false—it's all *unconsciously* based on dramatic effect; whatever works to meet the immediate felt need. False allegations can be made quickly, but getting the full facts can take months or even years.

4. High-conflict disputes with a Histrionic often look like two HCPs fighting, even when there's just one. From the outside, it could look like two people who like to bicker. Whenever you point out that the HCP is lying, he or she will simply reverse the allegation and say you're lying.

5. Eventually, those near the dispute start to understand: one person is acting inappropriately and the other is being falsely accused. Once this conclusion is finally reached (which can sometimes take months or years), the conflict typically stops escalating and the Histrionic person moves on to find new listeners.

Trying an Intervention

Maria was seeing a therapist to help her cope with the stress of Carlos's emotional demands and high-conflict behavior. Her therapist suggested an Intervention, which is an approach that's been used for many years in getting alcoholics and addicts into treatment. This approach is just beginning to be used in getting those with personality disorders into treatment (U.S. Journal Training, 2007).

An Intervention is done with a mental health professional who directs a very structured meeting with the disordered person and all of the closest people in his or her life. A famous example of an Intervention occurred in the 1970s with Betty Ford, the wife of President Gerald Ford. This Intervention got her into alcoholism treatment with great long-term success. During that Intervention, everyone in her close family shared their love for her as well as their sadness and concern for her disordered behavior (alcoholism and pill addiction). They required her either to immediately go into a treatment program or to lose their support.

An Intervention requires a lot of pre-planning. The mental health professional must take time to explain the process to the family and friends who will be participating. Then they practice what they're going to say so that it is supportive and non-blaming, but focused on the facts of the person's behavior that needs treatment. There usually is a plan for immediately going into an in-patient treatment program. This is so that the person doesn't have time to change her or his mind before going into treatment.

Unfortunately, at this time, in-patient treatment programs are not available for treating personality disorders unless there is also another mental health problem, because in-patient treatment programs are very expensive and health insurance plans don't pay for treating personality disorders (yet!). But there are some outpatient programs, such as Dialectical Behavior Therapy (DBT) for Borderline Personality Disorder. An Intervention may help if you know of a program to send the person to in your area.

An Intervention is a strong approach for setting limits on strong problems. No one attacks the person—they share their love and the hopes they have for the person if the person gets treatment. But they explain that they can't continue to support the person's behavior if they don't get treatment. They also state that, without immediate treatment, they may withdraw all financial and personal support, and possibly social contact. Successful Interventions are fully prepared for either outcome—full cooperation or total non-cooperation—with a plan of action for each possibility.

I have explained the basics of this approach, but it shouldn't be used with an HCP unless you have the assistance and guidance of a mental health professional who understands the issues, resources, and potential problems that can occur. You generally have only one shot at an Intervention.

Maria's Invitation

Maria: "Carlos, I want you to meet with me and Mom and my therapist. It'll just be an hour, and I can give you a ride."

Carlos: "What for? I don't need a therapist, you do."

Maria: "You're right, I need this therapist and if you come to meet with us it will help me in my therapy. It's just for this one meeting."

Carlos: "What the hell kind of meeting do I need? You're killing me, Maria, by not letting me move back in with you—just for a little while. Probably just a month."

Maria: "It's just one meeting, for just one hour, to help me in my therapy."

Carlos: "You don't get it, Maria. I don't need your %#$"+* meeting. You're the one who needs help. You really have to choose if you're with me or you're against me. It sounds like you're not with me, so you must be against me."

Maria: "Would it help if I picked you up and gave you a ride?"

Carlos: "Not at all. I still have a car. These gas prices are killing me, too. After my last paycheck, I'll probably have to start walking everywhere. And then I'll be living on the street. DO YOU WANT ME LIVING ON THE STREET, MARIA? IT WOULD BE YOUR FAULT!"

Maria: "So, you don't want me to give you a ride? Okay."

Carlos: "Of course not. You don't think I can take care of myself enough to drive around town? Maybe that's it, I'LL LIVE IN MY CAR, MARIA."

Maria: "Okay, that's enough for now. I'm going to get off for now. If you want to talk further about a meeting with me and Mom and my therapist, give me a call. Goodbye, Carlos."

Maria did pretty well at being persistent and setting limits on what she would discuss during that phone call. She expected she would have to keep her request firm and consistent. Carlos provided a good example of a Histrionic with one emotion rapidly shifting to the next, constantly changing subjects as he went. Getting Carlos to therapy wasn't working, so Maria dropped the subject. She didn't want to lock in his resistance. When you push too hard or too long with an HCP of any type, you build up more and more resistance and resentment. Don't fight battles you can't win with HCPs. Get in to the discussion and then get out of the discussion.

Does Carlos have an "Always Dramatic" Personality?

Is Carlos's way of speaking and writing filled with high-intensity, shifting emotions? It sure seems that way. Look at how he answered her question about needing a ride by yelling at her that he'd be living on the street. The drama and escalation of blame are very fast, and then he's on to his next topic.

Does he lack detail and have a hard time focusing? We have very few details about what's happening for him. He says he'll have a severance package from his job, but then jumps to the conclusion that he'll be living on the street. He gives no explanation of how these events are connected. He does stay focused on wanting to live with Maria, but she has already said no and he's having trouble focusing on other alternatives.

Is he exaggerating or fabricating events? It does seem that he makes himself into a helpless victim very quickly. Sometimes, Histrionics complain so much that they start to believe their complaints, or the line gets blurred and they defend them as if they were true. The shakier Carlos' story, the more he'll add drama to make it sound true.

Is he trying to be the center of attention? When he talks with Maria or emails her, his emotions rule the day. He's not at all interested in what's going on for her. No questions asked. Instead, he uses his comments about their childhood against her—whether they're accurate or not. It certainly seems like he's the center of attention in all their interactions, and his emotions certainly keep it that way.

You might ask: How is Carlos different from a Borderline? His anger is fleeting and loud, though he's not raging and focused, which Borderlines can be. But that's a good question. He does have a lot of anger, but he's not likely to be organized about taking action against her if he feels abandoned. If he was a Borderline, she might need to worry about him attacking her more viciously for not letting him live with her. But this is rarely clear-cut. Maybe he has Borderline traits.

You might ask: How is Carlos different from a Narcissist? He's self-centered. He doesn't seem to care about his relationship with Maria. He just wants to stay at her house. He wants special treatment because he's been a victim of his employer, he says. But he doesn't seem so much arrogant as pleading and dramatic. He doesn't seem to act superior, he just wants what he wants. In fact, he blames Maria for thinking she's superior because her life is well-organized, while his is not. Of course, he could be projecting his own sense of superiority. Maybe he has some Narcissistic traits.

These are interesting questions, but not essential to handling Carlos. Remember my cautions at the beginning of this book. You're not being trained in diagnosis here. I'm just letting you know some common HCP patterns so you can be aware that they exist and that you're not alone in dealing with them. Also, many HCPs have traits of two or more personality disorders. However, using the four approaches described in Part II of this book should help regardless of which or how many of these four high-conflict personalities you are facing. When in doubt, you can usually use Empathy, Attention, and Respect to calm down any High Conflict Person.

In handling a Histrionic, it is especially important to choose your battles. Otherwise, you'll become exhausted. It's natural and almost unavoidable. If you realize you're exhausted, start choosing your battles. Even though you'll be tempted to respond to every emotionally intense complaint, you don't have to. In fact, you don't have to respond to any of their emotional complaints. You can choose your battles.

A Question

Maria was exhausted. She couldn't decide what to do next, so she wrote down a list of her options. Which option do you think is the most realistic for Maria?

A. Tell Carlos that he can move back into her home.

B. Tell Carlos that she never wants to see him again.

C. Tell Carlos that she'll only talk with him at her therapist's office.

D. Simply stop talking or communicating with Carlos.

E. Give Carlos money for 3 months' rent.

If you said "C," I'd agree with you. By keeping the door open to communication, she's not cutting him off if he takes this positive small step. Yet she's also setting a clear limit by not talking to him by any other means. This is also less likely to trigger his sense of danger in being cut off.

A. Tell Carlos that he can move back into her home. Giving in and letting Carlos move in will only reinforce his emotional pressure because it will have worked again. It will encourage Carlos to keep badgering his sister in the future if she says no to him – as she did at first in this case. And she will regret every day that she lives with his emotional intensity right in her face in her home.

B. Tell Carlos that she never wants to see him again. Given how ambivalent Maria has felt, she's unlikely to stick with such an extreme option as telling Carlos she'll never see him again. This is also not necessary, as "C" has the same effect but leaves him with the opportunity to resume contact if he goes to the therapist's office. This announcement will definitely trigger his Mistaken Assessment of Danger because he's so dependent on Maria.

D. *Simply stop talking or communicating with Carlos.* If she stops talking or communicating with Carlos, it'll have the same effect as "B." She's unlikely to stick with it. This approach is unnecessary and undesirable if he takes the positive step of going to the therapist's office. While it's certainly understandable that she might feel like taking this all-or-nothing step, it'll escalate his Mistaken Assessment of Danger and he's likely to engage in Behaviors that are Aggressively Defensive (such as camping on her doorstep), which will make her life even more difficult.

E. *Give Carlos money for 3 months' rent.* Giving Carlos money would be another reversal for Maria that reinforces the problem, as described in "A." However, sometimes it's a realistic choice (although a less desirable one), especially if she can stick with it and limit the amount to three months as she has said. My experience is that providing money for consumer needs would have no helpful impact because he hasn't changed his behavior to receive this money, and unless he changes his behavior his problems will continue unchanged. Better to provide money for a therapist or treatment program, as that's an investment in his future behavior change and he'll have to put energy into making changes to keep that money coming.

Maria's Choice

Since she couldn't get Carlos to go to her therapist to try an Intervention, she decided to choose "C." She would tell Carlos that she'll only have contact with him at her therapist's office. She talked it over with her therapist. She talked it over with her mother, who she knew would disagree. But Maria decided that it was time to set a firm limit with Carlos and to protect her energy. Throwing away endless energy and sleepless nights on him was doing her no good.

While an in-person conversation might have seemed more sensitive, Maria had a lifetime of experience with him. She knew he was an expert at yanking away a subject that was important to her and changing it to his next dramatic tale. So she informed him in an email.

"Dear Carlos: I love you as a brother, but I've decided that I can't have any contact with you at this time, unless it's at my therapist's office. Her name and address are below.

You've not taken any of my suggestions, so there's no point in me listening to your problems, if you won't listen to my solutions. You seem to have some problems that could be helped by meeting with a therapist of your own. I'm willing to even help pay for it, and it can still be totally confidential. I don't need to know what you discuss.

But until you accept some real help, or take responsibility for some of your problems, I can't help you. And until you meet with me, and my therapist, I can't handle any more of our conversations or respond to your emails.

So, until you meet with me and my therapist, I'll no longer talk to you, no longer answer my door if you're there, no longer respond to your emails or letters, and I will not give you any money.

I know if you get the proper help you can make your life work. Many people have the kinds of problems you have, and they've gotten help and are much happier now.

Good Luck. Love, Maria."

Maria forwarded the email letter to their mother and also to several other relatives. She expected Carlos would complain to everyone about her. She wanted them to hear what she'd said directly. She knew she'd be blamed by Carlos, and even by their mother, but the rest of her relatives would probably be supportive. After all, everyone knew about their personalities from a lifetime of personal experience.

The next day, she got an email from Carlos. She couldn't help but read it.

"MARIA:

YOU KNOW THAT YOU'RE WRONG TO DO THIS. WHY ARE YOU TREATING ME SO BADLY? SO UNFAIRLY? WHAT HAVE I EVER DONE TO YOU TO DESERVE SUCH RUDENESS; SUCH INSENSITIVITY? LOOK, MARIA, I THINK I FOUND A PLACE TO LIVE. MY SEVERANCE PAY SHOULD HELP ME THROUGH THE FIRST TWO MONTHS. I'M GOING TO LOOK FOR A JOB. BUT I NEED TO KNOW THAT I CAN STILL TALK TO YOU.

YOU'RE KILLING ME. MAYBE I'LL KILL MYSELF SOMEDAY. IF I DO, YOU KNOW IT'LL BE ALL YOUR FAULT! PLEASE TALK TO ME. I NEED YOU DESPERATELY. YOU'RE THE ONLY SISTER I HAVE!

LOVE,

YOUR LITTLE BABY BROTHER"

Maria felt horrible. What if he killed himself? Would it really be her fault? Could she do something now to stop him? She decided to discuss it with her therapist. He'd never attempted suicide before, but he'd made these kinds of statements before. He didn't say he was going to kill himself, and he seemed a little optimistic with his new place to live and his severance package. Just to be safe, she decided to call her therapist.*

*Author's note: Calling a therapist or any mental health professional or suicide prevention hotline is always a good idea when anyone makes statements threatening suicide, even if they don't seem credible. Most suicidal people make a statement to someone before they commit suicide, and in many cases it didn't seem serious—until it happened. Many HCPs make suicidal statements as another part of their high-conflict drama, but some of them later commit suicide. These comments should always be taken seriously. These four personality disorders—Borderline, Narcissistic, Histrionic and Antisocial—all have a higher rate of suicide than average.

Maria also felt manipulated. Carlos had pulled all of her heart strings. She wasn't trying to hurt him! And he was also the only brother *she* had! But she'd been through a lot, and he wouldn't do what she asked. She had *set a limit* of not talking to him, except at her therapist's office. He ignored her request, yet he put such dangerous comments in his email that she felt forced to respond. She'd have to give him information about how to get help if he was truly suicidal. She'd have to go get him, if he was truly suicidal. She'd have to violate the limit she set with him, she thought.

However, when she met with her therapist, they came up with a different plan. Her therapist had a list of hotlines and suicide prevention services. Rather than having Maria respond to his vague threat and violate the limit she'd set, her therapist would respond to his email. Her therapist sent the following email back to Carlos:

"Hi, Carlos. I'm Maria's therapist. She's very concerned about you. She loves you, and really wants you to come meet with us at my office. You have the address.

I also want you to know that if you're ever feeling like hurting yourself in any way, that you should feel free to call me, or one of the following hotlines and suicide prevention services. You can also call 911, or go to any hospital.

Maria cares about you very much, and I hope to meet you some day."

The next day, Maria's therapist got an email from Carlos:

"I'm never talking to you, so you can just get out of my life. Don't bother me again."

Maria was glad to hear that. She was glad that Carlos had at least communicated with her therapist, even though he said he wouldn't talk to her. He probably didn't even see the irony in that. And did you notice that he didn't use bold, underlines, or capital letters? Maybe he can control his extreme emotions if he makes a strong effort. Maybe he would talk to the therapist again and get some help someday. At least there was a connection he might use in the future. In the meantime, Maria would do her best to focus on maintaining her own life, to resist initiating contact with Carlos, and to prepare to be firm and friendly in response to whatever Carlos's next move would be.

A Question

Three months later, Maria hadn't heard directly from Carlos. However, her mother told her that she and Carlos were in regular contact, and that Carlos had a new girlfriend, with whom he was very much in love. "The poor dear," Maria said to herself. "Maybe I should warn her about him," she wondered.

What do you think? How should Maria deal with Carlos's new girlfriend?

A. Call her up and tell her that he's very charming, but will quickly become very difficult.

B. Call her up and schedule a meeting in person.

C. Write her a letter explaining how histrionic Carlos can be.

D. Do nothing, and leave her and Carlos alone.

E. Talk with her therapist about it.

As you know, there's no perfect answer with HCPs. However, I think "E" may be the best answer. Maria seems worried about the situation. She needs to talk about this with someone, and her therapist would be the best choice. Otherwise, she's likely to talk about it with Carlos or his girlfriend, even if she doesn't plan to do so. The therapist can help her "let go."

"D" is also a good choice, although I think "E" is better. The main thing is that Maria is trying to let go of responsibility for her brother. If she volunteers to help his girlfriend, then she feels responsible somehow. This is Maria's issue. If she volunteers today, she'll have demands on her in the future. The best approach is to avoid getting started. Many family members who become Negative Advocates for their relatives get stuck this way. They think they're reaching out in a normal way to a normal person, but with HCPs the social rules are different. The HCP will take over your life if you open those doors in the first place.

"A, "B," and "C" are not wise choices. They would be destructive to all the progress Maria has made for herself.

The Histrionic Employee

The following 2007 published court case describes someone with a Histrionic Personality Disorder in a dispute with her employer. As with all published legal cases, I know only the facts presented and I'll never know if the court got it right. However, the explanation, if true, has many common characteristics that fit the behavior of people with Histrionic Personality Disorder.

> Camille Kotowski, age 56, worked for DaimlerChrysler from 1986 to 1999 as a benefits administrator. In 1999 she became disabled and began to receive Social Security Disability benefits.
>
> She explained her disability as follows to her attending physician, Dr. Abbasi, during her appointments:
>
> On September 9, 2002, she described her "daily activities" as follows: "Don't do much. Lay on couch most days. Getting dressed can take 3 to 4 hours. Try to do light work around house, but don't accomplish anything. Husband helps with meals and cleaning house."
>
> ....

On March 4, 2004, Ms. Kotowski also reported disability due to depression, anxiety, and panic attacks. She described her daily activities thus: "Not much. Usually sit or lay down most of day. Frequent doctors. Husband helps with meals and cleaning house. **Always overwhelmed — causing screaming and yelling fits.**"

Ms. Kotowski's complaints were initially supported by a number of medical opinions. The first opinion contained in the record is that of Dr. Calmeze H. Dudley, a board-certified psychiatrist who performed a medical examination at the request of DaimlerChrysler. Dr. Dudley determined that Ms. Kotowski suffered from severe anxiety. At the time of the examination, she was taking two doses of Xanax per day plus other medication as prescribed by Dr. Abbasi, and was seeing Dr. Abbasi once every two months. Ms. Kotowski told Dudley that her symptoms had not improved, and she stressed that, for her, **the simplest task was virtually impossible.** Among other things, she stated that **she "hates people"** and has trouble even picking up food from a drive-thru window. Ms. Kotowski told Dr. Dudley that she doesn't drink alcohol but admitted that she smokes 1.5 packs of cigarettes per day. (Kotowski v. DaimlerChrysler, 2007, 3-4) (Emphasis in bold added; slight edits for easier reading)

Dr. Dudley diagnosed her with "Borderline and Histrionic Personality Disorder, her main diagnosis." But he also said that she had Panic Disorder with Agoraphobia (meaning she had difficulty leaving the house and interacting with others) and General Anxiety Disorder. This means that he believed she truly had anxiety problems, but he also believed that her personality disorder was the main problem.

Notice the dramatic statements in bold. These statements may be true with some people, but with Histrionics they're the types of statements that have no supporting facts. It's all drama, and only drama.

Also note that she was diagnosed with a Borderline Personality Disorder, but Dr. Dudley appeared to conclude that her Histrionic Personality Disorder was the main problem. It's not uncommon for people with one personality disorder to have another personality disorder. Dr. Dudley concluded:

In summary, within a reasonable degree of medical certainty, I find her to be totally but temporarily disabled, both due to her anxiety, apparent recurrent panic attacks, and **most particularly her personality disorder.** While the **personality problems are not likely to benefit from any medication,** the other entities could certainly be improved upon were appropriate medication offered. I will suggest 1 final period of medications of a 2-month duration followed by another independent medical evaluation examination, assuming my recommendations can be put into place. If at that time no change has occurred, I would render total and permanent disability. (Kotowski v. DaimlerChrysler, 2007, 5-6)

Dr. Dudley pointed out that personality problems aren't really treatable with medications. This is important to know, as many other problems—including anxiety—generally can be treated with medications. As Dr. Dudley suggests, if her anxiety can be brought under control with medications, she might be able to work again. Keep in mind that personality disorders aren't legally considered a disability that would prevent someone from working. So her anxiety is the basis for her disability payments.

In 2004, DaimlerChrysler had another doctor, Dr. Wolf, examine Ms. Kotowski. In 2005, her doctor appointments were described as follows:

With Dr. Abbasi: On June 13, 2005, Ms. Kotowski reported the same disabling conditions and describing her daily activities in much the same fashion: "Sleep or lay down most of day. **Always overwhelmed,** so don't do much at all—being overwhelmed causes panic attacks. Go to doctors. Husband helps with house cleaning and meals." (Kotowski v. DaimlerChrysler, 2007, 4)

With Dr. Wolf: On June 20, 2005, Dr. Wolf examined Ms. Kotowski again. Today she claimed that she has experienced absolutely no symptomatic improvement whatsoever since last seen by me four months ago. **She rather theatrically stated, "Maybe I just need to accept that my life is over." Several times she yelled at this examiner in a rather dramatic fashion.** When asked what she does at home in an average day, she stated, "Nothing. All I do is sit on my back porch once in awhile and on Friday mornings between 6:30 and 7:00, I go to the grocery store so that I don't have to deal with anybody." Ms. Kotowski stated that she has difficulty driving, so that her husband drove her to this appointment today. (Kotowski v. DaimlerChrysler, 2007, 12-13)

Even Dr. Wolf commented on her theatrical and dramatic statements. But now it gets much more interesting. For some reason, DaimlerChrysler became suspicious and authorized the secret videotaping of her activities. They apparently suspected her of "malingering," which means presenting false or exaggerated symptoms of physical or psychological illness intended to get a benefit, such as disability payments. This is what the videotape showed during May 2005, *before* the last two doctors' visits above:

The surveillance footage, which was made part of the administrative record, consumes about three hours of video, and **there is no real dispute over its contents**. Beginning on the morning of May 16, 2005, Ms. Kotowski was seen walking her dog outside her home, and then driving to a tanning salon. Ms. Kotowski left the tanning salon after fifteen minutes and made her way to a drive-thru ATM. After completing the transaction, she went back home and remained there for four hours. At 1:45 p.m., she got back in her car and drove to a McDonald's restaurant, purchased a meal through the drive-thru lane, and went back home for the night.

On May 17, 2005, Ms. Kotowski was seen driving to a Lowes home improvement store at 8:00 a.m. She retrieved a shopping cart and spent approximately forty minutes in the store. After leaving Lowes, Ms. Kotowski drove immediately to Meijer's. She spent forty-five minutes in Meijer's and left with five bags of groceries. Ms. Kotowski apparently ran some more errands until noon, but the surveillance team lost her in traffic. They caught back up with her at her home, where she remained until 2:00 p.m. At 2:00, Ms. Kotowski left her house and drove to a bar in Sterling Heights named "MacKenzie's Tavern." The surveillance team followed her into the bar and watched as she drank beer, smoked cigarettes, and talked with other patrons until 6:00 p.m. The surveillance report states that she talked to "several adult males" and "drank between 4 to 6 beers." According to one of the surveillance personnel, Ms. Kotowski complained to one individual that, since her husband had retired, "all he wanted to do was to sit and watch TV." She arrived back home at approximately 6:30 p.m., and no other activity was recorded that night.

On May 18, 2005, Ms. Kotowski was observed walking into her backyard at around 12:40 p.m. She cleaned up a number of "dog deposits" and pulled weeds around the base of her pool. Ms. Kotowski spent the rest of the day indoors. On May 30, 2005, the investigators filmed her tending to plants outside for roughly one-half hour, after which she sprayed down the pool and patio for a few minutes. Ms. Kotowski performed various other gardening tasks, and fifty minutes later she returned to her home. Surveillance was resumed on June 20, 2005, when at 10:00 a.m. Ms. Kotowski traveled to Wal-Mart with her husband. They spent fifteen minutes in the store, and then traveled to a building supply store in Southfield, where they remained for around forty-five minutes. Then they drove to "Brady's Burgers" in Hazel Park, picked up some lunch, and headed back home. They spent an hour and a half inside, and then at 2:00 p.m. they drove to MacKenzie's in Sterling Heights, where they remained for over two and a half hours. While inside, Ms. Kotowski sat at the bar with her husband and drank several beers, had several conversations with her husband and other patrons, and played several games of Keno. (Kotowski v. DaimlerChrysler, 2007, 8-11) (Emphasis in bold added; slight edits for ease of reading)

So, she lied! She easily left her house. She did yard work. She did the drive-through at McDonalds. She bought five bags of groceries and brought them home. She spent four hours sitting and drinking at McKenzie's bar. This is pretty good for someone who says she can't go out or be around other people. There goes the Agoraphobia diagnosis. But is she still depressed?

After the June 20th appointment, Dr. Wolf saw the videotapes. Here are his new conclusions:

Based upon the information currently available to me, it is my opinion that Camille Kotowski is fit for duty without restrictions, in a full time capacity, as of the date of this appointment. The videotape clearly indicates that the history that Ms. Kotowski presented to me in interview, at least today if not during my previous evaluations of her, is, at the very least, grossly exaggerated. **She either fabricates symptoms or severely exaggerates the extent of her symptomology since in interview she claims that she is essentially immobilized by depression, while the video clearly reveals that this is not the case.** This appears to reflect a conscious effort on Ms. Kotowski's part to mislead the examiner and present herself as being more ill than in fact she is. Once again, based upon this information, in my judgment, she is fit for duty as of today's date. (Kotowski v. DaimlerChrysler, 2007, 13-14) (Emphasis added)

So, they determined that Ms. Kotowski was dramatic to the point of fabricating her disability. Drama and fabricating stories fit with Histrionic Personality Disorder (Ford, 1996). But malingering (fabricating illness or disability) fits more with Antisocial Personality Disorder, which will be described in the next Tip of this book.

So you can see that having one personality disorder may mean having two or three, and they may be hard to tell apart. This isn't important for you to know. What's more important is to understand the *possibilities* of these disorders. With Histrionics, don't get emotionally hooked. With Antisocials, don't get conned. With anyone who appears to be an HCP, you can apply any or all of the tips in this book.

What happened next was typical of all of these high-conflict personalities. They are rigid and uncompromising, repeating failed strategies, even when they are self-defeating and the evidence is obvious.

When Ms. Kotowski was confronted by DaimlerChrysler, she had lots of excuses: "she attempted to tell them that they had happened to videotape her on days when she had to run errands and other chores because her husband was so sick he was unable to do so." (page 15). Of course, he'd been taped **with her** some of the time. But she didn't give up.

Based on this series of events, DaimlerChrysler terminated the plaintiff's claim for long-term disability benefits on August 1, 2005. DaimlerChrysler stated that Ms. Kotowski was not "totally disabled because of disease or injury so as to be unable to engage in regular employment or occupation with the Corporation." DaimlerChrysler terminated the plaintiff's employment on August 23, 2005 for "a violation of DaimlerChrysler's Standards of Conduct," to wit, "providing false or misleading information to the Corporation."

On September 22, 2005, Ms. Kotowski filed a timely appeal of the benefits denial. Attached to the letter of appeal was a document signed by Dr. Abassi and therapist Judith Willis reporting that Ms. Kotowski was still "clinically depressed and unable to work." However, the report does not make mention of the surveillance video or otherwise suggest that Dr. Abassi and Willis had seen it.

On October 24, 2005, DaimlerChrysler denied Ms. Kotowski's appeal. In reaching this decision, DaimlerChrysler relied on a comprehensive report. The report was evidently drafted by a registered nurse, but the identity of this individual is not set forth in the document. In any event, after setting forth the narrative in a manner essentially consistent with the facts described above, the nurse-evaluator concluded that Ms. Kotowski had been malingering. The nurse dismissed the apparent suicide attempt and criticized Ms. Kotowski for not agreeing to treatment recommended by Dr. Wolf. She recommended upholding the decision to terminate benefits.

Following the denial of her appeal, Ms. Kotowski commenced the present action on November 29, 2006 to recover benefits under her employer's disability plan. On March 12, 2007, Ms. Kotowski filed a statement of procedural challenge **alleging conflict of interest** because DaimlerChrysler both funds and administers the plan, **bias** on the part of Dr. Wolf because he may be inclined to deny claims based on his relationship with DaimlerChrysler, **and an incomplete review** on the part of Dr. Wolf because he only watched 39 to 40 minutes of the three hours of surveillance video. (Kotowski v. DaimlerChrysler, 2007, 17-18)

So, Ms. Kotowski ignored the reality of a videotape showing her lying, and instead appealed her loss of disability based on conflict of interest, bias, and an incomplete review. This is typical of cases I've seen with HCPs. This is their high-conflict thinking: wishful thinking, tunnel vision, and emotional reasoning, at the very least. Don't expect evidence to matter. In many ways they're blind to the highly likely outcome. And the result is that you can read all about her case in the public record. Embarrassment or remorse is often lacking in these cases. It doesn't make any sense, unless you understand their high-conflict thinking. What's her fear? I can't say for sure, but Histrionics fear being ignored. Repeatedly going to court is one guaranteed way of getting attention in today's society.

Lastly, we may find an example of projection:

> The final argument offered by Ms. Kotowski alleges improper "shopping" for a medical opinion. **Divorced from the facts,** Ms. Kotowski's **argument has superficial appeal:** a corporation should not be able to subject an employee to a battery of evaluations by a multitude of doctors in the hopes that a finding of fitness to work eventually will turn up. When analyzed in context, however, Ms. Kotowski's argument has no support in the record. First, she was only seen by two doctors at the request of DaimlerChrysler, Dr. Dudley and Dr. Wolf. Second, and far more significantly, Ms. Kotowski's **argument ignores the fact that Dr. Wolf had a very good reason for changing his opinion.** Ms. Kotowski paints a picture of the defendants forcing her to see Dr. Wolf a number of times, just waiting for Dr. Wolf to eventually render an inevitable opinion of non-disability according to the law of averages. However, **there was nothing random or inevitable about Dr. Wolf's decision;** he consistently concurred in the finding of disability until he saw the surveillance video. There was no impropriety on the part of the defendants to seek further evidence of Ms. Kotowski's continuing disability and provide it to Dr. Wolf.
>
> The Court finds that there is a reasonable explanation for the administrator's decision to discontinue benefits in this case in light of the plan's provisions and the evidence contained in the administrative record. (Kotowski v. DaimlerChrysler, 2007, 29-30) (Emphasis added; slight edits for readability)

This may be an example of projecting, because Ms. Kotowski is the one who seemed to be shopping for a doctor who would support her, although she blamed the company instead. After Dr. Wolf saw the videotapes and changed his mind about her, she's the one who submitted "a document signed by Dr. Abassi and therapist Judith Willis reporting that she was still clinically depressed and unable to work." It seems that she was shopping for opinions that supported her, without giving them full information, even after the videotape was known and obvious to all of the other decision-makers.

As the bolded words point out, she *ignored the facts* in her arguments and hoped that the court would do this as well. This is very common with HCPs, in and out of court. As I explained in Tip #2 of this book, high-conflict thinking is not about facts and logic—it's about defensiveness and denial of reality so that one can keep fighting the battles they feel inside. Unfortunately, there are victims of this probably unconscious process. There are Targets of Blame they fight against. While it may be hard to have a lot of empathy for a large automobile corporation as a Target of Blame, remember that consumers are the ones who ultimately paid the cost of her lawsuits *and* her social security benefits.

Don't Get Emotionally Hooked

Whether you're dealing with someone like Carlos, who is highly dramatic and probably sincere, or someone like Ms. Kotowski, who is highly dramatic and lying, the key issue with Histrionic HCPs is getting emotionally hooked into their drama. Given their constant exaggerations and emotional demands, it's hard to avoid getting hooked. Even if you resist for awhile, you still might finally give in—if you're not careful. Remember, even Ms. Kotowski's doctor believed she had a Histrionic Personality Disorder, but he still believed her stories! That is, until the videotape showed otherwise.

You have to choose your battles with Histrionic HCPs—although this is a helpful tip with all HCPs. They're so emotional and demanding of attention that you hardly have a chance to breathe—or think. Yet they're also fascinating and tell wonderfully dramatic stories you could listen to for hours, especially when you first meet them. Generally, you'll catch on pretty quick that you're dealing with a Histrionic, but sometimes they'll still fool you, as Ms. Kotowski's doctors discovered.

In most cases, Histrionic HCPs are sincere, but intensely dramatic types, like Carlos. It's the emotional intensity and drama that characterizes these HCPs. This is what I describe handling below. The conning types may also have Antisocial Personality Disorder, which I will describe in the next Tip.

You can probably think of someone in your life who is Histrionic. They can be hardest on their families, but they're present everywhere, including at work and in your neighborhood.

Handling Histrionic HCPs

1. **Focus on what is most essential, if anything.** Before (or during) contact with a Histrionic, plan to focus on no more than one to three very small tasks that you want to accomplish. I expect to get only five minutes of meaningful work done in an hour with a Histrionic. So, if you have a neighbor who needs to have a talk, a co-worker who has a project, or a relative who needs to do some chore, think of the most important next tasks that you need to get done and how you're going to present them to the Histrionic.

2. **You have the right to interrupt an intensely emotional person.** There's an unwritten rule of social manners that says you shouldn't interrupt someone in the middle of feeling deeply painful emotions. This is a good rule and it helps people help each other heal from terrible losses and crises. But Histrionics manipulate this rule (mostly unconsciously) by keeping the deeply painful emotions going for hours. Remember, Histrionics' emotions are superficial and fleeting. In most cases, it's a drama and not a moving experience. They're not moving through their feelings and they're not healing—they're exaggerating their feelings for a desired effect: remaining the center of your attention. This doesn't mean they don't feel intense pain—it just means that listening to it won't really help them.

3. **Empathize with their pain, but don't buy into their stories.** They'll seek your sympathies for their terrible crises and events. They'll cry, scream, exaggerate, and make up details for dramatic effect. The more you seem to agree with their tales of being victims, the more they'll expect from you in the future. Try to be neutral about what happened while being empathetic: "Wow, it sounds like you were really frightened." Try to avoid saying things like: "What they did to you is terrible. They should be sued for that." You'll never know what really happened, and you may inadvertently escalate a high-conflict dispute.

4. **Avoid trying to change them or tone down their responses.** This is a battle many people get hooked into. Unless you're a therapist working with Histrionics you're unlikely to change their dramatic nature. Remember, these are personality disorders or maladaptive personality traits you're facing, which have existed for decades. Don't bother. Don't choose this battle. You can't win.

5. **Suggest realistic small tasks to solve specific problems.** Histrionics generally believe they're powerless and relatively helpless. Don't buy into their efforts to get you to do what they can do. Point out realistic tasks they can

do to solve a problem. Remember, Maria suggested Carlos look in the newspaper. While it seems obvious to everyone else, Carlos was so absorbed in his emotions at the moment that he might not have thought of that. Later, he says he found a place. Perhaps this was a helpful suggestion.

6. **Avoid trying to protect the person or those around the person from reality.** You could exhaust yourself trying to protect a Histrionic from himself or herself. You could also exhaust yourself trying to protect other people from a Histrionic. If you're setting limits to protect your own energy, this needs to include avoiding endless involvement with others with whom the Histrionic comes into contact. They'll always find someone else, and they usually move quickly from person to person, as they're used to burning out everyone around them. So Maria shouldn't feel responsible to interfere and "warn" her brother's new girlfriend—the girlfriend will catch on soon enough. Exceptions to this would be if he is potentially dangerous, such as having a history of domestic violence. Another exception would be if the girlfriend starts spreading rumors on Carlos's behalf, in which case Maria would need to take action to respond to those rumors with accurate information. In any case, she should get the advice of a professional (therapist, attorney, law enforcement officer) if she feels that someone may be in danger.

TIP #5 SUMMARY

Don't Get Hooked By Histrionics

Characteristics

1. For Histrionics, fear of being ignored is a driving force.

2. Histrionics are very dramatic, theatrical, and superficial.

3. Histrionics have high-intensity, shifting emotions with few facts and little focus.

4. Histrionics exaggerate and sometimes fabricate events.

5. Histrionics have difficulty focusing on tasks or making decisions.

Managing Histrionic HCPs

1. Focus discussions on what is most essential, if anything.

2. You can interrupt an intensely emotional person.

3. Empathize with their pain, but don't buy into their stories.

4. Avoid trying to change them or tone down their responses.

5. Suggest realistic small tasks to solve specific problems.

6. Avoid trying to protect the person or those around the person from reality.

Tip #6: Don't Get Conned by Antisocials

CHAPTER

6

"I gotta tell ya, these embezzlement convictions raise a red flag."

Tip #6
Don't Get Conned By Antisocials

Michael worked the evening shift, so he decided to go to an early movie one weekday afternoon. It was an action-packed thriller, but nothing he would really remember, especially after what happened next.

As Michael was leaving the mostly empty theater, he gently pushed the exit door and suddenly heard a scream from the other side.

"Hey! Look what you've done! Somebody help me!" a woman screamed.

"Are you OK?" Michael asked the woman who'd fallen down on the floor and was holding her head.

"Somebody help me! This man pushed me down!" the woman screamed.

A man suddenly ran up to Michael, pushed him against the wall and screamed, "Stand still! Right there!"

"Hey! I didn't do anything!" Michael said, in a loud voice. He pushed the man who was holding him against the wall. It was easy, Michael was 6 foot 3, and the other man was 5 or 6 inches shorter.

"What's all the commotion?" a theater attendant said, walking quickly to the area. It was the first time there was an official present.

"This big man here," the woman said, "pushed ahead of me, and slammed me with the door. He knocked me down. I hit my head and it really hurts now!"

"That's a bunch of crap! I didn't do anything to her!" Michael exclaimed, starting to get red-in-the-face angry. He turned to the man who had pushed him against the wall, "She's lying and she's manipulating you to think I hurt her. I didn't push ahead of her—I just came out of the theater, and she pretended to fall down and be hurt."

"Ma'am, do you need a doctor—or an ambulance?" the theater attendant said, eying Michael nervously.

"Yes, I think I do. Ohhhh, this hurts!" the woman said. Michael would find out that her name was Darlene, as it was written on the Summons he was served for the court case against him. She listed a man, Jonathan, as a witness. He must have been the man who pushed Michael up against the wall, Michael thought. How did he fall for her scheme?

Antisocial HCPs are Con Artists. They see other people and the law as challenges for manipulation and domination. They can lie more persuasively than you can tell the truth. They look good on the surface and sometimes have a very good reputation. Beware, because Con Artists do good deeds as "sugar-coating" to distract you from their bad deeds.

Antisocial HCPs don't care about you or the rules of society. You can sense this before you consciously see it. Maybe you get a cold feeling about them—such as their "sincere" words don't match their nonverbal behavior. Maybe you feel a little afraid of them, but you can't figure out why. In fact, Con Artists are known for getting you to doubt yourself and believe in what they tell you. This way, you develop confidence in them (that's the "con"), while they prepare to take advantage of you.

The common pattern for Antisocial HCPs includes the following traits:

• Try to dominate and manipulate others, because of a fear of being dominated

• A willingness to hurt others for their own personal gain

• Strong disregard for social rules and laws, and a lack of remorse

• Aggressive energy, risk-taking, and reckless disregard for danger

• Constant lying and deception, even when they can be discovered

There are a wide range of Antisocials in the world today, from minor family manipulators (who steal from their own families) to major robbery schemers and serial killers. Many meet the criteria for Antisocial Personality Disorder (ASPD), which is approximately 3 to 4% of the general population (APA, 2000; Grant, 2004). Of these four high-conflict personality disorders, this is the only one that includes the additional criteria that the person must have shown antisocial behaviors in adolescence. It seems that Antisocials always have a "history."

They're also known as sociopaths, and a small percentage are known as psychopaths—those who are extra vicious in harming others. Most Antisocials (those with the disorder or just traits) are men, but about one in four are women (Grant, 2004).

Antisocials fear being dominated and therefore they desire to dominate and control others—it gives them a reassuring sense of power in the world. They often have a drive to hurt others to get what they want, as compared to the other personality disorders, which primarily involve *self*-sabotage and *inadvertent* harm to others. This drive to dominate others usually encompasses taking advantage of other people, such as the con man who marries several women at the same time for their money or the psychopath who feels comfortable killing you because he wants your coat.

Antisocials are skilled at fooling neighbors, spouses, legal professionals, and even mental health professionals. They're often found in cases involving criminal charges, and appear to make up a substantial portion (frequently estimated at about 50%) of the prison population.

Causes and Treatment

Antisocial Personality Disorder appears to develop out of a combination of biological and environmental factors. However, in contrast to the other personality disorders, ASPs (those with the personality disorder or just traits) appear to have a much stronger genetic link. Studies indicate that children with an Antisocial parent have a greater risk of developing an Antisocial personality. Even if an Antisocial's child is adopted by people without a personality disorder, the child may grow up Antisocial, because of the strong genetic factor (Ford, 1996). This finding is supported by anecdotal reports I've heard from criminal defense attorneys regarding cases where the children of their criminal clients were raised from very early childhood by normal parents and still developed Antisocial Personalities.

Some research indicates that the biological differences of Antisocials may be based in the person's central nervous system. They get less upset about negative events, during which they're less likely to feel fear or guilt. Research shows their heart rate actually decreases in a fight (Dutton, 1998). They sweat less too. Perhaps for these reasons, Antisocials can often lie effectively without being detected on police polygraph tests.

Despite the genetic link, early life experiences and environment can't be ignored. It appears that chaos in the household and inconsistent reinforcement of social values may train a child for antisocial behavior. Children of severe alcoholics and addicts may experience this inconsistency, as they absorb the antisocial behaviors of addicted parents into their own personalities. Ironically, parents who become recovering alcoholics or addicts may stop showing signs of antisocial behavior (such as lying, violence, or lack of remorse), but the child may have already learned them as permanent behaviors.

While most alcoholics and addicts don't have Antisocial Personality Disorder, a large proportion of Antisocials are alcoholics or addicts. Under the law, drug addicts are engaged in antisocial behavior. However, most addicts in recovery don't engage in other antisocial behaviors. Addicts with Antisocial Personality Disorder, on the other hand, will continue to engage in high-risk and illegal behaviors even after they are clean and sober.

Some research has indicated that learning to lie extensively in childhood may be a strong predictor of antisocial behavior in an adult. As the DSM-IV-TR criteria explain, antisocial behavior in the form of a conduct disorder prior to age 15 is a necessary requirement for the Antisocial Personality Disorder diagnosis, and lying is one of the core criteria of a conduct disorder (APA, 2000).

Antisocials may be the hardest of these four personalities to treat and change. For those who have traits but not the full personality disorder, some cognitive therapy methods have been successful (Beck & Freeman, 1990). However, for those who are diagnosed with the full disorder, treatment is difficult because they have many qualities that make them antagonistic to personal change and to bonding with therapists—or with anyone.

Extremely low or extremely high intelligence are factors that decrease the likelihood of successful treatment in an ASP (Meloy, 1997). This would make sense, given the lack of insight for low-intelligence ASPs and the strong ability of high-intelligence ASPs to manipulate others.

However, group therapies have had some success. Some examples are groups for treating perpetrators of domestic violence, long-term therapeutic communities for hard-core drug addicts, and prison treatment groups for child molesters. These programs are all based on direct confrontation by peers who share many of the same characteristics and therefore can see through the cons and connect with the vulnerability and fears they feel deep beneath the surface.

While groups appear to be the preferred treatment for ASPs, the success rate seems far more limited than for other personality disorders. This would make sense, given the inability of ASPs to form interpersonal bonds—in contrast to BPs and NPs, who form bonds—even though they're negative and conflictual bonds—upon which positive treatment can be based.

High Conflict Dynamics

The good news is that most of the Con Artists you deal with in neighborhood, co-worker, or family disputes aren't violent and don't have Antisocial Personality Disorder. The bad news is that the Con Artists you meet are so manipulative and smooth-talking you may not know you're being cheated or robbed until it's too late.

With their life-long skills at deception, Con Artists know how to make their stories sound credible. Often, the people who are most easily conned are truly nice and sincere people. They like to help others and Con Artists play on their goodwill. Even people dealing with Antisocials in a professional or business relationship, rather than a personal or emotional one, can be easily conned.

Surprisingly, many Antisocial HCPs are comfortable bringing false claims to court. They may pursue a claim against a former partner in crime, a business partner, a family member they wish to harm using the legal system, or even against a stranger who looks like an easy Target. One example is the Con Artist who brings a fabricated charge of domestic violence against a spouse or partner, when in fact he or she was the one who was abusive and violent. By focusing the court on other people (the Targets of Blame), Antisocials distract everyone from their own behavior.

If you become involved with people you suspect may be Con Artists, you should attempt to gather independent information to verify anything they ask you to believe, before you believe them or assist them in any of their many plans and "projects." Better yet, just try to avoid them as much as possible.

The Finger in the Soup

In 2005, people were shocked when Anna Ayala, 39, reported biting into a 1½ inch-long human finger in her bowl of chili at a Wendy's restaurant in San Jose, California. My first thought was to be skeptical. My second thought was, does she have a "history" of reports like this?

As her case received international publicity, the woman filed a lawsuit against Wendy's national franchise. The restaurant checked with all its employees at that particular store and all of its suppliers, and found no one with a finger missing. They offered a $50,000 reward for anyone who had verifiable information about the origin of the finger. Not surprisingly, the restaurant's sales declined.

As I suspected, within two weeks, a history of six lawsuits in the San Francisco Bay area by Ms. Ayala came to light, including suing another fast food restaurant, an auto dealership, and her former boss for sexual harassment. She was successful in the other fast food lawsuit, in which she acknowledged receiving a settlement for medical expenses when her daughter got sick on the food.

Within a couple of months, the truth came out. The finger originally belonged to one of her husband's co-workers, who accidentally severed it at work in Las Vegas—where Ayala and her husband happened to live. Ms. Ayala and her husband pled guilty, but Wendy's reportedly lost $2.5 million and was forced to lay off many workers.

Interestingly, one report of this story mentioned that the couple's attorney said they were "remorseful" about the incident, and were sorry that workers were harmed by their actions (www.blottered.com). If they are truly Antisocials (which I can't say absolutely, because I haven't met them and done a clinical interview), saying they're remorseful is a reflection of their continued "conning," not a reflection of their true remorse. After all, this was at least the seventh lawsuit Ms. Ayala had participated in. The pattern of lack of remorse and continued questionable behavior was unchanged.

One of the first things you'll hear from Antisocials after they are caught (and many are) is that they are "truly sorry." They know it's the right thing to say, and they say it all the time—but only after they get caught. It has nothing to do with a change of heart, but if they have Antisocial Personality Disorder it fits right into their conning behavior.

Mistaken Assessment of Danger

You might wonder how Antisocial HCPs are acting out of fear. They're the toughest to empathize with because they're so calculating in their conning. From my experience, the Antisocials I've dealt with believe that *everyone* lies and cons. They appear to think that's how you survive and get ahead in the world. They think if they don't con others, they'll be conned themselves. Yet they don't have real friends and appear to be fearful in the world, *except* when they're conning.

Further, they put the blame on their Targets for allowing themselves to be conned. For example, a man was recently sentenced to prison for marrying several women at the same time, without these women knowing about each other. After he was caught, he was interviewed on television and seemed surprised that people were critical of him. He thought the women should have been more careful, and that they got what they deserved for being so gullible. He appeared to think of this as a dog-eat-dog world in which everyone is a con artist and you're a fool if you're not conning somebody. It's not a happy world for Antisocials, as their personality pattern of behavior is repeatedly self-defeating for them as well as their Targets.

Behavior that is Aggressively Defensive

An example of self-defeating dynamics is the man who believed he could con a jury. While the news article describing his story did not say that he's an Antisocial, he appears to have some potential traits.

Omar Ageel, age 29, was on trial for killing his wife by stabbing her 34 times. At trial, his attorneys argued that he was under the influence of methamphetamine at the time, which he claimed was slipped into his drink by his wife. Mr. Ageel told the court that he wanted to testify.

His attorneys and the judge, apparently out of hearing of the jury, told him that he would open up his entire legal history if he described himself as a good, law-abiding person who would never kill his wife. He still insisted that he be able to testify in his own defense. His aggressive pursuit of this opportunity to defend himself was his Behavior that was Aggressively Defensive. Since he had the legal right to do this, the judge had to allow it.

During his testimony, he basically said he had a history of being a good, law-abiding citizen who would never kill his wife. The judge then ruled that Mr. Ageel could be questioned by the prosecution about his history, which the judge had previously ruled off limits. Mr. Ageel was then questioned about his 1994 manslaughter conviction, his two recent assaults on sheriff's deputies while in jail, and about 40 other violations. This information apparently had a dramatic impact on the jury, including one member whose jaw reportedly dropped when he heard about the prior conviction.

Mr. Ageel was convicted with the maximum sentence of 36 years to life (Jones, 2004).

This is an example of typical Antisocial "con artist" behavior. They *think* they can talk their way out of anything. When I've taken depositions from people I think have Antisocial traits, it always amazes me that they have convincing answers at one point in the deposition and then contradict themselves with convincing answers about another point. They truly think they can fool anyone on the spot with their believable stories. But what they don't realize is that they're often being asked different questions at different times for exactly this purpose.

For most Antisocials, their preoccupation is the story in the moment, and they don't think ahead about overall consistency—or getting caught. Remember, they're risk-takers and aggressive, and full of confidence when they're conning. This isn't a question of intelligence, as Antisocials have the full range of intelligence, from very low to very high. It's the personality traits that make them act this way, even when it causes them to sabotage themselves. It's unconscious and embedded in their personalities.

Like Small Children

In many ways, those with Antisocial Personality Disorder are like small children who want instant gratification and can't tolerate frustration. They may get into legal trouble due to an overwhelming impulse to have some object, which they can only obtain immediately through theft or violence (Ford, 1996).

However, they may be able to plan ahead to accomplish a short-term criminal scheme. It's the long-term consequences that Antisocials have difficulty imagining—even after being caught in the past. For example, a bank robber may be highly effective at pulling off the robbery, but unable to understand the risks of engaging in the same behavior at six different banks in the same city around the same time.

Since Antisocials are in a constant state of child-like desire, there's frequent irritability at delayed gratification. This may lead to violence or aggressive interactions with those close to them. In addition, the biologically heightened aggressive energy that's characteristic of Antisocials appears to keep them engaged in antisocial behavior.

As indicated, there's usually a long history of physical fighting for one reason or another. Yet, in contrast to the Borderline or Narcissist, the Antisocial's physical confrontations are usually not highly emotional—instead, they're simply the means to an immediate end. For example, when an Antisocial engages in domestic violence, there may be an internal calm as he focuses on accomplishing a task through power and control, with no remorse following it. In contrast, when a Borderline engages in domestic violence, it's likely to be an impulsive, short-term release of tension followed by a period of remorse.

Since Antisocials are absorbed with themselves and with immediate gratification, they have little awareness of others and little concern for them. This allows for reckless disregard for consequences to themselves, as well as to others. For example, speeding in cars, high-risk drug use, and other dangerous activities can be particularly attractive to them.

In families, Antisocials may have their children removed from their care because of neglect or abusive behavior. Further, they may have difficulty maintaining employment and frequently get into trouble for not paying debts and fulfilling normal financial obligations.

Michael at the Theater

"Sir, you stay here and don't make a move!" the theater worker said to Michael.

"Hey, I didn't do anything!" Michael said, heatedly. "And I have to get to work!"

"Yes, he did. I saw him! He pushed her with the door!" said the man who had pushed Michael against the wall. "I heard him tell her to get out of the way, he was there first! Then he slammed the door against her in anger!" Michael found out later that his name was Jonathan.

The movie worker called on his walkie-talkie for help. Several theater workers came over to the scene. "We've called an ambulance, ma'am, they should be here right away. Just stay still." The theater manager was now clearly in charge.

"So what happened here?" the theater manager asked. Immediately Jonathan said, "That woman on the floor was walking up to the door and that big man over there pushed ahead and said that he was there first. He swung the door open and it knocked her down and she hit her head against the wall. I saw the whole thing."

"That's a total lie! I was coming out of the theater after seeing the movie, and I didn't see her there. I just pushed the door open gently, as usual. Nothing I did could have knocked her down!" Michael insisted.

"Do you remember what happened?" the manager asked the woman, as she lay there on the floor. "Can you talk?"

The woman moaned, but she said, "Yes, I can talk a little. What the man said is true. That big man pushed ahead of me, swung the door open. It hit me and knocked me down. He made me hit my head against the wall, like he didn't care at all. Owww! It still hurts!" she stopped talking and held her head.

Finally, an ambulance and police car arrived. The police officer asked everyone what they'd seen. A small crowd had gathered, all of them angry at Michael.

He thought to himself, "I can't believe they believe this jerk about what happened. And no one is listening to me. I didn't do anything wrong." He figured he could prove he was coming out of a movie, and not going into one, by showing his ticket stub for the earlier show. But he felt in his pocket and it wasn't there. He remembered he'd thrown it in the trash with the soda cup he'd finished. With hardly anyone around, he couldn't prove he was coming out and not going in. But why were the woman, and this man, saying it was all his fault? He'd become a Target of Blame for a whole group of people. People who'd just met each other.

Is Darlene a Con Artist?

Darlene and Michael are strangers to each other. Did Darlene know that her explanation wasn't true? Did she simply jump to the wrong conclusion? For some types of high-conflict personalities, this could be a regular and sincerely believed occurrence. Her cognitive distortions could cause her to leap to the wrong conclusions and then defend them.

However, in this case, Darlene is lying in order to get money from someone—any Target will do (because she doesn't care). If you're going to learn how to handle High Conflict People in everyday life, you need to believe this possibility with some strangers in today's world. They'll easily take advantage of you with no remorse.

Darlene has fabricated a story of assault and battery and she's going forward with criminal charges, with the unaware assistance of a Deputy District Attorney. Does this sound like high-risk behavior to you? Remember, Antisocials believe they can con anyone—including legal professionals.

Does she have the energy and confidence to promote this deception all the way to a trial? If she has Antisocial traits or Antisocial Personality Disorder she does. She'll get excitement and a sense of dominating many people from this experience. Does she appear to have any remorse about spending tax-payer dollars to use the District Attorney and the courts to promote this scheme?

Does she want something for which she's willing to promote a criminal scheme? Actually, she wants $10,000. Not a bad sum for a creative story and some bad acting.

You might wonder whether she has a Histrionic Personality Disorder, or some traits. That's a good question, and she might. She seems to enjoy being the center of attention and she's fabricated an exciting story. However, it doesn't really matter exactly what her diagnosis might be because you just want to get some idea of how Michael might handle his case. All that matters is that you understand that it's high-conflict behavior, whether it is antisocial, histrionic, or both. In any case, use the approaches described in Part II, or seek the advice of a therapist, attorney, or law enforcement officer.

The Summons

Two days later, Michael was served with a Summons. The District Attorney was bringing charges against him for assault and battery for injuring Darlene. It was a felony charge because she had a physical injury to her head as a result.

Michael was advised to get an attorney, and he did. The attorney advised him that since Darlene had a credible, unrelated witness (Jonathan), and Michael didn't, it was likely that Darlene would win the case. Also, since Michael was 6 foot 3 and Darlene was 5 foot 5, a jury would certainly be more likely to believe her.

Michael was encouraged to settle the case by his defense attorney and by the District Attorney. Darlene made an offer—she would drop the charges if he would pay her $10,000. When she had her head examined, there wasn't any obvious signs of an injury to her head other than a small bump. She was considered fortunate to have escaped serious injury, but she had incurred costs for the ambulance service and a CAT scan of her head.

"I think it's a good deal, given the total picture, Michael," his attorney advised him. "If you don't make this settlement, and the District Attorney prosecutes you, you're risking one to three years in jail. Furthermore, even if you win, my fees to defend you in a criminal trial could easily be $10,000—or more!

Michael felt devastated. He knew he'd done nothing wrong. He knew that Darlene was making the story up. But he didn't know why Jonathan was acting as a witness, saying he saw the same thing. Michael wondered if they were in it together somehow. He'd heard of phony car crashes, where one driver pulls in front of a car and another driver rear ends the middle car pushing all three together. Then the person in the first car makes a claim for whiplash and gets a lot of money from the car insurance company for the second (the Target's) car.

But Michael didn't know how he could investigate whether there was any relationship between Darlene and Jonathan. Maybe Jonathan was just easily influenced by a woman "in distress." Michael was a Target for Jonathan now, and Jonathan had already started convincing others that Michael was to blame for Darlene's injury. If they were working together, Jonathan would be careful not to be found out.

What Should Michael Do?

Michael had a busy life and a good reputation at work. If he paid Darlene $10,000 and the charges were dropped, he'd have no criminal record. He'd also not have a public criminal trial, which would hurt his career, regardless of the outcome. Besides, the District Attorney and his own attorney were telling him that he was likely to lose a trial because Darlene had a witness and he didn't.

What would you do if you were in Michael's shoes? Would you pay the money and end it now?

Jonathan's Letter

Michael received a passionate, handwritten letter from Jonathan, demanding that he quickly pay Darlene for the assault at the movie theater. It was his first contact from Jonathan. The letter said:

"I know it's none of my business, but you should do the honorable thing and pay this woman for her injuries! NOW! I don't want my life held up by a trial, just so you can pretend that you're innocent of this brutal act. I was there and saw what you did. Just because you don't want your friends and family to believe the truth about you, is not a good enough reason to delay this any further. DO THE RIGHT THING, NOW! Respond within 7 days."

Michael showed Jonathan's letter to his attorney. "I want to stop him from sending me letters like this. What can you do?"

His attorney responded, "Well, actually I recommend that you settle with Darlene. Jonathan's right; you could look bad to your relatives and friends. You have no evidence on your side, and Jonathan is a credible witness. It could cost you $10,000 in attorney's fees to fight this, and you're likely to lose. I wouldn't recommend going to court. I recommend you settle, pay her, and be done with it. That's how I would suggest responding to Jonathan's letter."

Michael didn't want to give in. He at least wanted to do some more research before he would pay. He decided to get a second opinion. He met with another attorney (let's call her Attorney B), who seemed more compatible with Michael.

Attorney B said, "I'm suspicious of Jonathan. Something stinks here. He's taking a very strong role on Darlene's behalf. I would suggest that I write back to the District Attorney and point out how aggressive Jonathan is. I'd encourage the D.A. to investigate what's in it for Jonathan."

"Of course, you realize that you could end up spending $10,000 fighting this, and still lose. On the other hand, if you don't fight this, it'll look like you're guilty. This could leave a cloud of suspicion over you, which may hurt you in the future, especially if someone else tries to fabricate another assault. If you pay Darlene, word could get around to others like her. But I can't promise you anything. Are you sure you want to hire me, with this approach?"

"Definitely," Michael said. "There has to be some kind of consequence for her making this up. I'm willing to fight it all the way."

Attorney B said, "Well, let's not decide everything all at once now. Let's just try this assertive approach for now and see what happens. We don't want to fight just for the sake of fighting. If we hit a dead end, I might suggest you settle. But for now, we need to assert ourselves and look for more information. Sometimes if you take a strong approach, the other party in the case will act so aggressively that it provides us with valuable information and shows *how* they're lying. Not just reveal that they were lying. We just have to keep our eyes open."

Attorney B wrote a letter to the Deputy District Attorney handling the case:

"Jonathan seems **highly** aggressive on Darlene's behalf. This makes me suspicious. I hope it makes you suspicious too, because if he's an unreliable witness you could end up being on the wrong side in this case. Michael has no history of violence against anyone. Also, please advise Jonathan to never again approach my client directly, either by phone, by mail, or indirectly through anyone else. All contact should be from you to me. I'm surprised he doesn't realize that."

There are several good things about this letter. First, it's as assertive as Jonathan was aggressive. Attorney B is arguing concerns about Jonathan without making assumptions. She's simply saying she's "suspicious," rather than jumping to conclusions or personally criticizing his character (as Jonathan did about Michael in his letter: "so you can pretend that you're innocent"). The assertive approach doesn't attack a person's character, but focuses on information gathering, information sharing and setting limits. (More on this in Part II of this book.)

Second, Attorney B has done some research and is providing accurate information to the District Attorney. She'll present accurate information to the D.A. every chance she gets, since the D.A. may be emotionally hooked into believing Darlene without question.

Third, she's attempting to set limits on Jonathan, through the District Attorney, by making it clear that no one involved in the case should contact Michael directly. No contact is standard procedure between the defendant and witnesses against him, but HCPs ignore standard procedures and try to cut corners all the time. Jonathan may be acting on Darlene's request or on his own initiative, but Attorney B's letter will probably inspire the D.A. to stop him. If not, it will show the D.A. how inappropriate his star witness is.

Suddenly, in the middle of the night, Michael woke up and said, "I'll bet Jonathan is a Con Artist too! He was very aggressive at the theater. He was very demanding and manipulative in his letter asking for money for Darlene. And I had this cold feeling about him. Maybe he has a legal history. I'll research him too! I wonder where he was born?"

The Investigation

Attorney B's investigator didn't find anything unusual in Darlene's Internet records, but he did find that she was born and raised in Washington State. Michael decided to research the court records in her county, as they were too old to be in the computer system.

Michael discovered that Darlene had been the victim of a rape back in high school. The boy was 18, so he was tried as an adult. Usually the victim's names were kept confidential, but in her case she wanted everyone to know about it, saying she didn't want it to happen to others. She gained a lot of respect for that, and Michael couldn't blame her for it. Rape is a terrible thing and he could identify with her for a moment because of the violations he was feeling in this case. At least my case isn't as serious, he thought. After he found out about the rape, he felt bad that he was so angry with her.

Then he read more newspapers from that period. Michael discovered that Darlene had sued the young man in civil court, and the case was suddenly dismissed on the agreement of both sides. The paper indicated that the boy's family paid Darlene a confidential settlement.

This made Michael suspicious. Did she get an appetite for legal settlements out of that experience, or did she fabricate the original story? He would never know. Of course, nothing about this would help him prove that Darlene was lying now, he thought.

Jonathan was his next research subject. Neither Darlene nor Jonathan had an arrest record in any of the 50 states. That was confirmed by the investigator. However, he found out that Jonathan lived for a period of time in Washington State as an adult—apparently after Darlene left the state. Could there be some connection between the two? Michael had hit a dead end.

"Look at what I found," Michael told Attorney B. "Darlene was involved in another case with a settlement for injuries years ago. Does that help?"

"Well," she said, "It doesn't prove anything. It may even make her more sympathetic to a jury. She may be able to keep that out of evidence, unless she wants to bring it in. We might want to object. Do you still want to look further? If you believe Darlene and Jonathan have a "history," can you think of any other place they might have been? We've exhausted all 50 states."

"I know! What about Canada? Which province is above Washington State?"

"Oh, that's British Columbia. Vancouver's the big city near the border. Maybe one or both of them spent some time up there. We could research that."

"Let's do it!" Michael said.

Michael's Outcome

Michael hit pay dirt! Jonathan was arrested once in Vancouver on a domestic violence charge. When the police arrested him, they asked him if he had any weapons in the house. Apparently he knowingly lied to the police. The police report said that after being specifically asked two times, and insisting he had no weapons in the house, the police found a gun, which Jonathan owned. Michael brought this information back to Attorney B.

"Jonathan is a liar. We have evidence now. And Darlene was involved in a rape case 20 years ago," Michael told Attorney B. "Does that help my case? I couldn't find anything connecting the two to each other in the past. Do I still need that?"

"Let me talk to the deputy District Attorney about this," Attorney B said.

A week later Michael heard back from his attorney, "Guess what! I've had several phone calls with the Deputy D.A. this week. It seems that Darlene lied to him about having no previous involvement with any legal case, including being a victim or getting a settlement. Your information, combined with them asking her that question, shows that she's a liar."

"Also," Attorney B continued, "They don't want to use Jonathan as a witness, since he has a record of lying to police. He's a liar too. So they're going to drop your case! No trial!"

"Yaaaa!" Michael exclaimed. "Now, will they go after them for conspiracy to commit extortion? They tried to get $10,000 from me."

"I suggested that, but the D.A. said no. They have no evidence this is what occurred. They just don't want to lose their case against you, because both of their only witnesses have a history of lying. This doesn't mean they think you're innocent. In fact, they think you're lying too. So, unless you can find evidence that there was a conspiracy to commit extortion, you're not going to get that satisfaction."

"Well, at least I can tell my friends and family that the charges are being dropped, and why. I'm innocent. I always have been, and now they'll believe me. But it cost me $10,000—and it didn't cost Darlene and Jonathan a dime. I hope the taxpayers know how much they spent on this case. I wonder when or where Darlene and Jonathan will try this next?"

Few Consequences

Antisocials get away with a lot. In Michael's case, there was no penalty for them. They lied to the D.A., but they didn't lie in court (which would have been perjury) because the case didn't get that far. In fact, there are rarely any penalties for perjury. Perhaps that's why there seems to be so much of it these days.

Antisocials often get away with a lot in the legal system because they know how to manipulate the system better than most people. Until people catch on, Antisocial HCPs will continue to use the legal system as they did in the case of Michael. There are skillful con artists, and they're willing to take risks. It may not happen a lot, but I have seen it happen too many times.

A Question

Michael is trying to decide whether to devote part of his life to catching Darlene and Jonathan. Which do you think would be his best approach?

A. Let go of this case all together and get on with his life.

B. Turn investigating Darlene and Jonathan into a hobby.

C. Try to meet with the deputy District Attorney to convince them he's not lying.

D. Bring a civil suit against Darlene and Michael, which has a lower burden of proof than a criminal case; he could possibly win.

E. Write and post an Internet article about his experience to inform others to watch out.

While there is no absolutely correct answer when it comes to dealing with HCPs, I think "E" is best. You might not believe that someone could go through what Michael did. Yet I know from my own experience as an attorney that similar events have happened. There are Antisocials out there who can fool anybody and everybody—at least in the short run. If more people like Michael shared their stories, perhaps people would realize how easy it is for an Antisocial stranger to turn anyone into his or her Target of Blame.

A. *Let go of this case all together and get on with his life.* This is certainly a good solution, since he would be "choosing his battles," and deciding not to focus on this case anymore, even though he feels frustrated.

B. *Turn investigating Darlene and Jonathan into a hobby.* This could also work, but Michael would have to be careful not to trigger any harassment claims or restraining orders. Of course, he could try to get a restraining order over-turned, but a court might leave it in place just to ensure that nobody got hurt in the future by getting too close to each other.

C. *Try to meet with the District Attorney's office to convince them he's not lying.* This is unlikely to be anything more than a waste of time. The deputy D.A. still believes Michael is lying, thinking that the evidence about the "history" of Darlene and Jonathan could be unfortunate and unrelated to the allegations against Michael. It sounds like the deputy D.A. may have become emotionally committed to the belief that Michael was guilty and won't change his belief.

D. *Bring a civil suit against Darlene and Jonathan, which has a lower burden of proof than a criminal case, which he could win.* This is an appealing option. But the D.A. is right—there's no evidence to support Michael's hunch that Darlene and Jonathan were involved in a conspiracy to commit extortion. It would be a long shot. If he pursued a civil case, his attorney would have the opportunity to take their depositions. As described above, Antisocials often contradict themselves in depositions. However, it may be difficult to prove a case with just these types of contradictions.

News Flash

January 8, 2008, a woman called in to a Harrah's Casino in San Diego County. She told the hotel operator that she had killed her husband because he'd gambled too much and lost several thousand dollars. She said she was going to kill herself. The SWAT team blocked off the hotel area and searched room-to-room. But they were unable to find her, or a victim.

I remember this story in the news in San Diego. I remember having discussions with friends about the weird logic of killing one's husband because he gambled too much. I didn't even stop to think or to be skeptical, because it sounded so realistic. Since families are under so much stress over the holidays, some spousal murders, sadly, don't surprise me. But I too was conned.

Apparently, her story seemed familiar and the police found out that a woman had made a similar phone call to Caesar's Casino in Atlantic City a couple of days earlier. That call was traced to a pay phone. She wasn't even in the casino.

Then it came out that Harrah's Casino security had asked this woman to leave several times, but she kept coming back. She was charged with a misdemeanor. The police know her name, but it hasn't been released. Apparently, in Atlantic City the police are familiar with her. She's made similar calls to 15 of Harrah's properties, including another casino in Mississippi. They say she has some psychological problems. Hmmm? I wonder if she fits the profile in this Tip. What do you think?

Don't Get Conned

While Antisocial "Con Artists" are the best at lying and manipulating information, all of the High Conflict Personalities lie some of the time. In your everyday life, from now on, you're wise to be a little more cautious with the information you believe—especially from strangers.

Handling Antisocial HCPs

1. **Be alert for unusual stories that require you to do something.** We naturally believe people who tell us they were victimized. The key point with Antisocials is that they want something from you. They'll say anything to get it. If someone's story requires you to make a leap of faith and make a donation or put your energy into something unfamiliar, say "I'll think about it"—and get more information.

2. **Pay attention to your gut feelings.** Antisocials will seek and find your soft spots. You'll feel uncomfortable around them before you consciously know why. Pay attention to your gut feelings and feel free to ask questions. They'll use many clever and fast words to distract you from your doubts about what they're saying. They'll try to put the burden on you, but only if you let them.

3. **Be skeptical when anybody tells you someone else is an evil monster.** Antisocials are constantly blaming others for terrible deeds that didn't occur, or at least not the way they describe them. Decide for yourself whether someone is not trustworthy, dangerous, or has made dramatic threats. Consider the source. People who speak in extremes are often projecting their own negative viewpoint onto others. People "get it backwards" more often than you realize.

4. **HCPs have distortions much of the time and lie some of the time.** This should be obvious, but people get fooled every day. There are people who will knowingly hurt you. Others honestly believe what they're saying, but it's false information. Be aware that this occurs.

5. **Remind yourself every day to maintain a healthy skepticism.** When we get fooled, most of the time it occurs because we didn't consider that this nice person could be insincere with us. HCPs are often in a lot of pain (with Internal Upsets) and very emotionally persuasive. It helps to remind yourself that you can be easily misled. Antisocial Con Artists chronically spin tales of being abused by their victims. Don't be misled.

Don't Get Conned By Antisocials

Characteristics

1. Antisocials routinely attempt to dominate others because they fear being dominated.

2. Antisocials show a strong disregard for social rules and laws.

3. Antisocials have lots of aggressive energy, high risk-taking, and disregard for others.

4. Antisocials constantly lie and deceive, even when they're easy to discover.

5. Antisocials have an extreme lack of remorse.

Managing Antisocial HCPs

1. Be alert for unusual stories that require you to do something.

2. Pay attention to your gut feelings.

3. Be skeptical when anybody tells you someone else is an evil monster.

4. HCPs have distortions much of the time and lie some of the time.

5. Remind yourself every day to maintain a healthy skepticism.

Tip #7: Don't Be a Negative Advocate

CHAPTER

7

DILBERT: © Scott Adams/Dist. by United Feature Syndicate, Inc.

Tip #7
Don't Be A Negative Advocate

"Maria! Either you're with me or you're against me! There's no in between!" Carlos said to his sister. "I need your help in persuading the Homeowners Association that my neighbors have been ruining my life."

One of the most shocking things about High Conflict People is how aggressively they seek (and find!) "Negative Advocates." Negative Advocate is a term I created after handling many high-conflict disputes. This term can apply to anyone who gets emotionally hooked by the HCP to fight their battles for them. Sometimes they are more aggressive than the HCP. And sometimes they have much more credibility.

Negative Advocates can be family members, friends, co-workers, neighbors, and even professionals. They join in HCPs' attacks against their Targets of Blame in a very emotional manner. They usually just want to help and aren't very well informed. But the high-intensity fear and anger of HCPs can be very emotionally persuasive.

There are several key issues with Negative Advocates:

- What to expect (Negative Advocates may be your biggest problem in any high-conflict case)

- Why negative advocates get hooked (The HCP's intense emotions are contagious)

- Why you should not become a negative advocate (The HCP will turn on you)

- What to do with negative advocates (When and how to respond)

What to Expect

Let's look at what happened when Carlos emotionally hooked his sister into fighting his battle. Maria explained the whole process to her therapist after she was caught by surprise by the realities of the situation.

I was all fired up because I was already frustrated by Carlos's problems everywhere he went. He told me that his next-door neighbor played the radio really loud, and that it kept waking him up. He complained to the Homeowners' Community Manager, who got angry and ignored him. Carlos says the Manager was friendly with the neighbor, so he didn't care about Carlos's problem. At least that's what Carlos said. I thought just because he's got problems doesn't mean that other people should get away with treating him this way.

Carlos asked me to come to his Homeowners meeting to put pressure on the HOA Board to make the Community Manager do something about this. This is what happened when I had a chance to speak. They only give you three minutes, so I was really feeling tense.

I said, "You people don't care about what happens to my brother. His neighbor keeps waking him up and your manager isn't doing anything about it. He pays huge Homeowners' Association fees and gets nothing for it. You people are inconsiderate and should be fired from your jobs. I'm sick and tired of people being irresponsible. Tell me what you're going to do about it. Now!"

Then the Board President, who was chairing the meeting, completely caught me by surprise.

"Ma'am," the President said, "I can really empathize with your frustration. We usually have more time at the end of the meeting to discuss these kinds of things in depth. But I'll take three minutes right now to let you know what I've found out about this problem. The manager told me that when the complaint was made they checked with the neighbors to see what was going on. Six neighbors wrote letters saying that the neighbor Carlos was accusing was gone, on vacation, for the last three weeks."

"We also found out that on one day, a house-cleaning person came in—during the afternoon. She admits she had the radio on while she was working. It's possible that your brother heard the radio on that one afternoon. However, all six neighbors say no one was there at night. And the house-cleaning person says she only came on one day—in the afternoon—during the three weeks the neighbor was gone."

"They're lying!" Carlos yelled at the President. "All of them. And so are you!"

"I respect your concerns," the President responded, calmly. "If you want to discuss this further, I can meet with you and the Community Manager after the general meeting is over. If you want to do that, just stick around. Now, I must let other people have their turn for three minutes—just as we let you and your sister have three minutes each. It's been our policy for several years, and I know it can be frustrating. But I also know that you want a peaceful community, and these procedures help with that. So thanks for your input, and we'll be available at the end of the general meeting. Now, let's hear the next speaker…"

Just like that, I realized I'd been a total sucker. I was completely humiliated to have stuck my neck out like that without really knowing what was going on. I swore I'd never stick up for my brother in public again, without a really, really good reason. I guess he can get me to feel so bad for him that I'll do almost anything to get him off my back. But sometimes it's a big mistake. That time it was a really big mistake.

Carlos just walked out of the meeting at that point, so I followed him. The next day, I apologized to the Manager and explained that I appreciated the President's calm explanation. She has a hard job, and I know what it can be like—having dealt with Carlos for so many years.

HCPs unconsciously seek Negative Advocates to justify their misperceptions and misbehavior and to assist them in blaming others for their problems. They feel driven to do this and it feels normal to them. In 30 years I've never seen a high-conflict dispute that didn't have one or more Negative Advocates who helped in creating, escalating, or perpetuating the dispute. HCPs are often too disorganized, emotionally distraught, or unbelievable to maintain a high-conflict dispute on their own. Yet they're especially skilled at drawing others in with their child-like charm, intense emotions, and false claims about their Targets of Blame.

Negative Advocates usually just want to help. They become convinced that the High Conflict Person is a victim of someone else's terrible behavior. They often fight harder than the HCP. That is, until they become fully informed about the true nature of the dispute. Then they often abandon the HCP or withdraw their active support—and try to avoid the Targets of Blame, because they helped blame them.

Negative Advocates generally have the following 10 characteristics:

1. They are misled by the HCP's *emotionally* intense charm, hurt, fear, and anger.

2. They sincerely want to help and become *emotionally* committed to helping the HCP.

3. They believe the distorted high-conflict thinking of the upset HCP *without question.*

4. They advocate *for* the HCP's negative behavior, negative emotions, and negative thinking.

5. They advocate *aggressively* against the HCP's perceived enemies.

6. They protect HCPs from the natural consequences of their negative behavior.

7. They take an "all-or-nothing" approach to problem-solving.

8. They join with the HCP in "splitting" those involved into "all-good" and "all-bad."

9. They often abandon or turn on the HCP when they become fully informed.

10. Some Negative Advocates have high-conflict personalities and identify with the HCP.

Like Enablers and Co-Dependents

In many ways, Negative Advocates are like the "enablers" for alcoholics and addicts. Enablers have been studied for decades in substance abuse treatment. They're the people who chronically cover up for the alcoholic, clean up their messes, call their bosses and say they'll be late for work, buy them their booze or drugs in hopes of controlling their use, pour out their booze or drugs in unrealistic hopes of separating them from their problem, and so forth. In short, they "enable" alcoholics and addicts to stay sick by protecting them from the negative consequences of their addiction.

Another common word for enablers is "co-dependents." They're "dependent" on helping the addict and this becomes the focus of their daily lives, just as addicts are "dependent" on drugs and focus their daily lives on getting and using drugs. I learned about all of this in the 1980s while running the Family Program for co-dependents in a hospital alcohol and drug treatment program for three years. Negative Advocates are very similar, although they often take a more public role and are often unaware of the true behavior of the HCP.

Maria exhibits all the signs of frustration and burnout that co-dependents have. Unfortunately, there aren't many support groups yet for Negative Advocates in recovery, like there are for those who live with an alcoholic or addict. However, if you're dealing with an HCP and recognize times when you have become a Negative Advocate, you can benefit from the books, support groups, and counselors who work with alcoholics and addicts. Also, there is a group called Co-Dependents Anonymous (CODA) which may be helpful in your area. Remember, you're not alone in dealing with HCPs!

Fortunately for Maria, her therapist helped her understand that she was "not the cause" and "not the cure" for her brother's disordered behavior. This helped Maria "let go" of being a Negative Advocate for Carlos.

Why Negative Advocates Get Hooked

Negative Advocates get unconsciously emotionally hooked by the emotional intensity of HCPs. This is why they take strong "protective" action before examining the facts of the situation. Let's take a look at the brain and how people operate in groups.

Human beings are social survivors. More than any other species on earth, we survive and thrive as a social group in almost any environment. We adapt as a social group. We build cultures and societies as a social group. We send people to the moon, build tall buildings, and discover cures for terrible diseases, all because of the teamwork of many, many people. And we protect ourselves as a social group. We are capable of speedy responses to almost any crisis, using our social group defenses. None of us could do this alone.

How do we do this so well?

Unlike all other living beings, we're highly connected and able to communicate nonverbally through our emotions—like a built-in wireless network (Goleman, 2006). Our emotions are contagious. We learn much of this in early childhood. For the first two years of our lives, the right hemisphere of our brains (the mostly nonverbal side of our brain) is developing. Our left hemispheres (the verbal and problem-solving side of our brain) start developing when we turn about two years old (Seigel, 1999).

This means that for the first most fundamental years of our lives, we're absorbing information and learning ways of behaving that are mostly nonverbal and unconscious. This is called Right-Brain to Right-Brain communication by some researchers (Schore, 2007).

This also means that we're highly attuned to the facial expressions and emotions of our parents or other caretakers. If our parent shows fear, then we know to be afraid and we adopt highly clinging behavior. If we're afraid and our parents are disinterested, we learn to express highly angry behavior. This gets their attention and irritates them enough to try to defuse our upset behavior by finding out what's wrong and fixing it.

Understanding how we learn socially and communicate emotionally helps us understand the impact that high-conflict people have on us and why we respond as we do. We're wired for high-conflict emotions. Emotions are the "instant messages" of this wireless network of human beings, as we quickly, nonverbally, and unconsciously receive important survival information from others before we have time to analyze the situation ourselves.

For Maria, her gut feelings told her she "had to" help her brother because of the negative emotions of guilt and fear she experiences if she resists his negative emotions. These emotions motivate us much more than we consciously realize.

Emotional Communication

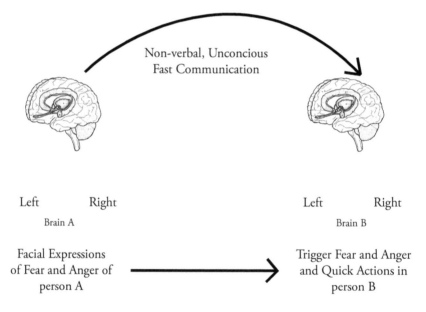

Non-verbal, Unconcious
Fast Communication

Left   Right   Left   Right

Brain A   Brain B

Facial Expressions of Fear and Anger of person A ⟶ Trigger Fear and Anger and Quick Actions in person B

This happens nonverbally, unconciously, and rapidly for quick protective group action.

Most of this emotional communication is fast and unconscious. We can override these quick assumptions if we can make them conscious and understand they're not signaling true emergencies.

HCPs frequently experience crises and intense emotions—much more than the average person. Thus, they get our attention and appear to be giving us social cues indicating a crisis and a need for quick, protective group action. It's human nature to respond emotionally—to get emotionally hooked—and to become an advocate for the person in crisis. But it may not be appropriate to the circumstances. It may actually make things worse for all involved, when the source of the crisis is the HCP's own Internal Upset and not a crisis requiring action against a Target of Blame.

Social Conclusions

Not only are our brains highly sensitive to the *emotions of others,* they're also highly susceptible to the *conclusions of others.* For quick survival action, our brains absorb expressions of fear, anger, and so forth in milliseconds—and become persuaded there's a need for action against a Target, as described by the fearful or angry person. Before we have time to question the conclusions of others, we can take quick, united action against the Target (Goleman, 2006).

Ideally, our conclusions about what actions to take in life come from logical, rational analysis of factual information. However, in emergencies our brains shortcut that process and shut down our slow, rational analysis (Goleman, 2006) and focus on extremely quick conclusions and actions. An individual's nonverbal, emotional assessment might be "There's a fire. My life's in great danger! I better run!" The person feels extreme fear and has great physical energy driven by this fear.

But an individual can pass this on socially. "The enemy's here. Our lives are in great danger! We better run!" Quick as a flash, the person and the whole group is running—before anyone has time to logically analyze the situation. If there is great danger, there may not be time to analyze the situation before you die. However, if there is no real danger, and it was the Internal Upset of an HCP, then there was a lot of running for no good reason, and perhaps for a bad reason.

Ironically, once we reach an Emotional Conclusion for action ("it just *feels right*"), we use our left hemisphere to analyze *how to* implement our emotional conclusion (I need to fight now!), rather than analyzing our emotional conclusion (do I really need to fight now?).

It appears that we're biologically programmed to help each other—to automatically and unconsciously come to each other's aid in a matter of seconds. It also appears that Carlos has learned (or was born with tendencies) to be highly emotional and therefore highly persuasive—regardless of the merits of what he's saying. He has all the nonverbal characteristics of someone in need of help: emotional intensity, guilt-inducing comments, demands for loyalty based on family relationships rather than valid needs, etc. Yet these are a manipulation, and shouldn't be the basis for Maria's decision.

These high-conflict personality traits seem to have survived for thousands of years. However, now that we live in a more interconnected, more rational world, we need to become more conscious of our unconscious social defenses. We need to learn how to manage the more extreme members of society so that we don't follow them into our own self-destruction.

Did Alison Have Any Negative Advocates?

In Tip #3, was Pat a Negative Advocate at any time for Alison? She encouraged Alison to "assert herself" with the first boyfriend she heard about, based on Alison's distorted information (unknown to Pat at first). But it doesn't appear that she advocated *for* Alison *against* her boyfriend. Instead, she backed off when she realized how aggressive Alison could be.

When Pat helped the first boyfriend clean up his bloody nose, was she being an advocate for him against Alison? I don't think so. Unfortunately, Alison took it that way. She became enraged with Pat for being disloyal. She had assumed that Pat was her Advocate because they were close friends. Since HCPs are blind to their drive to recruit Negative Advocates, Alison couldn't understand that it would have been *inappropriate* if Pat had refused to help her boyfriend. HCPs get it backwards, especially regarding loyalty issues and their negative behavior.

Was Mr. Johnson a Negative Advocate?

In Tip #4, Mr. Johnson confronted Jason with his alleged inappropriate behavior in the office. He suggested that Jason was upsetting Bob and other co-workers. Apparently Bob had emotionally persuaded Mr. Johnson that Jason was a problem. However, we know that Bob was projecting his own misbehavior onto Jason and making Jason his Target of Blame.

It appears that Mr. Johnson started out believing Bob. But there was a big difference between his approach and some of the others mentioned above. He wasn't emotionally committed to advocating for Bob. He didn't take an all-or-nothing approach, but instead told Jason he respected his work and would look at options for solving any problem. He was open-minded to feedback when Jason and other employees told him Bob was acting inappropriately. He was not emotionally hooked.

Mr. Johnson was tempted to become a Negative Advocate because he initially believed Bob. But I don't think he ever *advocated* for Bob against Jason. He raised his concerns and held off making any decisions until he heard back from Jason. He appears to be someone who was aware of the potential of becoming a Negative Advocate and therefore was much less likely to slip into that role.

Was Jonathan a Negative Advocate?

Remember Jonathan in Tip #6? He "protected" Darlene at the theater after she claimed that Michael knocked her down. He also wrote a letter to Michael, angrily demanding that he pay Darlene right away. Does he fit the characteristics of a Negative Advocate? Was he misled by her intense HCP charm, hurt, fear, and anger? His immediate protective action of restraining Michael would seem logical in a situation like that, and with a violent threat his action may be totally appropriate. It's what happens later that matters, when there's time to think and ask questions. By the time he wrote the demand letter, he appeared to entirely believe Darlene's story of being Michael's victim at the theater.

Did Jonathan strongly advocate *for* her negative behavior, emotions, and thinking? It sure seems that way. Did he advocate strongly *against* her perceived enemies? When you read his letter, there's no doubt about it. He's *emotionally* committed to helping her—not just favorable to her or objectively observing that she was in trouble. He's an advocate—a Negative Advocate.

Now, here's the big question: Does Jonathan know this is a hoax? Or is he simply a sucker? From the facts of the case, you can't know for sure and I encourage you not to "jump to conclusions." However, the speed with which he arrived at a very confusing scene and took an absolute position would suggest he knew in advance that this was going to happen. Plus, Jonathan had a "history"—he'd once lied to police about not having a gun in the house where he was staying. This alone would suggest he might be in on the hoax and that, if the case went to trial, more research on Jonathan would be highly appropriate.

If he was part of a hoax, would he still be a Negative Advocate? I believe so, because he fits all of the other characteristics: he was *advocating for* her negative behavior and high-conflict thinking. He was *emotionally advocating against* Michael, based on highly inaccurate information. It doesn't matter why people become Negative Advocates. What matters is that they take on the role of emotionally and strongly advocating for negative behavior, emotions, and thinking based on false or inaccurate information.

Negative Advocates in the Professions

When I first became an attorney 15 years ago, I was caught by surprise at how extreme some attorneys could be in advocating for their clients. After two or three years representing clients in several counties, I realized there were two types of attorneys who became Negative Advocates: the temporary Negative Advocates and the permanent Negative Advocates. I'll give you an example of each.

Mr. Jones: I represented the mother of a teenage boy in a divorce case. Mr. Jones argued hard in court and in negotiations for his client, the father, to take custody of the teenage boy away from the mother. She had been doing fine as the primary parent for over a dozen years, without complaint from the father. But when they got divorced, the father insisted on getting custody and he worked hard to convince the boy that this is what should happen. I told Mr. Jones that I had concerns that his client was highly manipulative and not interested in truly caring for the boy, but just wanted the title of "custodial parent." He insisted that his client was the better parent and was sincere about caring for him.

Despite my concerns, the mother decided not to oppose the father after he persuaded the boy to ask to move in with him. Soon after he became the custodial parent, he took a job that involved a lot of traveling and was gone for a lot of his custodial parenting time. Rather than tell the mother about this, the father left the boy home alone and swore him to secrecy.

After the divorce was over, Mr. Jones no longer represented the father and I no longer represented the mother. However, the mother contacted me one day and said that her son was living with her again at the boy's request.

Later, I ran into Mr. Jones at court and he apologized to me for believing his client was sincere and trying to persuade me that he was the better parent. He found out later that his client was a manipulator in many ways. I believe that Mr. Jones had become a temporary Negative Advocate. He had gotten emotionally hooked by his client, just as Maria was emotionally hooked by her brother Carlos in the example at the beginning of this Tip.

Mr. Brown: In this case, I represented the father in a divorce. The mother's attorney was extremely aggressive. He would send me two letters a day, each with a different demand. He scheduled numerous court hearings over unnecessary issues. He appeared to pride himself on being a bully and wouldn't return my phone calls. He advocated strongly against my client, claiming that he was threatening the mother by coming around their house. However, she had written in a declaration that he was staying away from their house. Either Mr. Brown was so emotionally hooked that he was making claims even his client didn't make, or he was knowingly lying. I wasn't sure, until I had other cases with this same attorney on the other side.

In another case, Mr. Brown represented the mother and I represented the father years after their divorce was over. My client had custody after the divorce without any problems and the mother was trying to get a change of custody to her. Mr. Brown argued that my client knowingly exposed their daughter to an abusive cousin—and he said that my client *admitted it* when Mr. Brown took his deposition. The judge looked critically at my client. I was caught by surprise because I thought it wasn't true, but I didn't have the transcript of the deposition with me.

Later, I re-read the transcript of the deposition and my client had clearly disagreed with Mr. Brown's suggestion that he had exposed the daughter to an abusive cousin. I later submitted that transcript to the court, showing the false statement, and it helped in winning sanctions against the mother for various other false allegations. Unfortunately, the sanctions law was written so that it was the client who had to pay sanctions, even when the attorney acted badly. However, the mother in this case earned the sanctions for herself with many of her own false statements. And my client retained custody of the daughter, who was doing fine in his care.

I might add that I also became a Target of this Negative Advocate. When we had to meet with the judge for some procedural matters in a different case, Mr. Brown told the judge that I was sending him two demand letters a day (which was his practice, not mine) and that he wished I would stop. The judge then looked at me and told me that I should stop doing that (without asking to see if it was true—perhaps she was emotionally hooked). Then, during our big trial in the case, Mr. Brown commented that he had tried to negotiate a settlement with me, but that I was difficult to work with and he couldn't understand it because he got along with all of the other attorneys (not at all true). The judge temporarily believed him, until she learned more about the case and about me. Later, after he was no longer in the case, his client was also ordered to pay sanctions for misleading statements to the court.

Overall, I would say that Mr. Brown enjoyed the role of being a permanent Negative Advocate. From my experience over the years, it appears that each county has a handful of attorneys like this. The good news is that most attorneys I've dealt with sincerely want to help their clients in a reasonable manner. The bad news is that many well-meaning attorneys become temporary Negative Advocates out of sincerely believing clients who are distorting or lying to them. I think the larger problem is this unconscious sincere advocacy, and the smaller problem is the group of permanent Negative Advocates—which is still a significant burden on everyone who deals with them and an embarrassment to the legal profession.

All occupations have some HCPs and Negative Advocates. This includes doctors (see Tip #4), therapists, scientists, artists, musicians, accountants, plumbers, and politicians. HCPs are often attracted to people in positions of power because they want them to use their power to advocate for them. Of course, people in positions of power may also want to be heroes.

The following case is an unfortunate and well-known example of a Negative Advocate who was a politician and attorney—and who also wanted to be a hero.

The D.A. vs. Duke Case

The alleged rape case at Duke University in 2006 wouldn't have become a high-conflict case at the university were it not for the District Attorney who apparently withheld evidence in the process of publicly targeting three lacrosse players. In this case, a young African American dancer and her friend went to a party for the lacrosse team at the university and afterwards alleged she was raped. The District Attorney, who was running for office in a significantly African American community, began the process of prosecuting three of the student players in a very public manner. This apparently triggered an intense conflict between the primarily white university and the African American community. It received national attention, with people on both sides quickly jumping to conclusions and escalating blame.

The case slowly came to a halt, when it was discovered that the "victim" kept changing her story, and her underwear had DNA samples from four different men—none of them matching any lacrosse team players. This DNA evidence (or lack of it) was apparently withheld from the defense attorneys, who had a right to have it to assist in their defense of their clients. The District Attorney was charged by the North Carolina State Bar with ethics violations for withholding important evidence—and the charges were eventually dropped against the students. The D.A. lost his license to practice law.

This case is a good example of many people becoming Negative Advocates based on very little information. Emotions took over the case, and the campus, as people jumped to conclusions, demonstrated all-or-nothing thinking and provided a powerful example of splitting people into all-good and all-bad. This is common when there's an HCP in a community, with half the people believing the HCP and half not—until the truth comes out.

- Did the District Attorney know the allegations had no basis, or was he easily persuaded by the emotional intensity of the "victim?" Whether he knowingly deceived the public and the defendants, or whether he became emotionally hooked by an HCP, he certainly acted as a Negative Advocate: He became *emotionally* committed to helping the HCP.

- He appears to have believed the distorted thinking of an upset HCP.

- He appears to have been misled by the HCP's intense charm, hurt, fear, and anger.

- He advocated *for* the HCP's negative behavior, negative emotions, and negative thinking.

- He advocated strongly *against* the HCP's perceived enemies.

- He may have a high-conflict personality and identify with the HCP.

From my experience, it appears unlikely that the District Attorney *knowingly* prosecuted a false claim, because sooner or later it would come to light in such a high-profile case. It's much more likely that he persuaded himself (as Negative Advocates often do) that she was truly a victim of a vicious crime, and he saw himself as her hero (as Negative Advocates often do).

This unconscious dynamic for prosecutors has been identified by those involved in the Innocence Project, which has won freedom for over 150 people wrongly convicted of crimes. Its co-founder has stated that experienced prosecutors sometimes simply go with their gut feelings and exclude evidence that doesn't fit. The director of the Center on Wrongful Convictions in Illinois, which was involved in the exoneration of 18 death row inmates, said that he had never seen a prosecutor intentionally prosecute someone he or she believed was innocent (Toobin, 2005).

I believe these cases are very likely examples of high-conflict people who emotionally hooked one or more professionals into becoming Negative Advocates. The professionals then jump to conclusions, have all-or-nothing thinking, and zealously engage in splitting by attacking the person who is all-bad in their eyes.

Negative Advocates Splitting Organizations

In the Duke case and the wrongful convictions cases, it's easy to see how Negative Advocates could escalate conflicts that are just under the surface, such as race relations and criminal prosecutions. But how does this happen when you have a group of people who are dedicated to working together on the same important cause?

In 2002, Amnesty International, the Nobel Peace Prize-winning human rights organization, found itself in just this kind of difficulty. A volunteer working for Amnesty International on a human rights project in Guatemala was found at the bottom of a set of stairs with her legs and arms tied up and her mouth taped shut. She said two men had attempted to abduct her. Nine months later, outside a small town in Washington state, a police officer found the same woman locked in her car with electrical tape over her eyes and mouth and wrapped around her legs. Her hands were tied behind her. She later said that in response to an article she had written and her work for the rights of prisoners she'd been receiving threatening phone calls and faxes and that knives were found in her apartment.

The Washington police detective's report said that she faked the incident. She took and failed a lie detector test. The result was that Amnesty International split into two or three factions. They intensely argued over whether she was a dedicated victim or a manipulative hoaxer. At times the "pro" wing of the board was barely speaking to the "skeptic" wing. Some people advocated strongly for her, while others wanted to distance from her. Her advocates demanded that a skeptical board member resign. Finally, her demands for organizational support and vindication were mostly approved and a newspaper advertisement was published supporting her, which she felt vindicated her (Parker, 2004).

Were her advocates Negative Advocates for her? Were the people who doubted her really Negative Advocates? Was she an unfair Target of Blame? Or was she an HCP? It certainly seems that, for nearly a year, this dispute took over many people's lives, in an organization known for its good work (which Amnesty reports was not interrupted by this organizational dispute). The emotional charge of these types of high-conflict organizational disputes can be devastating to those on both "sides."

I'm familiar with similar incidents in many organizations, including volunteer groups, religious organizations, colleges, hospitals, and other organizations that would ordinarily seem to be exceptionally "good" in their relationships and goals. One or more HCPs can escalate an "incident" into an intense and often bitter high-conflict dispute in almost any organization. Since I believe this is going to happen more and more, it's important to understand how people can resist becoming Negative Advocates.

Don't Become a Negative Advocate

Start by being aware of the existence of Negative Advocates and of how easily you can become one. It happens all the time. Look around, and I'm sure you'll see people who became hooked into believing an HCP's claims of abuse and victimization, people who helped advocate for an HCP's cause and made matters worse. Of course, this is totally different from helping a true victim of abuse. When in doubt, check it out—especially with a knowledgeable professional. It's vitally important to recognize that people are also true victims and to not make assumptions that a person is making false claims just because he or she seems extremely emotional or vague about an incident.

The difference between being a Negative Advocate and being a Positive Advocate is that Negative Advocates jump to conclusions and refuse to look further for information that may be either true or false. Keeping an open mind is essential when dealing with potential HCPs, who can also be true victims in some cases.

In order to resist becoming a Negative Advocate, it's important to consider doing the following:

1. Get lots of support. Otherwise, you'll be tempted to become too close to the HCP, because of their "charming" characteristics. They can charm anyone—for awhile. I think of many HCPs as "sugar-coated" personalities.

2. Regularly ask yourself if the facts you're operating on are true.

3. Keep an arm's length relationship with people who are high-intensity, highly demanding people.

4. Beware of HCPs who challenge your loyalty when you ask questions; they do this to divert you from the weaknesses of their "cause."

5. Talk to the people you believe may be Negative Advocates. Don't assume they agree with the HCP and are committed to being Negative Advocates. It may be just the impression the HCP wants to give.

Beware of Dual Personas

HCPs are often abusive (verbally, financially, legally, and physically) because of their frustrations. However, because this may be part of a chronic personality pattern, they've learned that they get into trouble for these behaviors. Therefore, many HCPs have developed a "dual persona" (Dutton, 1998), which means that in public they "appear" to be extremely charming, good, helpful, and generally the opposite of what they're really like in private. I think of them as "sugar-coated" HCPs.

So, you can (and will) be fooled by an HCP someday. They will appear to be the most sincere, honest, and victimized people you've ever met. Beware!

This is not to say that everyone who says they were victimized is lying. I want to repeat that there are many true cases of abuse. Even HCPs are true victims of abuse sometimes. Many of them were abused in childhood, which is when they got stuck thinking they are abused all the time.

However, an HCP with a dual persona can appear more persuasive while lying or exaggerating than an honest person can appear truthful. That's why so many people are emotionally hooked into becoming Negative Advocates every day.

Beware of HCPs Who Are Persuasive Blamers

Instead of adapting to their social group and current environment, HCPs try to get others and their environment to adapt to them and their point of view. This is a big reason they routinely get into conflicts and then escalate into "high-conflict" situations. They don't use the ordinary conflict resolution procedures of listening to and respecting others' points of view and making some adjustments (however small) in response. Because of their dual personas, they can be very persuasive.

There are at least 10 nonverbal, unconscious, social cues that HCPs generally use (mostly unconsciously, but sometimes consciously) that are highly persuasive to many people around them. Advertising researchers and negotiations experts call this "peripheral persuasion." It occurs on the periphery of people's consciousness and usually slips under their radar, highly influencing their thinking and actions. These 10 peripheral factors help persuade people in any type of dispute, even when the facts would indicate otherwise.

1. **Charm**—All human beings, including judges and juries, develop bonds with people, and these bonds can influence our view of the facts. HCPs are especially good at forming bonds temporarily with anyone. It's called charm. This is perhaps their strongest skill because they have to rely so heavily on others to handle their many interpersonal problems. They've spent a lifetime charming, manipulating, and pleading to get other people on their side. Ordinary, reasonable people usually don't put much energy into bonding with or persuading decision-makers, because they believe the truth will simply come out and resolve the dispute. Unfortunately, in a society based so much on persuasion, this is often not the result. Just as HCPs may have it backward because of their high-conflict thinking, they and their advocates often persuade others and decision-makers to also get it backward. Their Internal Upsets become external facts to those who bond with them.

2. **Heightened Emotions**—One of the first things people notice about HCPs is their high-intensity emotions: hurt, fear, anger, sadness, etc. These emotions can be almost intolerable to be around, so many people will agree with HCPs simply to get them to calm down. If you disagree, HCPs will escalate the situation more and more urgently. Finally, someone has to give in. HCPs usually outlast ordinary people, because to them the problem feels so urgent and absolute. Yet these emotions are highly persuasive. We tend to think that when someone is really upset it's because something upsetting happened. "That's awful. Something should be done about that." But with HCPs, especially the "Always Dramatic"

HCPs, it more likely comes from the constant emotional chaos of their Internal Upsets and is less likely caused by external events. On the other hand, the emotions of HCPs make them much more interesting than the average person, so they succeed at getting a lot of attention.

3. **Sense of Crisis**—HCPs are always experiencing a crisis, often triggered by some Internal Upset or by an exaggerated response to a relatively harmless external event. Yet in a crisis people often feel they can't take the time to fully evaluate the facts. They feel they must reach a decision and help out, with little information. They then make judgments based on presumptions. This means that HCPs can get a lot done in their favor in a very short period of time—as long as they can persuade others that there's no time to look beneath the surface. Many bad decisions are made in this context of crisis and urgency, which then take months or years to correct.

4. **Attractiveness**—Research confirms that attractive people do better in court, politics, and entertainment (Rieke & Stutman, 1990). It shouldn't be this way, but apparently it's true. It plays a huge role in persuading people to become Negative Advocates. Persuasive Blamers often dress nicely, smile at decision-makers and potential advocates, and are more respectful than they are in any other setting. They have learned to be appealing (sugar-coated). Unfortunately, this can be more important than the facts of any dispute.

5. **Size Matters**—In formal disputes, the number of advocates, the number of documents, the number of witnesses, and the number of arguments and allegations can make a big difference. These things intimidate and impress observers and decision-makers. If you've produced a lot of paper on the subject and gathered a lot of advocates, decision-makers may automatically assume you know what you're doing.

6. **Aggressiveness**—Research shows that in court cases the more aggressive attorney often wins. When people ask around for an attorney, they don't typically say, "I want a really knowledgeable attorney." They say, "I want a really aggressive attorney. I want to intimidate the other side." Most people know that court is often about drama and dominance, and many HCPs want their "day in court" (whether it's in real court, a Homeowners Association meeting, a workplace dispute resolution procedure, or some other setting). They want someone who'll dominate the other side and impress the judge or jury with energy and power. The facts may weigh a lot less than these impressions, except with experienced and skeptical decision-makers. The research also shows that assertive attorneys do equally as well in court, but don't get the same attention from the press (Rieke & Stutman, 1990).

7. **Simple Stories**—HCPs tell simple stories of being victimized by others. They're easy to understand and have an all-or-nothing, victim-villain quality. They're easy for the brain to process, so the decision-maker can focus more attention on what to do about the situation, rather than having to figure out what the situation is. "If it doesn't fit, you must acquit." Isn't that what attorney Johnny Cochran said in the O.J. Simpson case about the bloody glove from the crime scene that appeared too small on O.J.'s hand? I still remember that phrase. It was so simple it stuck in my mind. The jury that heard that statement acquitted O.J. of murdering his wife. However, later on, a civil jury found him guilty and ordered him to pay millions in civil damages because the burden of proof was lower and, perhaps, because the evidence was presented in a simpler manner.

8. **Fast Talkers**—People with high-conflict personalities are quick to act, quick to change their minds (or their arguments), and are fast talkers. They speak quickly, and you're so caught up in just keeping track of what they are saying that there's no time to process it. It's a neat trick used frequently by advertisers and con artists. Their point of view gets in under the radar. You sense something's not right in what they're saying, but you don't have time to stop and figure it out because they are already on to the next subject—still commanding your full attention. In one fascinating case, I discovered that the person was making a totally false statement, then quickly moving onto a reasonable conclusion and passionately arguing for the conclusion to keep attention away from the underlying false fact. "He was hitting the child and we need to stop this from happening in our community—there's just too much abuse to allow him to get away with this behavior. Don't you think you should do something about parents who abuse their children?" Now the focus is on what to do about abuse, rather than determining whether it happened in the first place.

9. **Body Language**—Tears, dramatic speech patterns, suggestive body movements, and nonstop talking are all part of the dramas that draw us in to an HCP's story. Facial expressions and hand-wringing can mean the difference between believing the story and not believing it. We get unconsciously hooked by these simple physical gestures because we identify with them so easily and they're part of our personal experience. We remember the dramatics much longer than the content of a dispute. We remember that he raised his voice and captured our attention, but we don't remember what it was about.

10. **Negative Stereotyping Labels**—When making an argument, HCPs frequently use negative labeling and catchphrases: Deadbeat Dad, Unfit Mother, Nosy Neighbor, Office Bully, Violent Man. These may or may not have anything to do with the facts of a case. But if you hear the negative label often enough, it seeps in under your radar and becomes part of your view of the person. Politicians and advertisers know this. Researchers have identified how children will adopt a highly negative view of a person and even generate nonexistent facts if an adult in authority promotes a negative stereotype of someone, then asks children questions about the "bad" person (Ceci and Bruck, 1995).

With these unconscious, nonverbal characteristics, HCPs are able to successfully recruit new Negative Advocates on a regular basis—at least for a short time. In responding to an HCP, you'll need to be alert to the existence of their Negative Advocates and how to deal with the misinformation they have. You'll also want to be very careful not to become a Negative Advocate yourself.

In the next Tip, part of the approach I describe includes responding to Negative Advocates. In the majority of cases, they're not HCPs themselves. They're generally much easier to deal with than the HCP because they're less committed to treating you as a Target of Blame—especially if you can provide them with real information.

A Question

Recognizing when you've become a Negative Advocate can be hard to do. Suppose you have a friend who's acted in an inappropriate aggressively defensive way with a Target of Blame, such as hitting, bullying, or spreading rumors. Which of the following behaviors do you think would be those of a Negative Advocate? (The answer may be none, one, or several of the following.)

A. Calm your friend by saying he or she was right.

B. Calm your friend by saying it doesn't matter and changing the subject.

C. Apologize to the Target for your friend's behavior.

D. Say nothing about the friend's behavior.

E. Withdraw your friendship.

If you chose A and B, I would certainly agree that these are Negative Advocate behaviors. If you chose C, D, or E, you are unlikely to be a Negative Advocate. However, in some cases choosing D (saying nothing about a friend's misbehavior) is considered the same as advocating for it.

Let's look carefully at each one of these.

A. *Calming your friend by saying he or she was right.* Agreeing with a friend's misbehavior against a Target is one of the worst forms of Negative Advocacy. Yet we see this all the time—at work, with neighbors, and even in our families. This encourages HCPs to escalate their misbehavior, and demoralizes Targets, who already feel isolated and abused. Perhaps as more people recognize the high-conflict thinking and misbehavior of HCPs, there will be less of this.

B. *Calming your friend by saying it doesn't matter and changing the subject.* Telling HCPs their behavior doesn't matter and changing the subject isn't quite as bad, but it still reinforces that their behavior is okay—which it isn't. Sometimes changing the subject, especially if you're also a Target (as Jason did in Tip #4), may be the best thing to do, but don't combine it with saying the misbehavior doesn't matter. Better to say nothing than endorse it in any way.

C. *Apologizing to the Target for your friend's behavior.* Generally, apologizing to the Target is not Negative Advocate behavior, because you're not advocating for the HCP nor advocating against the Target. Such an apology generally helps Targets feel better, as they know you think the HCP's behavior was wrong. Maria did this with the Homeowners' Association Board President, and it helped them both feel better and stronger. Of course, in some cases doing nothing about the HCP may be considered advocating for the HCP, so you have to use your judgment, as described below in the answer under "D."

D. *Saying nothing about the friend's behavior.* This is the biggest question in regard to Negative Advocates: Are you a Negative Advocate if you don't do anything when an HCP is acting aggressively against their Target of Blame? If you appear to be supporting the HCP, I'd say you are. If you appear to be truly neutral, then it may depend on the circumstances (for example, anyone at a violent crime scene is expected to help stop the crime, not just stand by). If you're a mediator and you ignore a few minor nasty comments in order to focus the disputing parties on the terms of a productive agreement, it wouldn't be considered advocating for the party who made the remarks.

If you choose to say something to your friend about his or her misbehavior, keep in mind the Cycle of High Conflict Thinking and that your feedback may be taken as Negative Feedback. The ability to give feedback productively with an HCP depends significantly on the strength of your relationship and the HCP's level of emotional upset. Sometimes it helps to say nothing at the time, then gently suggest a better way of handling things in the future without criticizing the past. This is a very tricky issue in our modern society and, as more people understand the dynamics of HCPs and their Negative Advocates, I hope there'll be a lot of discussion of it in the years to come.

E. *Withdrawing your friendship.* This may not be necessary in many cases. However, if your friend repeatedly engages in harmful behavior toward others, I would suggest that you try to get out of the friendship as soon as possible. You are at risk of becoming a Target sooner or later yourself. Of course, as a community member (at work, in your family, or in your neighborhood), you want to influence the community culture of conflict in a positive direction. (See Tip #11)

What to Do

First of all, don't attack Negative Advocates. They are usually uninformed and may abandon the HCP once they become informed. At times, they may even become friendly toward you and help you. I have seen this in divorce cases, where a new girlfriend insisted that my client's ex-husband would never be violent or abusive in any way. Then, a year later, the girlfriend split up with the ex-husband and admitted that he had become violent toward her too. She was emotionally hooked at the beginning of the relationship and became a Negative Advocate. But then she became informed by her own experience and turned against the ex-husband.

I know of another case where a divorcing husband discovered that his wife made the same false allegations against her previous ex-husband with the exact same details, word for word. When the husband and ex-husband compared court papers, they became good friends.

Second, provide accurate and full information when you can to the Negative Advocate. This is not always possible, but when it is this can make a big difference. Remember that Negative Advocates are usually emotionally hooked, but not factually informed. Don't assume they have an accurate impression of you. Don't assume that they support or even know what the HCP is doing.

Third, manage Negative Advocates in a similar way as you manage the HCP. Use the methods described in Part II of this book. You would be amazed at how many Negative Advocates respond well, even when they aren't HCPs themselves.

Be a Positive Advocate

Here are some characteristics of Positive Advocates—people who actually help HCPs focus on factual information, rational conclusions, and taking responsibility for problem-solving. There's more about the role of the Positive Advocate in Tip #12.

Positive Advocates:

- Don't make assumptions.

- Do investigate problems.

- Do provide support and information, without necessarily agreeing with the HCP.

- Don't take over responsibility for others' behavior problems or solutions.

- Don't do more work trying to solve the problem or conflict than the HCP.

- Don't get in the way of others' feedback and natural consequences.

- Do help the HCP get into a program of change, such as therapy or a treatment program.

This may be the most important Tip of this book, as it is usually easier for Negative Advocates to stop their own uninformed behavior than it is for HCPs to stop themselves. They're just not self-aware, but they usually back off from their Behavior that's Aggressively Defensive if no one will support them.

TIP #7 SUMMARY

Don't Be A Negative Advocate

1. HCPs constantly seek Negative Advocates to help fight their many battles.

2. HCPs can be Persuasive Blamers and unconsciously persuade others to be their Negative Advocates against their perceived enemies—their Targets of Blame.

3. Negative Advocates reinforce an HCP's negative behavior, emotions, and thoughts.

4. Negative Advocates often have more credibility and fight harder than the HCP.

5. When fully informed, Negative Advocates often abandon or turn against the HCP.

Managing Negative Advocates

1. Negative Advocates can be anyone who is "emotionally hooked" by an HCP, including family members, friends, neighbors, co-workers, and even professionals.

2. Remember that most Negative Advocates aren't HCPs themselves, but have been persuaded by the HCP's complaints about you out of loyalty, fear, or anger.

3. Don't attack Negative Advocates or assume they're committed to being Negative Advocates. They may be skeptical themselves, but feel pressured to go along temporarily until they become more fully informed—possibly by you.

4. Calmly provide as much accurate information as you can to Negative Advocates.

5. Handle Negative Advocates the same way as HCPs, including using your E.A.R. and the other methods in Part II.

Part II: Handling High Conflict People

Now that you know that High Conflict People repeatedly blame others, get things backwards, lack self-awareness, and rarely change, you may be wondering if there's any way you can handle them. While no one can control another person's behavior, there are methods you can use to *influence and contain* their behavior.

Since it's often hard to think when you're around the intense emotions and blaming behavior of high-conflict people, I've developed a simple four-step approach you can use in most high-conflict situations—or in any conflict situation. You don't even have to figure out whether the person has a high-conflict personality. It's fairly easy to remember, even under pressure. It's called the **C.A.R.S. Method™**.

C- CONNECT using your E.A.R.

A- ANALYZE your realistic options

R- RESPOND quickly to misinformation

S- SET LIMITS on misbehavior

Generally, this approach is best used in a step-by-step manner, but you won't necessarily need to use all four steps. Start with Connecting. Sometimes, this step alone eases or resolves the conflict. Next, take some time to Analyze your realistic options so that you don't just react too quickly. Then, check to see if there is any inaccurate information you need to Respond to with accurate information. Finally, decide whether you need to Set Limits on the HCP's misbehavior, and, if necessary, who can help you. Thinking about these four steps will help you have a strategy ready—especially when you are under a lot of stress and it is hard to think.

In the next four Tips I'll describe each of these steps in detail, with examples. The next page shows a set of questions you can ask yourself when using the C.A.R.S. Method.

You can write out your answers on your own or with another person acting as a Positive Advocate for you, which I'll also explain in Tip #12. This can be anyone, such as a friend, family member, neighbor, or even a professional, such as a therapist, attorney, or a person experienced in conflict resolution. Ideally, this is someone who has had some training.

There are no absolutely right or wrong answers to these questions, as each situation is different. However, based on the information in this book, some answers will be better than others. See what works for you, and change what you're doing if it's not working. Remember, you don't have to do all of these steps. Just do what fits your situation. Simply thinking and writing about these problems can go a long way towards reducing stress in a conflict.

THE C.A.R.S. METHOD™ OF CONFLICT RESOLUTION

Please feel free to make photocopies of these C.A.R.S. Method™ pages FOR YOUR OWN USE. However, do not give photocopies of these pages to anyone else, except for your C.A.R.S. Conflict Consultant™ when he or she is working with you. (Feel free to use another piece of paper to make a larger list.)

1. **CONNECT** with your E.A.R.

    A. How can I show Empathy for the other person?

    _____

    B. How can I pay Attention to the other person's concerns?

    _____

    C. How can I show my Respect?

    _____

    D. Is there a reason this is not appropriate in this situation (danger, etc.)?

    _____

2. **ANALYZE** Realistic Options:

    A. What are three or more options I have for handling this dispute, realistic or not?

    (1)_____

    (2)_____

    (3)_____

    B. Is there any high-conflict thinking (theirs or mine) that makes any of these options unrealistic?

    (1)_____

    (2)_____

© 2008 Bill Eddy

(3) _____

C. What option will I try first?

_____

3. **RESPOND** Quickly to Misinformation:

A. Is there any inaccurate information? Does it need a response?

_____

B. What is my more accurate information?

(1) _____

(2) _____

(3) _____

C. Who should I provide with the more accurate information?

(1) _____

(2) _____

4. **SET LIMITS** on Misbehavior:

A. Is there any behavior that needs to be contained?

_____

B. What power do I have to Set Limits?

_____

C. What resource in my community could be used to Set Limits?

_____

D. What will I ask the community resource to do?

_____

Tip #8: Connect Using Your E.A.R.

CHAPTER

8

"Look, mother, this section should interest you."

Tip #8
Connect Using Your E.A.R.

The first thing that most people feel like doing when they're blamed or attacked is to attack back—to retaliate. To say, "No, it's not all my fault. It's all YOUR FAULT!" While this might get a reasonable person to stop and assess the situation, with High Conflict People this simply escalates their emotions and their Mistaken Assessment of Danger (M.A.D.). This escalates their Behavior that's Aggressively Defensive (B.A.D.). It influences them to be more difficult, not less.

Instead, it's helpful to respond to the other person with Empathy, Attention, and Respect (E.A.R.). Rather than yelling at the person, running away from the person, or giving the person Negative Feedback (which is interpreted as any feedback about their behavior), focus on showing *Empathy,* giving your full *Attention* (even if it is brief), or telling the person something that you *Respect* about him or her.

This is very difficult to do at first. However, from my experience (especially after doing it wrong many times), I have learned that Empathy, Attention, and Respect generally calm the high-conflict person down right away, at least briefly. I'm not saying that it causes a long-term change in their behavior or their personality. But it calms them down enough to use their problem-solving skills for awhile. This gives them the chance to work *with you* rather than against you for a few minutes to solve the problem. In some cases, E.A.R. alone turns the conflict around and makes it manageable.

The reason that E.A.R. works is that it soothes the HCP's unconscious defenses enough to calm their fear of you and allows them to see you as less of an enemy and more of an ally in solving an objective problem. All of us find it easier to solve problems with someone who cares—even a little bit—than with someone who doesn't care.

My Group Experience

Years ago, when I worked in a psychiatric hospital, I was a therapist doing group therapy with patients with long-term mental illness. Most of them had schizophrenia, which is a mental disorder causing delusions and hallucinations. The purpose of the group therapy was to help them cope with daily life. Most of them were on medications that helped reduce their hallucinations and anxiety.

One day, I was leading the group therapy and somehow the patients got on to the subject of their hallucinations. "Bill, you don't know what it's like to have someone else's voice in your head telling you what to do, or telling you that you're a bad person." Trying to help them feel better, I said, "Don't worry, those voices aren't really other people, but part of the problem in your mind. You take medications to hopefully quiet the voices or make them stop."

In response, several of the group members said, "No, Bill! You don't understand! These voices are real! They're not just made up in our heads. These voices are real! And they're very upsetting."

I tried to explain that research showed the voices were not real, but the group got angrier and angrier with me. Then I realized that the issue for them was *how upsetting* it was and how it made them feel helpless to have these voices in their heads. So rather than arguing about the truthfulness of the voices, I switched to empathizing with them.

I said, "I don't really want to argue with you. I can see how difficult it is and I really empathize with you for having to deal with this problem. Whatever is happening, I can imagine how frustrating and distracting and discouraging it must feel to have this happening."

To my surprise, they immediately calmed down. That's what they really wanted—empathy. They wanted me to understand and care about how they felt, and I really did. I'd worked with them for many weeks and their battles within their own minds were heart-rending. They wanted me to know that their lives weren't easy. They wanted me to know that it was a daily struggle to ignore these voices and do what they planned to do that day. It was a great learning experience for me about respecting and empathizing with people who were different, because I learned that they experience the same human emotions that all of us do.

How Do You Give Empathy, Attention, and Respect?

E.A.R. requires some emotional self-discipline with HCPs. In the face of someone being angry with you, this means you don't get angry back. In the face of someone blaming you, this means you don't blame them back. In the face of someone giving you feedback that is negative and possibly filled with misinformation, it means you don't challenge their point of view. Instead, you first give them your Empathy, your Attention, and your Respect.

Empathy

Empathy is the ability to sincerely identify with and care about another person's feelings and life experience.

For example: "I can empathize with your sadness at the death of your mother."

For example: "I can empathize with the frustrations you're having with your noisy neighbor."

For example: "I empathize with your desire for an answer before Monday, and I wish I could let you know sooner."

Attention

Paying full attention to someone involves brief, uninterrupted listening, followed by repeating the essence of what you heard so the person feels that you were paying attention (and not just thinking of a response).

For example: "I heard how important it is to you to get the parking lot lights fixed by the weekend."

For example: "I understand this tree is threatening to drop a branch on your roof and you're concerned for your safety."

Respect

Let the person know something that you truly respect about him or her.

For example: "I really respect how hard you've worked to gather information about this issue and notify us of this problem."

For example: "I respect your concern that you won't get a response from us, so let me reassure you this is important to us too."

When you give someone your empathy, attention, and respect, make sure that it's sincere. These aren't just words. These are natural human feelings we all have and that are meant to be shared with others. You don't need to exaggerate or think of something big. A small amount of E.A.R. can go a long way.

Keep in mind that you must do all of this honestly. If you don't truly empathize with or respect the HCP, he or she will sense it and become more angry with you for your dishonesty—which "proves" that you don't care. Instead, only empathize as much as you really do. Don't lie about having empathy for the person, and don't make an empty statement. Instead, find something human about the other person that you can connect with, and show them your empathy, attention, and respect. It doesn't have to be all of these, and you don't have to use those exact words.

Perhaps you can empathize with their struggles in life, or mention something about a time when you've been in a position like theirs. You might find something about their pain you can empathize with because you've had a similar pain at some point in your life. Most people experience empathy and learn to empathize with others in early childhood. But some people (including many HCPs) don't get much empathy growing up because of abusive relationships or traumatic experiences.

Therefore, they may not know how to give empathy or ask for it directly. Many of those with high-conflict personalities are so preoccupied with their own distress that they don't have awareness of the pain of others. Therefore they don't have much empathy. However, you can still empathize with them, regardless of their ability to empathize or not.

Keep in mind that empathy, attention, and respect are what high-conflict people want more than anything. This is part of human nature—as necessary as eating and breathing. HCPs want this more than most people because they get less of it in daily life as a result of their Behavior that's Aggressively Defensive. They push people away without realizing it. It doesn't cost you anything to empathize with them.

The same goes for attention. In today's world, there's so much activity and so many people around that it's hard to get attention. High-conflict people are desperate for attention, and they may not have gotten enough positive attention as their personalities were developing. They'll often behave in totally inappropriate ways, just to get attention. Even getting negative attention appeals to them, since it's at least some attention. Of course, this backfires because they don't like the negative attention they usually get. What they really want is positive, full attention, as described above.

Respect is also in short supply these days. High-conflict people are desperate for respect, yet they don't know how to get it. They often escalate their conflicts in an effort to get others to be impressed with them—to think they're especially tough or smart or important. Yet there is something you can respect about most people. So just give it to them. It doesn't cost you anything.

Ashley Smith's Example

You might have a hard time imagining giving your empathy, attention, and respect to a High Conflict Person. You might think that you shouldn't have to give your E.A.R. to someone who's acting badly. However, the amazing story of Ashley Smith may help you realize that this can be done even under extreme stress.

On Friday, March 11, 2005, in Atlanta, Brian Nichols was in court for a trial on a rape charge. He somehow grabbed a court deputy's gun and killed the judge and two other people. He then escaped from the courthouse and killed a federal agent before eluding the authorities.

Around 2 a.m. the next morning, Brian took Ashley Smith hostage at her new apartment in a neighborhood outside of Atlanta. He told her he wouldn't hurt her if she did what he told her to do. She realized who he was because she had heard on the radio that there was an escaped prisoner who had killed some people at the courthouse that morning.

She begged him not to kill her. She told him that she needed to live to raise her six-year-old daughter, whose father was stabbed to death four years earlier. Her daughter was staying with her aunt because of Ashley's on-and-off struggles with drugs, but she was supposed to meet her in the morning.

Brian tied her up and made her sit in the bathroom while he took a shower. She knew that he was on trial for raping his former girlfriend. She feared he would rape her after his shower and kill her too. But he covered her head with a towel so she wouldn't have to see him naked.

She tried to strike up a conversation with him, and he started talking a little bit. He explained how he was treated badly in the jail, and she empathized with him by telling him that she'd been in jail a few times, just a few hours each time for driving under the influence of alcohol. She said she could relate to how hard it is to be in jail.

After his shower, he moved her to the bedroom. He seemed quiet and tense, and she knew at any minute he could rape her and kill her. She kept talking to him. He eventually removed the tape and the extension cord that he had used to tie her up. But she made no effort to run because he had shown her the three guns he had and she knew he would use them.

She continued to make every effort to "connect" with him (her word). She kept telling herself to feel what he was feeling so she could help him stay calm. She pictured him as a lonely, helpless little boy who had gotten himself into some very big trouble. They discussed his former girlfriend, his parents, his newborn son, his church, and God.

She kept bringing their short conversations back to her daughter. She hoped that he would feel empathy for her daughter, now that he had a son. She wanted him to understand how terrible it would be if both of her parents were killed. He looked at pictures of her daughter and her family. She specifically told him she needed to leave in the morning to go see her daughter at 10 a.m.

As the night wore on, she felt that she had enough of a connection that he might actually let her leave in the morning. She built up her confidence and decided to try to persuade him to give himself up to the police in the morning too. She pointed out to him that the people he killed had families who would be devastated, just like she was devastated when her husband died. She told him that God wanted people to do their best and that he needed to pay for his actions by turning himself in. He said he just wanted to stay at her apartment for a few days. He knew there was a huge search on for him in the Atlanta area, because he turned her TV on from time to time.

Around sunrise, she offered to cook breakfast for him. He was impressed that she gave him pancakes using real butter. He said if they had met under different circumstances, he felt they could have been friends. Finally, when the time came for her to leave for her meeting with her daughter, he let her walk out of her apartment and told her to tell her daughter he said hello.

Once she was far enough away, she called the police and they came and arrested him without a struggle. For more information about Ashley's experience, see her book: "An Unlikely Angel: The Untold Story of the Atlanta Hostage Hero," by Ashley Smith with Stacy Mattingly (2005).

None of the news reports stated that Brian Nichols had a personality disorder, but he clearly had some high-conflict behavior. Ashley connected with him by talking to him gently, by cooking him pancakes with real butter, and by describing her concerns for her daughter.

Several aspects of the way of she handled him stand out:

1. Her actions communicated empathy, attention, and respect. It didn't matter what the words were.

2. She apparently created a sense of connection by describing her concerns about her daughter. He then began to share that connection and told her to tell her daughter "hello for me."

3. Her actions may have only calmed him down a little, but it was enough for him to let her go.

4. Her matter-of-fact, calm conversations helped her build enough empathy with him to persuade him to turn himself in without a bloodbath.

It's hard to imagine a situation more frightening than Ashley's. Yet she was able to keep herself calm and to communicate that calm to him. This is an excellent example of not giving negative feedback so that he didn't have a mistaken assessment of danger.

If you think of situations in which you don't feel like giving another person Empathy, Attention, or Respect, just remember Ashley's story. Brian's behavior certainly wasn't her fault and was clearly caused by his own Internal Upset. She would certainly have been justified in yelling at him, cursing him, and blaming him, or withholding any empathy or respect. However, even though the problem wasn't caused by her, she had to handle it and she handled it well.

Azim Khamisa's Example

Another powerful story of connecting with empathy is that of Azim Khamisa, a successful international businessman.

In 1995, Azim's only son Tariq was a student at San Diego State University. He had a part-time job delivering pizza. One night he couldn't find the address he had been given for a pizza delivery. While he was walking around searching for it, someone walked up to him and shot him to death.

The shooter was a 14-year-old new gang member, Tony Hicks, who was instructed by an 18-year-old gang leader to kill someone as a gang membership requirement. They phoned in a false order for a pizza, and then ambushed and killed Tariq while he looked for the phony address.

Yet Azim did not seek revenge and retaliation. Instead, he thought that there were two victims of this senseless crime: one was dead and the other was in prison. He says that he will mourn the death of his son forever. However, he became committed to making a change in the society in which children were killing children.

Azim formed the Tariq Khamisa Foundation to honor Tariq's life. He reached out to Tony's grandfather and guardian, Ples Felix, and together they have spoken to tens of thousands of school children across the United States about using the "power of forgiveness" to end youth violence.

When Tony was sentenced to prison, he gave an emotional speech about asking for forgiveness and taking responsibility for what he had done. He is eligible for parole in 2027. Azim has visited Tony and they have developed a respectful relationship. Azim says that there will be a job for Tony at the Tariq Khamisa Foundation when he gets out. For more information about the work of the Tariq Khamisa Foundation, go to their website at www.tkf.org (Khamisa, 2007).

For their work in violence prevention education, Azim and Ples were given the National Crime Victims "Special Community Service Award" in Washington, D.C. in 1997. They were also given the Peacemaker of the Year award by the National Conflict Resolution Center in San Diego, where I work.

Several aspects of this example stand out:

1. Everyone would have understood if Azim had sought revenge and retaliation. Instead, he showed enormous empathy for Tony Hicks as another one of America's lost sons in addition to his own son.

2. Azim uses the power he has to help others, rather than giving up and becoming isolated and depressed—or blaming. He really connects with people. I've seen him speak to groups several times.

3. Azim is a devout Muslim. Ashley Smith, in the example above, is a devout Christian. In today's world there is a lot of fear and criticism of people from different faiths, and a lot of talk of retaliation rather than forgiveness. I

hope that examples like Ashley and Azim will show that people—regardless of differences of faith, politics, or race—can get along and have empathy, attention, and respect for others, even under the most extreme circumstances.

How To Connect With Your E.A.R.

Connecting with your E.A.R. is less about listening and more about what *you* communicate to the other person. For you to connect, you need to do more than just say "I hear what you're saying." It's more than reflective listening, in which a person "reflects back" what they heard. An example of reflective listening is "I heard you say that you're upset about such-and-such." While reflecting back can be a very useful method to use with most people, it generally isn't enough with HCPs.

With HCPs, you need to really *connect*. You need to make efforts to say or show your E.A.R.: "I *care* that you're upset about such-and-such, and I want to help you. I *respect* the efforts you've made to solve this problem." It's a *giving* process from you to the other person, to help create a connection. It's not just a neutral reflection back to the person, because that's not usually enough to help HCPs feel connected.

This connection is what HCPs are mostly looking for. That's why showing your E.A.R. usually calms them down so effectively. They desperately want empathy, attention, and respect and aren't used to getting it. The average person doesn't need you to care to help them solve a problem—they already feel cared for and can get that from other important people in their lives. But HCPs are desperate for E.A.R. and get into conflicts with those close to them in an effort to get it. They often don't have real friends and don't feel really connected anywhere else in their lives. So they go from conflict to conflict, trying to find someone who will give them their E.A.R.—someone who will at least respect them as a person, despite their flaws.

Homeowners Example

Linda is a member of a homeowners association, and she lives near a tennis court that is managed by the association. One of two light bulbs has burned out over the tennis court and it's 4:50 p.m. on Friday. She calls up the Homeowners Association Community Manager's office to complain and gets Betty, the office assistant. Betty is sick and tired of Linda's complaints about one little thing after another.

Betty: "What is it this time, Linda? You know I have to leave at 5."

Linda: "The light bulb's out over the tennis court. You have to do something about it."

Betty: "It can wait until Monday!"

Linda: "No it can't! It's dangerous out there! You never know if someone dangerous might try to sleep there in the dark. What are you, stupid? Anything could happen over the weekend."

Betty: "Isn't there another light out there? It's not totally dark and you know it. Don't exaggerate! Don't lie to me about it being dangerous just to satisfy your latest impulsive demand!"

Linda: "You can't talk to me that way! Where's your boss? I insist that I talk to him right now, or I'm coming over there."

Betty: "Let me put you on hold for a minute." Betty took a deep breath. Her boss was already gone and she knew the conversation wasn't going well. She decided to try another approach.

Betty, in a calm and soothing tone of voice: "Hi Linda, I'm back. He's not here now, but I can really empathize with how frustrating it must be that the light has burned out. I'll put a call in to our groundskeeper, who was planning to stop by in the morning to pick up some paperwork. Hopefully, he'll be able to fix it because we need his tall ladder. That's what I can do now to pay attention to this problem. There's a chance that he'll be able to come by tonight, but I can't guarantee it. I'll check back in with you on Monday. So you have a good weekend, okay?"

Linda calmed down a bit after hearing that Betty empathized with her situation: "Are you sure he'll be here tomorrow?"

Betty: "I'm pretty sure, because he said he planned to be here briefly on Saturday. I can't guarantee it, but it's the only way it can get fixed before Monday. I'll check back with you on Monday. That's what I can do for you. You take care."

Linda: "Okay, I guess."

Some thoughts to consider about this conversation:

1. Betty caught herself, took a very short break and changed her tone of voice. You can often start over again like this with an HCP and still have some success, although it's harder if you have already negatively influenced the HCP with Negative Feedback (like "Don't exaggerate" or "Don't lie to me"). But don't give up. Try a little E.A.R.

2. The words you use don't really matter. Your tone of voice and effort to treat the person with respect will come through no matter what the words are. The main message is that you *care* about their problem and *want to help* solve it.

3. Betty emphasized the positive. "That's what I *can* do for you," rather than emphasizing the negative by saying something like "I can't do this" or "I can't do that." Remember, you're trying to have a positive influence on HCPs, who tend to focus on the negative—especially if you do too.

4. This doesn't always work. Sometimes you have to listen a little longer, then give some more empathy and respect. If the person criticizes your words ("I don't want your empathy, just fix it!"), explain that you're just trying to help them. It's hard for them to disagree with that, and they sincerely do want help. HCPs are constantly in so much distress that they are often glad to receive help in any way they can.

5. This takes practice. Don't expect it to be perfect. But realize that you're influencing the HCP one way or the other. So try to make it a positive way.

When Not To Use Your E.A.R.

Under some circumstances, E.A.R won't be appropriate. If it would be dangerous to talk to the person or to communicate with the person by mail, telephone, or email, then don't do it. If you're a victim of violence by an HCP, the best thing to do may be to get away from the person completely. If there's a restraining order against you communicating with the person, then don't do it.

If you can't find any empathy or respect for the person, then don't use this approach. You shouldn't fake this. However, I encourage you to search for *something* you can empathize with about the person, such as Ashley picturing Brian as a lonely, helpless little boy facing some very big consequences. Finding empathy may open the door to resolving or at least managing your conflict.

Likewise, find something you can respect about the person. It's very difficult to resolve or manage a conflict with a person you don't respect. And HCPs are very sensitive to being disrespected. Just picture the HCP as an abused child. In many cases, this is true.

"I Don't Feel Like Using My E.A.R.!"

Of course you don't *feel* like using E.A.R. with an HCP. HCPs constantly trigger our own unconscious defensiveness, which tries to protect us by taking an aggressive position ("fight") or a passive approach ("flight"). However, these approaches generally don't work and E.A.R. generally does work. Try it and you may be surprised.

The challenge to you is to develop some emotional self-discipline so you can use E.A.R. when your unconscious defenses don't "feel" like doing it. In fact, our natural feeling is to withhold empathy, to not pay attention, and to show disrespect to others who treat us poorly. You see this happen every day, especially in the news, and in the movies, where it's seen as desirable or funny to disrespect people.

It may briefly feel good to disrespect someone and withhold attention and empathy, but that good feeling doesn't last very long. In fact, it doesn't feel good to the other person and they'll escalate their efforts to get your empathy, attention, and respect. Even it if means trying to harm you. Remember that HCPs are preoccupied with feeling safe and confident by putting other people down or harming them.

"Do I Have To Listen For Hours?"

No. What is different about handling HCPs is understanding that they don't think you'll give them empathy, attention, and respect, so they talk to you with great emotional intensity for a long time because they think they have to fight to get your E.A.R. As soon as you give HCPs sufficient E.A.R., they usually calm down immediately. They no longer need to talk to you for an hour. Five or 10 minutes may be sufficient, or even a minute if you have to keep it really short and are good at giving your E.A.R.

Generally, listen for a few minutes or even just a minute if necessary. Then, tell the person you can Empathize with them, that you'll pay Attention to their concerns, and that you have Respect for them. This way you skip their usual flow of desperate emotion and information and get directly to what they really want and need.

Remember, an ordinary person doesn't need to get empathy, attention, and respect from you (they already get enough of it somewhere else), so they can just give you the basic information about the conflict and then they can stop. You can tell sometimes that people are HCPs because they regularly talk on and on and on and have high-intensity emotions with any subject they're discussing. Therefore, with HCPs you want to *interrupt* their flow fairly soon and let them know that *you already have* empathy, attention, and respect for them, rather than waiting until they are done. Because they're rarely done. They rarely feel that anyone cares – because most people truly don't understand that underneath all of the HCP's intensity and misbehavior their needs are actually very simple basic human needs.

Of course, if you have time, you can encourage them to take their time to tell you everything that concerns them. This openness to them communicates that you're paying Attention to their concerns, and often they don't need to talk all that long after you tell them you'll listen.

After you've listened, communicate your empathy, attention, and/or respect for them (or their concerns) in words that feel comfortable to you. Sometimes you can use one of these three words, but other times you should use other words such as *caring* about them or their problem, or *wanting to help* them with their problem.

"But I Don't Agree With Them!"

One of the concerns people have about using E.A.R. is that HCPs will think you agree with them about the dispute. Using E.A.R. and agreeing with the content of their complaints are two very separate things. It's important to remain neutral about the issue and the details. You don't need to agree with an HCP's point of view, or anyone else's point of view. Instead, *empathize with the person, not the complaint.* You can make a neutral statement about the issue, such as "I'll never know what really happened, but I care about you and want to help you solve this problem." Or, "I find it helps to focus on what to do now, rather than what happened in the past." Or, "We'll probably always see this differently, so let's try to focus on what we can do together about it."

It takes awhile to develop this balance of E.A.R. and factual neutrality. You don't have to point out that you don't agree with the facts they're presenting. Instead, point out that you want to solve the problem as quickly and easily as possible, with empathy and respect for each other, focusing on the future, not the past.

Maintain Good "Boundaries"

Even though you're going to show your E.A.R., this doesn't mean you should try to be buddies with HCPs when they calm down. Most HCPs will spontaneously start up their high-conflict thinking soon enough and you'll be the Target of Blame again if you're too close or start doing favors.

One of the key issues for HCPs, especially Borderline HCPs, is trying to get too close to you too quickly. Try to keep an "arm's length" relationship that is not too close and not too rejecting (which triggers fear and anger). You can be gentle about saying when you can talk and when you can't, when you will do a favor and when you can't, and when you can be flexible and when you have to be firm. Just do it all in a manner that is respectful and shows empathy, if possible. Your life will be much easier than if you try to have a relationship that is too close with someone you already know is an HCP.

Business Examples

In his book, Working with Emotional Intelligence, Daniel Goleman (1998) gives two examples that seem to show the importance of empathy, attention, and respect in business and the workplace.

In 1985, Gerald Grinstein became CEO of Western Airlines, which was in serious financial trouble. In an effort to reduce expenses, he got to know his employees by spending time with them in the planes, at the counters, and in the areas where they moved the baggage. In this manner he paid a lot of attention to his employees, he respected their work, and appeared to feel a lot of empathy for them. Eventually, they agreed to cutbacks in pay and tougher work rules in exchange for a greater interest in a successful company. After only two years, Grinstein was able to sell the company for $860 million to Delta Airlines.

He was highly regarded as being tough *and* empathetic.

In contrast, there is the story of Ronald Allen, who became CEO of Delta Airlines in 1987. In 1991, he bought Pan American World Airways, which quickly plunged Delta Airlines into a tailspin because of its huge debt, at the same time that profits were diminishing for airlines in general. Allen took a get-tough approach. He criticized managers in front of their employees. He humiliated and eliminated those who opposed him. By 1996, half of the employees were hostile to him as a leader. His response was to say "So be it." This alienated them further. Ironically, even though his cuts made the company profitable again, he was fired by the board as primarily responsible for causing serious damage to the company's reputation and workforce morale.

These examples show that even in hard times you need to use empathy, attention, and respect in an organization—even while "setting limits" on costs. Interestingly, it looks like the Delta board eventually set limits on the CEO who didn't take this approach!

A Question

Rochelle's boss, Phil, is a Narcissistic HCP. He's arrogant and insensitive. She never knows when he'll blame her for his mistakes. "This report was filled with mistakes. This was your responsibility and you blew it! You should have caught these errors. That's what you get paid for."

Phil is supposed to give Rochelle her annual evaluation soon, and she wants it to be as positive as possible, since she's seeking to move out of his department (he doesn't know this). Whenever he has a managers' meeting, he wants to bend her ear about how incompetent the other managers are. "You wouldn't believe the stupidity I have to put up with at those meetings!"

Then he'll get angry with her for not getting her work done because she was listening to him.

Rochelle wondered, "How can I get a decent evaluation out of him, if he's so difficult? Sometimes I want to just scream at him, 'Can't you see what an arrogant jerk you are?' I'm thinking of going to his boss and telling her what a jerk he is. Maybe I can get her to do my evaluation."

What should Rochelle do?

A. Go to Phil's boss, explain how difficult Phil is, and ask her to do the evaluation instead.

B. Try to show empathy toward Phil, even though she has no empathy for him.

C. Listen to Phil, then ask him if he wants her to get back to work on his projects.

D. Tell Phil she respects some suggestions he has given her that have actually helped her.

E. Quit her job because it's not safe to give him any empathy, attention, or respect.

I would recommend C or D or both.

C. Listen to Phil, then ask him if he wants her to get back to work on his projects. By paying Attention to Phil, she may calm him down and influence him to be positive toward her. Limiting the time she spends listening by asking *him* if he wants her to get back to work on *his* projects may allow him to feel okay about letting her stop listening.

D. Tell Phil she respects some suggestions he has given her that have actually helped her. By mentioning that she respects (honestly) some of Phil's suggestions, he (as a Narcissistic HCP) will probably feel flattered and more positively toward her.

I would not recommend the following, at least not at this time.

A. Go to Phil's boss, explain how difficult Phil is, and ask her to do the evaluation instead. Unless Rochelle has a strong positive relationship with Phil's boss and is certain that the boss understands her predicament, it wouldn't be wise to go over Phil's head. This is generally discouraged in most companies as threatening the power structure. Many employees have innocently done this and had it backfire on them, when the boss's boss calls them both in to openly discuss the employee's complaint as though they were equals, when they aren't. Then the employee's boss retaliates and the company often doesn't care. There are many HCPs in management positions who are supported by their companies well beyond their usefulness because the company doesn't want to deal with them.

B. Try to show empathy toward Phil, even though she has no empathy for him. Remember, if you don't truly feel empathy for someone, don't pretend. On the other hand, if you think hard enough about it you may find a way to feel empathy, in which case that's okay. But if you don't truly feel empathy, consider showing Attention or Respect, which are often easier.

E. Quit her job because it's not safe to give him any empathy, attention, or respect. There's nothing in this scenario to indicate that it's dangerous to give Phil empathy, attention, or respect. They have contact every day, so he's hard to avoid.

When I described dangerousness earlier in this Tip, I meant physical or serious emotional danger and removing yourself from the HCP entirely. However, you can always choose to skip this step in the C.A.R.S. Method. You don't have to quit your job. You can focus on using any or all of the other three methods described in the following Tips. Of course, you could quit your job, but plan it out first rather than just up and leave in frustration. Remember, Rochelle wanted a good evaluation.

Let's see what might have happened in Rochelle's case. Suppose Rochelle thought about it and decided to try E.A.R. with Phil.

"Wow," Rochelle said to Phil the next time he wanted to talk her ear off. "It's just amazing what you go through at those managers' meetings. Sounds really frustrating. I guess it must be hard being a manager these days—with all those pressures coming down from above. Oh, Phil, you wanted me to get that report to you by the end of the day tomorrow. Do you want me to get back to work on it right now?"

"Oh, yeah. Of course. You better get that done by tomorrow," Phil replied.

"All right, boss! I'm on it! And thanks for your suggestions yesterday about how to do the report."

Rochelle spent only a couple of minutes giving Phil her full Attention about his manager's meeting. She heard his complaints, then she gave him some quick Empathy ("sounds really frustrating") and some Respect ("thanks for your suggestions"). She also showed respect by asking him if she should get back to work on his assignment to her. She used a little humor by saying "all right, boss!" This might not have worked with another supervisor, but in this case Phil felt special and flattered because she called him "boss." He liked that word.

Rochelle laid the groundwork for a more positive relationship with a Narcissistic HCP by not putting energy into taking his behavior personally. Instead, her goal was to do a good job while keeping him happy with her. It just took a few moments—and she felt a lot better too. When you give an HCP your E.A.R., it usually relieves a lot of tension. At least for awhile.

Rochelle decided to work on her relationship with Phil and to try to get a good evaluation from him. In the meantime, she decided to work on building a relationship with his boss. If she didn't get a decent evaluation from Phil, then she would be in a position to go to his boss and ask for help. Lastly, she knew she intended to leave soon anyway, so she wasn't stuck and had lots of choices in dealing with this situation. By trying to connect with her E.A.R., she would have experience she could apply to any new situation.

TIP #8 SUMMARY
Connect Using Your E.A.R.

1. HCPs are desperate for empathy, attention, and respect.

2. Think of something you can empathize with, and honestly show your empathy in words or deeds. However, if you can't feel any empathy for the HCP, then don't do this.

3. Pay full attention to the HCP by listening without interrupting or thinking about something else. Tell the HCP the essence of what you heard, and that you'll pay attention to their problems or concerns. But don't necessarily spend a lot of time listening, unless you have the time available. The most important part is to communicate that you'll pay attention to the HCP and his or her concerns.

4. Think of something that you respect about the person and let the person know that you respect that quality in him or her.

5. Focus on what you can do to connect with the person. Don't place the burden on HCPs by asking lots of questions before you have shown Empathy, Attention, and Respect. Connecting with your E.A.R. is something you give to an HCP in order to build a connection.

6. Remember that you will still need to keep your boundaries in using your empathy, attention, and respect. E.A.R. doesn't mean that you agree with the content of what the person is saying—just that you want to help. It doesn't mean that you have to listen for hours, unless you have the time and want to spend it that way. It doesn't mean that you have to be close to the person. You can keep an "arm's length" relationship and still use your E.A.R.

7. If it is not a safe situation and you can get away, focus on getting to a safe place first. If you are safe, try hard to find a way to show empathy, attention, or respect. This reduces many unmanageable conflicts to a manageable level. However, if this just doesn't fit your situation, move on to the next steps.

Tip #9: Analyze Your Realistic Options

CHAPTER

9

"I've arranged our options according to their legality."

Tip #9
Analyze Your Realistic Options

The next step is to figure out **what to do** about the whole situation. In this step, I want to help you focus your thinking. Remember, the High Conflict Thinking of High Conflict People will often distress you and influence you to take strong action without thinking. And such actions usually make things worse. So instead, you're going to use your analyzing skills.

This analyzing step has three parts:

A. Write a list of 3 to 10 options, realistic or not.

B. Check each item for high-conflict thinking—the HCP's and your own.

C. Check which is the most realistic choice to try first.

(Just think of this as the "Santa Step": You're making a list and checking it twice!)

So, slow down and think. Make a list of options you have for handling this situation. For now, don't worry about whether they're realistic options. You just want to get a list down on paper. Write at least three ideas; the more the better. From my experience, my lists grow as I write down one idea and another suddenly pops into my mind. They can be absurd, funny, and even totally impossible. But once I get going, it gets easier and easier.

Remember to actually *write* your list, rather than just thinking about your options. Writing generally engages the problem-solving part of your brain and calms down the part of your brain that just wants to react immediately.

Sometimes I start out writing in really big letters if I'm really angry about a situation. Then, after I've written down two or three ideas, my writing gets more normal and my ideas become more realistic. Get started now! Write a list of 3 to 10 ideas—silly, extreme, impossible, whatever—just start writing a list! You can do it right here, or on separate sheet of paper.

"What are 3 to 10 options I have for handling this dispute?"

1. _____

2. _____

3. _____

4. _____

5. _____

6. _____

7. _____

8. _____

9. _____

10. _____

Now, before you look closely at this list, let's look at what Rochelle did.

Rochelle's Example

Remember Rochelle from the previous Tip? She had the narcissistic boss she was trying to handle. She tried E.A.R., and it helped some. But now she wants to look at the big picture of "What to Do." She decided to write out her options and came up with six:

A. Write a list of 3 to 10 options, realistic or not.

1. Quit working there tomorrow!

2. Try to get Phil fired!

3. Wait and see how the annual evaluation turns out.

4. Start looking on the Internet for another job while waiting.

5. Talk to Phil's boss to see if there's a future in another division.

6. Move in with my boyfriend and stop working.

Notice that some or most of these ideas aren't realistic—yet. But they may help trigger Rochelle's thinking of an idea that she'd never considered before. It's okay to write any idea down at this point.

"That wasn't too hard," Rochelle said to herself. "Now, what's next?"

B. Check each item for high-conflict thinking—the HCP's and your own.

To examine each option for high-conflict thinking, let's look at the Tip #2 list of types of High Conflict Thinking:

- All-or-nothing thinking

- Jumping to conclusions

- Personalization

- Emotional reasoning

- Mind reading

- Wishful thinking

- Tunnel vision

- Exaggerated fears

- Projecting

- Splitting

Here's Rochelle's list, as she checked it once:

1. *Quit working there tomorrow!* Well, that's my All-or-Nothing thinking. Emotional Reasoning, too. I might quit in the long run, but I don't really feel desperate yet.

2. *Try to get Phil fired.* When I think about it, Phil will really Personalize this and try to ruin my career. I'm also probably Splitting, if I think that it's all Phil's fault and getting him fired would solve everything. I think my part of this problem is that I still need to learn how to manage a boss better. Then I can stay or go.

3. *Wait and see how the annual evaluation turns out.* If I do this, I'll have a better idea if I'm ready to leave this job. Maybe, if I learn to manage Phil better—like using a lot of E.A.R.—I can tolerate it longer. That's Realistic, unless something worse happens.

4. *Start looking on the Internet for another job while waiting.* This is the best idea, I think. It's Realistic.

5. *Talk to Phil's boss to see if there's a future in another division.* After I look on the Internet, I'll decide if I want to talk to Phil's boss. Realistic.

6. *Move in with my boyfriend and stop working.* I think this is entirely Wishful Thinking—but I'll suggest it to him and see how he reacts—as a joke!

Rochelle re-read the options list and her Analyzing list. She chuckled at a couple of her answers. Somehow, it didn't feel as overwhelming as it did before. She realized that she could manage this situation after all. She had lots of choices—she just hadn't realized that at first.

Then she checked it again to decide what action to take.

C. Check which is the most realistic choice to try first.

"I like #4 the best. I'll start looking in the papers and on Internet job sites," Rochelle decided. "Actually, I'll look at the job board at work, too. Then I'll decide whether to talk to Phil's boss about other possibilities in the same company.

Maybe, if there's nothing any good out there, I might try harder to work things out at this job. Then, I'll (4) wait to see how the annual evaluation works out after trying more E.A.R. with Phil. Then I'll (6) talk to Phil's boss to see if there's a future in another division. If not, I'll be ready to leave the company because I'll know what jobs are out there."

When Rochelle went back and checked the list, she realized she could have added another idea to the list if she wanted to—especially if none of her original ideas were realistic. Even when she checked it the second time to choose one, she could have revised her choices. For example, she could have decided: *Look on the Internet for another company doing similar work, and visit that company to speak with someone about their company vision and workplace environment.*

The main idea here is to:

A.   Make a list of options without any restrictions on your thinking.

B.   Check the list for High Conflict Thinking. Add as many new ideas as you want.

C.   Check the realistic items and decide on one to try first. Then revise if necessary.

A few comments about Rochelle's experience:

When Rochelle made her list, then checked it twice, she started to feel less trapped working under Phil. She realized that she'd been limited in her thinking—like thinking about getting Phil fired or quitting her job. She felt better about herself and started to think more about the company where she worked. "You know, it's not really about me," she thought to herself.

She realized that the problem might be a little bigger—that upper management wasn't paying much attention, so that bosses like Phil were able to get away with a lot.

Perhaps another company might be a better place to work. That idea hadn't entered her mind until she was writing her list. The idea developed even more when she picked "looking for another job" as her first choice.

This example shows that writing a list can calm down your emotions and help you focus on creative problem-solving rather than "fight" or "flight." Rochelle immediately felt better and became more creative. She started to see a bigger picture than when she was just grumbling to herself.

This is also highlights a reality: In many companies upper management isn't paying enough attention to the issue of HCP managers and employees. They ignore the problem and just hope it'll go away (Wishful Thinking?). "Maybe he'll change. Maybe she's just having a bad week," they think. They can't tell the difference between an HCP manager like Phil and a manager having a bad week. This is because the company doesn't know the patterns of HCPs and they don't realize that these patterns rarely change. Yet HCP managers can drive good employees, such as Rochelle, out of a company.

Your Example

Let's return to the list you wrote out (or didn't write out) at the beginning of this Tip.

"I couldn't think of anything to write down."

When you're just starting out with the C.A.R.S. Method, this can be a common problem. That's why I suggest writing any idea down that comes into your head. For example, a common idea is to quit and leave the situation. That was Rochelle's first idea. This could mean leaving a workplace, a neighborhood, a committee, a relationship, your family, etc. Even if this turns out to be unrealistic, it may lead to a good idea, such as taking a break for a couple of days, looking at other jobs or neighborhoods, or reducing contact with certain family members.

On the other hand, it's common to think about getting the other person to leave the situation. Write that down. (You can always destroy your list after you're done checking it twice.) Sometimes this is a realistic option. Even if it's not a realistic option, it may lead to some good ideas, such as encouraging the person to take a different job for their own benefit, providing incentives for the person to change neighborhoods, or motivating an unmotivated family member to move out or pay rent.

Ask someone to help you think of ideas for this list of options. (There will be more about using someone as a consultant in this process in Tip #12.)

"I couldn't find time to write anything down."

Nowadays, with computers and email, it's easy to type out a list of 3 to 10 items. Or you could write it out on a Post-It™ note, or on the back of an envelope. If none of that will work, you can think of 3 to 10 ideas in your head. While I said writing is better, just thinking is still better than just reacting.

"I can't stop writing my list. I have 37 ideas now."

That's why I suggested stopping at 10 ideas. Most people don't have this problem, but if you do, just stop now. If you need help, go to Tip #12 to read about using a coach, who can help you stop writing the list and help you start checking for High Conflict Thinking and picking a realistic option.

"I don't know if I'm identifying the right High Conflict Thinking."

In this exercise you don't have to worry about getting it "right." If it helps you in any way, then you're doing it well. The goal is to stimulate thinking of good options. By looking back at the ones you've written, you'll generally know whether an option is realistic or not. If it's unrealistic, but you can't think of which type of High Conflict Thinking it is, just put "Unrealistic" after it. Many ideas have two or three types of High Conflict Thinking in them. For example, Rochelle's idea of quitting tomorrow was both All-or-nothing thinking and Wishful thinking.

"All of my ideas are very unrealistic."

You may want to keep writing to see if some new ideas are more realistic. Perhaps you're being too critical of your ideas and some of them can be realistic. Perhaps you feel guilty and won't even consider being more assertive in your situation. Or perhaps you're very afraid and have good reason to feel afraid. You may want to talk with someone who can coach you about creating realistic options in your case.

"I've picked my most realistic option, but now I'm afraid to try it."

Sometimes fear is a good thing—warning you of realistic dangers. Sometimes it's left over from situations that you're no longer in, so it's safe now. Perhaps you can write down your realistic option in very small steps and see if it becomes more doable. Again, don't hesitate to get support and consultation from someone who can coach you in facing this situation—or help you decide if it's too dangerous. If it's too dangerous, then one of your realistic options may be leaving the situation. Another realistic option may be to get help from professionals or people in responsible positions in your community, workplace, or family. The main point is to think it through, rather than just react.

"Just writing ideas down helped me feel so much better that I don't need to do anything else now."

Sometimes this happens because, generally, you'll feel better just making your list. It moves you out of feeling trapped, helpless, or immobilized because you're doing something physical—whether it's writing it down on paper or typing your list in your computer. It is also stimulating the creative problem-solving parts of your brain rather than the parts of your brain that want to react without thinking.

It's often okay to stop at this point. There may be nothing else you really need to do, now that you have a different attitude about the situation—and feel better about yourself ("Whew! It's not about me!").

Often the biggest step in dealing with a High Conflict Person is to stop taking them personally and avoid giving them feedback. Once you feel better and understand this HCP problem, you can disengage from the emotional intensity of the situation. You can even do this with an HCP in the next cubicle. Keep your distance by remaining sufficiently friendly (E.A.R.), but not engaging in discussions of the many "issues" that he or she brings your way. You might not need the last two steps of the C.A.R.S. Method, although you may need to watch out for inaccurate information that the HCP may spread from time to time.

The Picture-Taking Neighbors

An increasingly common high-conflict dispute these days has to do with residents who videotape their neighbors. They often feel that they "have to" to protect themselves from rotten neighbors, who they think are getting away with bad behavior. In some cases, it may be true. But in many cases I've read about, it's the videotapers who are out of line. Let's look at a couple of examples. Then we'll try Analyzing realistic options for someone in a similar situation.

One example is the Michigan case of Gordie Howe, also known as Mr. Hockey, one of the greatest ice hockey players ever. A September 2007 new article stated that Dr. and Mrs. Dorfman, neighbors of Mr. Howe (who was 79 years old at the time), had been taking his picture every few seconds. Up to 17,000 photos a day. Apparently, they believed that he was running a business out of his house in violation of their Homeowners Association rules and other local laws.

Perhaps this was a case of *Jumping to Conclusions*, because the Dorfmans, also in their 70s, saw a lot of hockey memorabilia in his garage one day when the door was open. The attorney for Mr. Howe indicated that Mr. Howe was moving his commercial office and stored some items in his garage briefly before moving them to his new office.

The Dorfmans claimed there were several cars parked at his house, which also showed he was operating a business. Gordie Howe's son said that his car was there frequently because he visited his mother, who has had dementia for several years and needs extra care. Nurses also came to care for Mrs. Howe. However, the Dorfmans believed the nurses were part of a plot to bring in commercial products hidden in their food bags and indicated this on one of their photos.

After more than a year of photos, Gordie Howe obtained a temporary restraining order against the Dorfmans from taking any more photos, videotaping, or tape recording of Mr. Howe (Maki, 2007).

Since I don't know anything more than what was contained in this news article, I won't try to draw any conclusions of my own. But after more than a year, it's likely that this is a high-conflict dispute that may have had one or more high conflict people involved. Dr. Dorfman didn't deny taking the pictures, but stated that the Homeowners Association encouraged him to gather evidence. Perhaps the association contributed to the problem, or perhaps Dr. Dorfman misinterpreted what he was told.

From the outside, it's very important not to jump to conclusions in these cases. If you're on the inside of such a dispute, it's very important not to act like an HCP; otherwise, those who read about you in the press may think that you're the HCP driving the dispute.

The Videotaping Neighbor

Ron Hinton, age 51, has been videotaping his neighborhood in California in an effort to show illegal gang behavior. However, a May 2007 news article about him indicated that he hadn't yet seen or videotaped any illegal gang behavior. In fact, the police say there are no gang members or hangouts in the neighborhood. Instead, Mr. Hinton has been criticized for harassing families in his neighborhood, especially minority teenagers. He feels he's doing a public service and named himself the "Neighborhood Watch Gangbuster from Hell."

The local school was photographing the boys' volleyball team when Mr. Hinton showed up. He confronted the team, asking if they were "gangbangers." Their coach stepped in and apparently asked him to leave. But Mr. Hinton claimed he could go anywhere he wanted. Mr. Hinton then posted the video on YouTube, which was particularly upsetting for the teachers and parents.

In contrast to Mr. Hockey, when the family of one of the teenagers that Mr. Hinton was filming filed for a temporary restraining order to get him to stop videotaping, the videotaper won. Taking pictures in public on its own is apparently not illegal. However, if he puts false statements with them (like saying that someone is a gang member who isn't), then he could be liable for defamation. Also, he may be violating people's civil rights if he's harassing them because of their race or ethnic group.

Interestingly, Mr. Hinton has a history. He was arrested for suspicion of misdemeanor battery in his 20s, was once found not mentally competent for awhile, and in 1992 pled guilty to possessing methamphetamine. In 2004, he sued the police department and lost. On the other hand, some of his neighbors say he's helped clean up the neighborhood and that his watchful behavior is a good thing (Davis, 2007).

As I do not personally know this situation, I can't make any conclusions about the individuals involved. However, it appears to be a high-conflict situation that may involve one or more HCPs.

Analyzing a Neighbor Dispute

Suppose that a new neighbor moved in next to you a couple of months ago, and he's a real bully. He lets his dogs run free and they make deposits on your lawn. You can hear him swearing at his wife and children, and sometimes he swears at you. He lets his trees grow over your fence and they drop their leaves in your yard.

No one likes him, although one neighbor seems to have a connection with him because they have the same kind of car.

A couple of days ago, when you complained to him about the leaves, he yelled "F--- You!" and walked away. Today there was a small branch with a dozen leaves on it in your yard. The only explanation is that he threw it over the fence.

Let's analyze your realistic options.

A. "What are 3 to 10 options that I have for handling this dispute, realistic or not?"

Here's my list, off the top of my head:

1. Throw the branch back into his yard!

2. Organize the neighbors to tell him to move!

3. Move out of the neighborhood!

4. Contact the local zoning board and find out the rules about dogs and trees.

5. Talk to the neighbor who seems to get along with him.

6. Ignore him.

7. Set up a loud stereo system and whenever he yells loudly, turn it on loud!

8. Call the police next time there's yelling next door.

9. Call the local mediation center to try to have a mediation with him.

10. Videotape the dog when he poops on the lawn.

11. Try giving him some empathy, attention, and respect.

If you made a list, you probably found that it wasn't too hard. Your list could be completely different from mine. That's fine. The idea is to get thinking—whatever ideas come up may lead to some good ideas. Now, let's check for high-conflict thinking.

B. "Is there any High Conflict Thinking that makes any of these unrealistic?"

Here again, is the list from Tip #2 of types of High Conflict Thinking:

- All-or-nothing thinking

- Jumping to conclusions

- Personalization

- Emotional reasoning

- Mind reading

- Wishful thinking

- Tunnel vision

- Exaggerated fears

- Projecting

- Splitting

Try writing your own analysis, picking out one or more of the above types of high-conflict thinking for each option you wrote down. Then, read on.

Here's my analysis. Remember there are no right or wrong answers. It's figuring out what's realistic and what's not in *each specific situation* that matters.

1. *Throw the branch back into his yard!* This will probably trigger his *Emotional reasoning* and *Projecting* onto me. Rather than realizing he was "over the line," he'll project that *I'm* over the line. He may come right back at me in greater anger. Given that he's already violated the boundaries of our fence (with the branch), our lawn (with dog poop), our peace and quiet (with his yelling), etc., he may cross other boundaries and become physically dangerous or violent against me. I think this idea of throwing the branch back into his yard is *Wishful thinking* on my part and a dangerous idea.

2. *Organize the neighbors to tell him to move!* This may also be a bad idea, for the same reasons: *Emotional reasoning*—he's not really thinking logically, but emotionally. *Projecting*—he'll probably think it's all our fault instead of seeing that he's driving the problem. Again, I think this is *Wishful thinking* on my part. The more neighbors I have organized against him, the more defensive and angry he'll probably become, not more cooperative.

3. *Move out of the neighborhood!* This seems to be my own *All-or-nothing thinking*. I like the neighborhood in general and don't want to have to move, although I might consider it someday if this keeps going or gets worse.

4. *Contact the local zoning board and find out the rules.* I really like this idea. This is *Realistic*.

5. *Talk to the neighbor who seems to get along with him.* This is also *Realistic*. I get along okay with this neighbor. In fact, I'm sure he's concerned about the bully also.

6. *Ignore him.* I think this is also *All-or-nothing thinking*. Something needs to be done, as it can't keep going on like this.

7. *Set up a loud stereo system!* I really feel like doing this, but I think it's *Emotional reasoning*—it feels like a good idea, but it isn't really. It's also *Wishful thinking*, because it will influence him to be angrier, rather than more cooperative.

8. *Call the police next time there's yelling next door.* This may be *Realistic*. However, it may just set him off again. I think what I'm going to do is go have a talk with someone at the local police station and ask them what they suggest.

9. *Call the local mediation center.* I recently heard about this mediation center and I think I'll call them too, to get some ideas of what happens in mediation. I'm not sure if it will make a difference, but it doesn't hurt to ask questions. This is *Realistic*.

10. *Videotape the dog when he poops on the lawn.* This may trigger more *Emotional reasoning* on his part. It may be *Wishful thinking* on my part. I've heard that this can backfire, as neighbors who are seen videotaping each other are often seen as the high-conflict person.

C. "What realistic option will I try first?"

I need to check over the list of realistic options again:

4. *Contact the local zoning board and find out the rules.*

5. *Talk to the neighbor who seems to get along with him.*

8. *Call the police next time there's yelling next door.*

9. *Call the local mediation center.*

I think I'm going to do some research. First, I'll call the zoning board and the mediation center for advice, then I'll talk to the police and see what they suggest. In the meantime, I'll just try to be friendly and show him my empathy, attention, and respect—even though I don't think he deserves it! But maybe it'll calm him down a little while I figure out what to do next. I don't have to initiate any conversations to show him a friendly and respectful face.

Don't Make This Complicated

This step of Analyzing is supposed to help, not get in the way. So do it in a way that works for you. If you want to just do it in your head, then just ask your-self to think of what might work, then whether these options are realistic. Just thinking about What To Do Next will help you feel and think better.

If you want to make a list without checking for high-conflict thinking, then just do that. The idea is to think it through so that you don't simply react and make things worse. The more you think about it, the more realistic your next step will be.

The best approach is to practice, practice, practice. Write out several scenarios of high-conflict situations and see how you'd analyze them using this method. Then, when a conflict arises, it should be simple to Analyze Your Realistic Options. And, if I'm right about HCPs increasing in our society, you'll be one of the fortunate people ready to handle them well, regardless of where they appear.

A Question

Mark's mother is known as an extreme "helicopter" parent. She hovers around him and tells him what to do in dealing with school, jobs, and his relationships. In fact, she's known as a Blackhawk helicopter parent, ever since she tried to get his college professor to change his grade. Mark is now 29. It's not unusual for her to yell at him and occasionally embarrass him at his job by showing up unannounced. Then she calls him to apologize and wants to take him out to lunch to make it up to him.

He's having a hard time setting limits on her contact with him. He has a new girlfriend, Samantha, who is nice and successful at her job. But his mother doesn't like her and seems dedicated to breaking up the relationship. She drops by Mark's apartment when she knows Samantha's over for dinner.

What do you suggest Mark do?

A. Call Mom and yell at her to leave him alone.

B. Stop taking her phone calls.

C. Move out of town to an unknown location.

D. Invite her to have a meeting with him and Samantha to discuss reasonable boundaries.

E. Meet with a therapist and his mother, give her a list of do's and don'ts, and discuss it.

If Mark analyzed his realistic options, he may come up with these possible results.

A. *Call Mom and yell at her to leave him alone.* This feels like *Emotional Reasoning*, because I'm just reacting emotionally. I feel like doing this, but I expect that she'll react by *Retaliating* and probably show up at my apartment to argue with me about yelling at her. (Mark added Retaliation to his list of High Conflict Thinking because his mother used that a lot and he recognized that it was not logical, but a defensive automatic reaction of hers.)

B. *Stop taking her phone calls.* This looks like *All-or-nothing thinking.* Once again, it will influence her to *Retaliate* and probably show up at my apartment.

C. *Move out of town to an unknown location.* This seems like another *All-or-nothing* solution. If nothing else works, I might have to do this someday, but not yet.

D. *Invite her to have a meeting with him and Samantha to discuss reasonable boundaries.* I'm not sure about this idea. It puts Samantha in the middle and it gives my mother equal power in my relationship with Samantha. I need to deal with this myself. I think this is *Wishful Thinking* that it'll make my mother back off. This will probably encourage her to be even more involved in my relationship with Samantha.

E. *Meet with a therapist and his mother, give her a list of do's and don'ts, and discuss it.* I like this idea. Maybe I can find a therapist who has adult children and who has set reasonable boundaries with them. Maybe I'll speak to the therapist first. I'll make a list of what I think are reasonable boundaries and see what the therapist thinks. Then I'll invite my mom. My mother can complain to the therapist, who can listen to her and empathize with her. This sounds *Realistic. I'll pick this option!*

I think by now you've got the idea of this Tip. Give it a try.

TIP #9 SUMMARY

Analyze Your Realistic Options

High Conflict People will often distress you and influence you to take strong action without thinking. Such actions usually make things worse. Instead, Analyze Your Realistic Options.

The Analyzing step has three parts:

A. *Write a list of 3 to 10 options for What To Do about the situation, realistic or not.*

This list can include ideas that are extreme, funny, or unrealistic. The point is to start thinking about the high-conflict situation. Often an unrealistic idea will trigger your creative thinking and you'll come up with new ideas that are realistic.

B. *Check each option for high-conflict thinking—the HCP's and your own.*

When you check for High Conflict Thinking, look at the list of 10 items below, but feel free to add new ones. The point is to think each option through to see if it's a realistic idea. Many ideas feel good until you think them through. Then you realize they're not realistic. The list below will help you screen out bad ideas. Feel free to get help with this step from someone in an objective position.

C. *Check the most realistic option to try first.*

If nothing on your list of options seems realistic enough, then write down some more. Once you've decided which one you're going to try, you're well on your way to handling the dispute and the HCP. Remember to learn from whatever you do so that you can keep refining your options as you handle the situation with the HCP.

Here are the 10 common types of High Conflict Thinking for HCPs, and for those trying to deal with them. Make sure to check for High Conflict Thinking that your plans may trigger in the HCP, and for your own High Conflict Thinking, which may make it unrealistic:

- All-or-nothing thinking

- Jumping to conclusions

- Personalization

- Emotional reasoning

- Mind reading

- Wishful thinking

- Tunnel vision

- Exaggerated fears

- Projecting

- Splitting

The Analyzing step gets easier the more you do it. Don't worry; it doesn't have to be done perfectly to be helpful. I encourage you to write down your options, but if you don't want to write them down, don't let that stop you. The goal is to improve your responses with High Conflict People to manage or end high-conflict disputes. The more you think these situations through, the more effective you'll be.

Tip #10: Respond Quickly to Misinformation

CHAPTER

10

"How accurate is our misinformation?"

Tip #10
Respond Quickly to Misinformation

Misinformation is very common in high-conflict disputes and is the result of High Conflict Thinking. Most often, High Conflict People don't realize their thinking is distorted. But some of the time they knowingly spread misinformation. They think they have to do so in order to protect themselves from the dangers they see around them. This misinformation is usually inaccurate for the situation, and a primary cause of their Mistaken Assessment of Danger. While you may feel angry about this misinformation, or feel that no one in the world could possibly believe it, you still have to deal with it. Ignoring distortions of information is often just as bad as over-reacting to it.

This step helps you consider the When, What, and Who of Responding:

A. When to respond: Is there any inaccurate information that needs a response?

B. What is my more accurate information?

C. Who should I provide with the more accurate information?

When to Respond

The first question is, "Do I really need to respond at all?" There are two main categories of answers to that:

1. *Is it just the HCP who has this inaccurate information?* If so, you probably don't need to respond. It's unlikely that you'll change the HCP's thinking— or the thinking of their committed Negative Advocates (such as a family member or close representative, like an attorney). Any response will most likely be taken as Negative Feedback. Even suggesting that the HCP could have made a mistake isn't tolerated well by any HCP. However, sometimes it's not a distortion. The HCP may actually have received inaccurate information, and may be open to a correction by you.

For example, Alison in Tip #3 had some high-conflict thinking. She believed that Pat had made her boyfriend split up with her. At first, Pat offered to explain to Alison what happened, but she got an angry reply to that idea. Once she realized (from Analyzing the situation) that Alison wouldn't benefit from discussing the reality of what happened, Pat decided not to respond further.

This was a wise decision. No one else was involved (yet), and she knew that she wouldn't change Alison's thinking. She also realized that confronting Alison was likely to escalate into more bad behavior, not less.

Please keep in mind that not responding to an HCP takes a great deal of personal strength. HCP Behavior that's Aggressively Defensive (B.A.D.) is often designed to hook you in to a negative engagement. Remember, our emotions are biologically "wired" to the emotions of others. So, by not responding, you'll naturally *feel* like you're not "standing up to injustice," not "setting her straight," not "winning the battle," letting the HCP "get away with it," etc. This is your defensive High Conflict Thinking, and you don't need to be defensive.

2. *Has the misinformation gone out to potential Negative Advocates or your larger community (workplace, neighborhood, extended family)?* If so, then you probably should respond, as soon as possible. You don't want the misinformation to settle into other people's minds without a challenge. They need to know they've been misinformed, otherwise they'll assume you agree with the misinformation.

    Also, misinformation based on the HCP's High Conflict Thinking usually has an emotional charge to it, which will shift the listener into High Conflict Thinking as well. As you know, once a person is using High Conflict Thinking, logical Analysis (Left Brain) shuts down and the person will become focused on taking Action (Right Brain) against you. Then it's much more difficult to get through with accurate information—especially if it comes from you.

    I've seen people allow misinformation to stand unchallenged in cases with HCPs. Unfortunately, it quickly becomes "fact" and a weapon in all future discussions for the HCP. Don't let this happen to you. Respond as quickly as possible to those who have received the misinformation. Also, if you can, provide verification of it by other credible people you know.

    We assume that people won't fall for the misinformation. Don't make this assumption. The High Conflict Thinking of HCPs can be very contagious (because of its emotional persuasion) and may provoke Negative Advocates to join in blaming you. Then you may become their Target of Blame as well. Soon people may repeat the misinformation to you and to others—with angry looks and words. I've seen this happen over and over again.

What to Say: B.I.F.F.

I recommend the B.I.F.F. approach to responding to HCPs and to their communications with others:

Brief, Informative, Friendly, and **Firm**. This is almost always done in the same medium (email, in person, by phone, letter, organizational newsletter, etc.) that the misinformation was first presented by the HCP and to the same person(s), at least.

In my experience, most of the serious misinformation spread by HCPs has been in writing: in emails, memos, letters, or even the newspapers. I designed B.I.F.F. for use in response to hostile emails, to help people avoid impulsively responding in anger. But you can and should use it in responding to any misinformation. Here's B.I. F.F. in a nutshell.

Brief

Keep your response brief. This will reduce the chances of a prolonged and angry exchange. The more you write, the more material the other person has to criticize. Keeping it brief signals that you don't wish to get into a dialogue. Just make your response and stop. Don't take their statements personally and don't respond with a personal attack. Avoid focusing on comments about the person's character, such as saying he or she is rude, insensitive, or stupid. It just escalates the conflict and keeps it going. You don't have to defend yourself to someone you disagree with. If your friends still like you, you don't have to prove anything to those who don't.

Informative

The main reason to respond to misinformation is to correct inaccurate statements that others might see. "Just the facts" is a good idea. Focus on the accurate statements you want to make, not on the inaccurate statements the other person made. For example: "Just to clear things up, I was out of town on February 12th, so I wouldn't have been the person who was making loud noises that day."

Avoid negative comments. Avoid sarcasm. Avoid threats. Avoid personal remarks about the other's intelligence, ethics, or morals. If the other person has a high-conflict personality, you'll have no success in reducing the conflict with personal attacks. While most people can ignore personal attacks or might think harder about what you're saying, HCPs *feel* they have no choice but to respond in anger—and keep the conflict going. Personal attacks rarely lead to insight or positive change for HCPs.

Friendly

While you may be tempted to respond in anger, you're more likely to achieve your goals by communicating in a friendly manner. Consciously thinking about a friendly response will increase your chances of getting a friendly or at least neutral response. If your goal is to end the conflict, then being friendly has the greatest likelihood of success. Don't give the other person a reason to get defensive and keep responding.

This doesn't mean you have to be overly friendly. Another word for this could be "civil." Just make it sound a little relaxed and non-threatening. If appropriate, say you recognize their concerns. Brief comments that show your empathy and respect will generally calm the other person down, even if only for a short time.

Firm

In a non-threatening way, clearly tell the other person your information or interests on an issue, including closing the discussion. For example: "That's all I'm going to say on this issue." Be careful not to make comments that invite more discussion unless you're negotiating an issue or want to keep a dialogue going back and forth. Avoid comments that leave an opening, such as, "I hope you will agree with me that ..." This invites the other person to tell you "No, I don't agree."

Sound confident and don't ask for more information. A confident-sounding person is less likely to be challenged with further emails or contact. If you get further emails, ignore them if you've already sufficiently addressed the inaccurate information. If you need to respond again, be even more brief, and don't emotionally engage. In fact, it often helps to just repeat the key information using the same words.

Example

Joe and Jane had a high-conflict divorce. The divorce is over, but the conflict isn't. Joe appears to be an HCP. Jane is trying to disengage from the conflict, using B.I.F.F. when she has to communicate with him.

Joe's email: "Jane, I can't believe you're so stupid as to think that I'm going to let you take the children to your boss's birthday party during my parenting time. Have you no memory of the last six conflicts we've had about my parenting time? Or are you having an affair with him? I always knew you'd do anything to get ahead! In fact, I remember coming to your office party and seeing you making a total fool of yourself! Including flirting with everyone from the CEO down to the mailroom kid! Are you high on something? Haven't you gotten your finances together enough to support yourself yet, without flinging yourself at every Tom, Dick, and Harry?" [And on and on and on.]

Jane: "Thank you for responding to my request to take the children to my office party. Just to clarify, the party will be from 3-5 on Friday at the office and there will be approximately 30 people there, including several other parents bringing school-age children. There will be no alcohol, as it is a family-oriented firm and there will be family-oriented activities. I think it will be a good experience for them to see me at my workplace. Since you don't agree, then of course I will respect your wishes and withdraw my request, as I recognize it is your parenting time." [And that's the end of her email.]

Who to Provide With the Accurate Information

In the example above, Jane only needed to respond to Joe. She kept it brief and didn't engage in defending herself. She didn't need to. However, if he involved other people, she would need to provide accurate information to them as well. In general, you want to inform the same people who've been misinformed.

Negative Advocates: Remember that Negative Advocates are usually misinformed ordinary people, not HCPs themselves. However, some people have become "committed Negative Advocates," such as family members or ongoing representatives like attorneys or other official advocates. Generally, there's no point in responding to misinformation—especially inflammatory misinformation—from committed Negative Advocates, because their opinions have already been influenced beyond your repair.

For example, highly blaming letters from a Negative Advocate attorney in the middle of a court case often don't need any response. In many cases, the letter is sent for no other purpose than to impress the attorney's client or to engage the other party with irrelevant emotional issues. Hard as it may be to resist an angry reply, there's usually nothing to be gained by doing so.

On the other hand, "potential Negative Advocates" should be given accurate information to discourage them from becoming Negative Advocates or to encourage them to stop being Negative Advocates. Remember, most Negative Advocates abandon their HCPs when they become more fully informed.

Your Community: If misinformation has gone out to your community (workplace, neighborhood, extended family, etc.), then it's usually very important to correct it. Often, at least one person in the community will get hooked by the misinformation, even if most people don't.

Jane's Example Again

After Jane's response, Joe decided to send their email conversation to Jane's extended family. He proudly cc'd his email to Jane because he believed that she would be embarrassed and pressured to recognize his point of view. HCPs often do this in an effort to get support from others for their high-conflict thinking. Someone will see the "truth" as they see it, they think, lacking self-awareness of their own distortions and isolation.

Therefore, Jane responded to the larger group with more information.

Jane: "Dear friends and family: As you know, Joe and I had a difficult divorce. He's sent you a private email showing correspondence between us about a parenting schedule matter. I hope you'll will see this as a private matter and understand that you don't need to respond or get involved in any way. Almost everything he's said is in anger and not accurate. If you have any questions for me personally, please feel free to contact me and I'll clarify anything I can. I appreciate your friendship and support."

And that's it: B.I.F.F. No one responded negatively to her and several family members complimented her on trying to stay disengaged from any battles. Inadvertently, Joe showed how inappropriate he'd been and how appropriately Jane had responded. But if she hadn't responded quickly, they might have believed that some of what Joe said was true—especially because of the emotional hooks of his HCP message.

These HCP dynamics are very similar in many high-conflict situations, whether with family, neighbors, or co-workers. Let's look at a workplace example.

Rochelle's Example

Rochelle's boss, Phil, sent an email to the manager of a major project they were working on, explaining that it was running late:

"Jim, I hope to have this project in to you by the end of the month. I know we're running about two weeks behind, so I wanted to give you the heads up now. Unfortunately, my assistant Rochelle has been dragging her feet in getting the statistical analysis finished. I've been trying to keep her focused, but she keeps getting distracted by other matters. I'm working with her on prioritizing. I'm not ready to fire her just yet, because she already knows the subject matter and the players. So, just to let you know, I'm doing the best I can under these circumstances. With best regards, Phil."

He copied this email to Rochelle as a matter of routine.

When Rochelle saw it, she immediately confronted Phil, although she caught herself and stopped short of calling him a jerk and instead said, "What's this all about, boss?"

"Oh, Rochelle. Calm down. Don't take it so personally. I just had to get something over to Jim. You know how it is," Phil said, laughing at her. "You're so emotional."

Rochelle was really angry now, but she just turned around and went to her desk. She took out a pad of paper, printed off the email, and went for a short walk. As she wrote down some options, she focused on responding.

A. Is there any inaccurate information that needs a response?

"Of course!" she thought. What he said in the email couldn't have been farther from the truth. She looked it over and decided that it contained enough misinformation that it definitely needed a response because it had gone out to the project manager—and whoever else had seen it by now.

B. What is my more accurate information?

Rochelle wondered if she should point out that Phil was blaming her for delaying the project. After some thought, she decided that focusing on Phil's misinformation would trigger Phil's high-conflict thinking, since he would have to see her memo, and the project manager might think she's too aggressive. Instead, she decided to focus on what she'd done for the project, how prompt she'd been in doing it, and how soon the project manager could expect the information.

C. Who should I provide with the more accurate information?

Rochelle decided to send an email to the project manager, with a copy to Phil.

"Hi, Jim, I just wanted to follow up on Phil's email from yesterday. Regarding the statistical analysis, it's almost finished. Everything is on time, according to the schedule, and I've even gotten some parts of the project completed before the deadline. Now that this is the top priority of our department, I expect you'll have the finished results by Friday. Let me know if you have any questions about the statistical information. Rochelle."

She also printed out the memo to Jim. She thought it was important to file it with other important papers of the project, rather than delete it as a simple email.

Phil was furious. "What are you doing!" he demanded. But Rochelle remained calm. "I just thought it was important for the project manager to know we're working hard on this project and that he'd have it soon. I think we'll look good to him, since we're addressing his concerns about the deadline by speeding things up. Say, do you have any plans for this weekend? Anything fun you're going to do?"

Rochelle resisted the urge to make her memo a personal attack on Phil. Instead, she kept the focus on what was being done, not what wasn't being done or what had been done wrong. Before Phil could get too upset, she changed the subject to his weekend plans—a subject that he loved to talk about. By being calm and giving him Attention, Rochelle was able to keep Phil from getting too heated up over her memo.

With many Narcissistic HCPs, changing the subject to something about him often helps keep him from getting stuck in his anger. Directly confronting his anger always escalates it. Of course, this doesn't always work, so you have to be careful in how you manage your HCP boss.

By *quickly* getting accurate information to the project manager, Rochelle managed to create doubt in Jim's mind before the misinformation settled in his mind as a "fact." Such facts could have quickly been passed on to other managers, so timing was very important. Putting it in writing was essential, so when someone looks back in the project's file, they'll see Rochelle's response right next to Phil's false allegations about her. The effect of this is to at least create doubt in the reader's mind—even if the reader doesn't automatically believe Rochelle. Without her written comment, a reader would take Phil's comments as unchallenged facts because they sound believable when woven into his email, which sounded reasonable.

Of course, an employee has to be careful in going over a supervisor's head. In general, it's considered inappropriate. But if you look carefully at the way Rochelle wrote her email/memo, it had several important characteristics that helped:

1. She didn't criticize Phil. She resisted the temptation to say he lied or distorted the facts.

2. She didn't indicate she was going over his head, she was merely "following up."

3. She said what she has done (she always was on schedule) to protect herself, rather than correcting Phil for falsely saying what she hasn't done.

4. She explained it to Phil as helping both of them in the eyes of the project manager.

5. She confidently changed the subject to Phil's weekend plans, which sometimes works with HCPs. Most HCPs are used to issues remaining unresolved—as they jump from subject to subject, emotionally reacting and over-reacting to new events. So they often allow you to change the subject because it helps them get unstuck. But I should warn you that this generally doesn't work with non-HCPs, who say, "Wait a minute. We're not done discussing this issue. I want to resolve it." This is because most non-HCPs do resolve issues. So decide whether changing the subject is likely to work or not in your own situation.

The Community Manager

Nancy is a new member of the ArrowWood community, and she's already had several problems with the home she just bought. She sought out Larry, the Community Manager for the Homeowners Association and who reports to the Homeowners Association Board. She wanted Larry to verify that: 1) her windows don't close securely, 2) the roof has a leak, and 3) the kitchen floor wasn't replaced, as promised by the previous owner.

Larry Sutter is very diplomatic and well-liked in the community. However, he disagrees with Nancy on all three issues. At her request, he walked through the house with her to address her concerns. He told her that all the windows he tried appeared to be closing securely. He looked, but found no evidence that the roof had a leak. He said the prior owner had briefly discussed replacing the kitchen floor when negotiating the sale with Nancy, but that it was never agreed upon. Nancy gave Larry a copy of the sales agreement for him to read. Larry said he would get back to her after he read it through.

Back at his office, Larry spent an hour reviewing Nancy's sales agreement, but he could find nothing that said she would get a new kitchen floor. So he wrote her a short letter stating his results, as well as putting in writing that he had discussed her concerns about the windows and roof, but found no problems.

Nancy took Larry's letter as an insult and an effort to undermine her efforts to resolve these issues with the prior owner. She sat down and wrote a long letter to Larry, and sent copies to every member of the Homeowners Association Board. It stated, in part:

Dear Mr. Sutter,

I am writing to you today to strongly object to your letter dated April 14th to me! You have been unethical and egregious in the manner in which you have handled my complaint! I am due a duty of due care!

You should have made much more serious efforts to evaluate my concerns and not write a conclusion until due diligence had been done. You were haphazard in opening and closing the windows to check them in my house, and did not take the time to see that they don't fully and properly close. Yes, the lock can be locked, but the space the window leaves is not secure. Any common criminal could easily slip something in there and force open my window.

I also object to your superficial inspection of the ceilings under the roof. Yes, it has leaked and I saw evidence of it, even if it wasn't there the day you came. You should have waited until it rained to check it again before you wrote your letter. You said you would take responsibility for this problem and you failed in your duty to me.

Lastly, the kitchen floor remains an outstanding issue. I distinctly remember the prior owner saying to me, "I will replace the kitchen floor before you move in. Trust me." I don't care if it's not written in the sales agreement, he owes it to me to have kept his word. And you owe it to me to do a more thorough inspection of my premises. I consider your lack of proper attention to these matters as a fraudulent misrepresentation of your job as Community Manager. As you can see, I have brought these serious concerns to the attention of your Board. Hopefully, they'll address these issues with more intelligence and complete discretion than you have!

Sincerely,

Nancy Graham

What should Larry do? He thought this was a case for responding to inaccurate information:

A. *Is there any inaccurate information? Does it need a response?*

Larry wrote: Nancy's letter is filled with inaccurate information and allegations against me. She can think that way all she wants, but I have to respond because she also sent it to my Board.

B. *What is my more accurate information?*

1. I haven't been unethical or egregious in any way. (Oops! That's not information, that's just me feeling defensive. I don't need to defend myself because it's not about me! It's about her and how to handle her.)

2. I am not a home inspector and I never suggested that I was. I just tried to see if I could help her out.

3. I did not say I would take responsibility for any problem of hers as Community Manager. I did not assume any duty to do anything. I told her I would look at her house and see if I could help her out in communicating her concerns to the prior owners, who I knew fairly well.

C. *Who should I provide with the more accurate information?*

1. I need to respond to Nancy, for sure.

2. I need to inform the Board of the accurate information. I need to put it in writing, since Nancy put her letter in writing.

Here's the letter he wrote to Nancy:

Dear Nancy, I'm sorry you were disappointed in my letter to you. I wanted to be helpful, but I realize now I should just stay out of the way since inspecting your home is not part of my role. I would suggest that you contact a home inspector if you have continuing concerns. Also, you should communicate directly with the prior owners if a home inspector finds any problems. I want to wish you all the best as you settle into our community. Sincerely, Larry Sutter

Does the style of that letter sound familiar? It should, because it's a B.I.F.F. letter. Larry was brief, informative, friendly, and firm. He was tempted to include several additional comments, but took them out before he sent the letter to Nancy.

1. "if a home inspector finds any real problems…" This would have insulted her and triggered her to retaliate in some way.

2. "I owed you no duty of care regarding inspecting your house." This would have been Negative Feedback because it was about a specific past statement she made. It was better to focus on a future positive action ("contact a home inspector"), rather than to counter the negative by saying no duty was owed.

3. "You should contact a home inspector…" The tone of this is more likely to trigger an HCP than what Larry decided to say: "I would suggest that you contact a home inspector…." HCPs react particularly negatively to being told what they "should do."

Here's the letter he wrote to his Board:

Dear Board Members:

You have received a letter from a new member of our community, Nancy Graham. She has a very different point of view on some assistance I tried to give her. I am enclosing my letter of response to her.

I also want to respond to some specific statements she has made that might have concerned you:

1. I am not a home inspector and I never suggested that I was. I just tried to see if I could help.

2. I did not say I would take responsibility for any problem of hers as Community Manager. I did not assume any duty to do anything. I told her I would look at her house and see if I could help her out in communicating her concerns to the prior owners, who I knew fairly well.

If you have any questions about my interactions with Ms. Graham, please feel free to call me. I don't think you need to respond to her letter to me, as it was addressed to me and I have responded. However, if she does address a letter or email to you, I would encourage you to contact me before responding, as she may have some information that needs clarification.

Sincerely,

Larry Sutter
ArrowWood Community Manager

When did Larry respond? He responded with both letters the next day. He didn't want his board to get hooked, and he didn't want to have them think that he had created any expectations that were inappropriate for his role.

He also spent a few minutes at the next Homeowners Association Board meeting explaining more about the situation. He encouraged the board members not to assume that her statements about anyone were accurate without getting more information. He also encouraged them to treat her with empathy, attention, and respect, regardless of how she spoke to them or treated them.

Larry also explained that sometimes organizations get "split" among their members when someone makes highly dramatic statements of wrong-doing. They end up fighting with each other until the full information comes out. Therefore, it would be essential for the board to discuss the full factual information before any one person took an action or made a public statement about a homeowner's complaint.

A Question

Suppose that Nancy Graham sues the homeowners association for a long list of problems that have no more basis than her complaints about her house. She files a 200-page complaint in court and provides a copy to the community newspaper about her lawsuit. The newspaper reporter calls Larry Sutter, the Community Manager, for a response to her complaints. What would you advise Larry to do?

A. Tell the newspaper "I have no comment, as it's a litigation matter."

B. Send the newspaper a 200-page explanation that addresses each of her complaints.

C. When he calls again, tell the newspaper reporter that, except for her, it is a great community and that her complaint has no basis.

D. Invite the reporter to the next homeowners association meeting in three weeks, when these issues will be discussed. At the meeting, explain that each and every one of her complaints has been investigated and none have been proven.

E. Call the newspaper reporter right back. Say that you have a lot of empathy for the complaining party's feelings of frustration, but that you have reviewed each of her concerns and strongly believe that her complaints are without basis. Add that you love the ArrowWood community and that you will not let this lawsuit be a distraction. Say "that's it; I have nothing else to add."

I would recommend *"E"* for the following reasons, which can be applied to most public situations with an HCP:

He responds quickly. That's important, because a story like this can grow into a major news event, which can often include many rumors and new inaccurate information.

He says that he empathizes with her feelings of frustration. This is good because he's letting Nancy and the community know that he's not against her, won't attack her, and won't escalate her dispute.

He doesn't use her name publicly. This helps Nancy and the community feel that it's not a personal attack, but simply a rational business matter being dealt with according to rational business procedures. This makes it less likely to be viewed as a "civil war" between them.

He says each of her concerns has been reviewed and is without basis. This is important information for the community. While he doesn't need to respond to each individual complaint (he will in the court case), he needs to let the community know that he disagrees with all of them so that they don't gain any credibility with potential Negative Advocates.

He says he loves the community and won't be distracted. This helps prevent concerns by those in the community that there really is something wrong or that it's a personal dispute between Nancy Graham and Larry Sutter. It also reinforces that Larry is providing caring and well-organized leadership, which is always reassuring to a potentially worried community when there appears to be a crisis.

His response was a B.I.F.F. response. He was brief (he said "that's it"), he was informative ("I reviewed all complaints and all have no basis"), he was friendly (he "had empathy"), and he was firm ("this won't be a distraction").

Here's some comments about the other answers:

A. *Tell the newspaper "I have no comment, as it's a litigation matter."* When a public official these days says, "No comment, it's in litigation," it allows the HCP's complaints to gain traction. While many other types of legal issues might merit a "no comment" statement, you take a big risk with HCPs—especially in public disputes. HCPs can be successful persuasive blamers and often generate community sympathy that's hard to overcome later. However, this isn't a bad response, just risky. If you say no comment now, you should stay on top of the public situation, as you may need to make a comment later, along the lines of "E." Of course, you should check with your legal counsel before making this decision and explain why an early response to an HCP may be a good idea.

B. *Send the newspaper a 200-page explanation that addresses each of her complaints.* A 200-page explanation will delay your response for weeks or months, which isn't advised with HCP situations that become public. It's also burdensome on you and is more likely to feed the controversy than to put it to rest. However, keep in mind that you'll need to respond to all of her complaints in your court papers, and that will be in the public record after it's filed, which is information the newspaper will have access to.

C. *When he calls again, tell the newspaper reporter that, except for her, it is a great community and that her complaint has no basis.* First of all, waiting for the reporter to call back risks too much time for the story to grow, similar to the "no comment" option. Avoid criticizing her publicly, like saying "except for her" it's a great community. That will escalate her and make you appear negative in the community. It risks making it look like a civil war between the two of you.

D. *Invite the reporter to the next Homeowners Association meeting in three weeks, when these issues will be discussed.* At the meeting, explain that each and every one of her complaints has been investigated and none have been proven. Inviting the reporter to the next Homeowners Association meeting is not a bad idea, although it carries some risks. It causes a delay that allows a negative story to grow unless you have already spoken to the reporter using the approach in "E." But it also shows an openness about the issues. The reporter can listen to what the community discusses at that meeting, which should be a thorough report of the ongoing issue with Nancy. Of course, if Nancy has gathered a following of Negative Advocates (which many HCPs do in homeowners associations), it may be a very difficult association meeting, so you might decide not to invite the reporter. But be prepared, as the reporter may show up anyway.

Conclusion

Remember, each situation is different and you need to use your own best judgment. However, from my experience and consultations, these general principles about Responding Quickly to Inaccurate Information seem to apply in many different settings, including extended families, workplace environments, government agencies, schools, healthcare systems, and other types of communities.

TIP #10 SUMMARY

Respond Quickly to Inaccurate Information

High Conflict People repeatedly distort information. They truly see it differently, and most of these distortions are honestly believed. However, many HCPs lie more than most people because they feel they "have to" in order to cope with their chronic fears.

A. Is there any inaccurate information that needs a response?

1. Is it just the HCP who has this inaccurate information?

2. If so, then you usually don't need to respond at all. You're not going to change the HCP's mind, especially since you're seen as an adversary (a Target of Blame).

3. Has the misinformation gone out to potential Negative Advocates or your larger community (workplace, neighborhood, extended family)? If so, then you'll usually want to respond, and as quickly as possible. An exception to this would be responding to committed Negative Advocates. They're unlikely to change their opinion. With information that has gone out to a community, be careful to take a balanced approach that reassures the community it's not a civil war between you and the HCP.

B. How can I best present my accurate information?

1. Always show empathy and respect for the HCP in public.

2. Depending on the situation, provide a detailed response or a general statement of disagreement.

3. Say you care for the community and won't be distracted.

4. In general, be Brief, Informative, Friendly, and Firm (B.I.F.F.).

C. If I'm responding, who should I provide with my accurate information?

1. Potential Negative Advocates are usually the most important.

2. Committed Negative Advocates are optional unless you're legally required to respond to them, such as to their attorneys.

3. The general community should be included, through the same means that the HCP has communicated, such as emails, bulletin boards, newspapers, and in-office memos.

4. Usually include the HCP, so that the HCP doesn't find out another way.

Tip #11: Set Limits on Misbehavior

CHAPTER

11

"To be frank, officer, my parents never set boundaries."

Tip #11
Set Limits on Misbehavior

In many cases, setting limits is the most important and most difficult step in handling High Conflict People. HCPs generally have less self-control, are more impulsive, less aware of the impact of their behavior on others, and often don't care if their behavior bothers or hurts themselves or anyone else.

Ordinary reasoning, persuasion, and logic don't apply. HCP behavior only makes sense when you understand that it's Behavior that's Aggressively Defensive (B.A.D.) based on their personality-based Mistaken Assessments of Danger (M.A.D.). Therefore, HCPs often need others to stop their misbehavior because they can't stop themselves.

In this Tip I talk about how individuals and communities can set limits. I use the term "community" broadly to mean a neighborhood, a homeowners association, an office workgroup, a whole business, an organization, a family (which can include one household or many households of aunts and uncles and cousins, etc.), or any other group of people in which you and the HCP are members.

Setting Limits

The process of setting limits has two simple steps:

Step 1:   You establish rules (policies, procedures, laws, etc.).

Step 2:   You provide logical consequences if the rules are violated.

Of course, as with everything else, this simple process is extremely difficult with HCPs. It's as though their personalities were built to break the rules, to avoid the consequences, and to aggressively claim that rules and consequences don't apply to them because they're "special." HCPs are the ones who "push the limits" and "con" people into making exceptions for them. They often argue that their Targets of Blame are so bad that anything the HCP does in response should be praised and tolerated without limits.

Therefore, in order to effectively Set Limits on HCP misbehavior you need to bear in mind several issues you don't need to consider with someone who isn't an HCP:

1. HCPs don't respond with ordinary logic or realistic self-interest!

2. What is your goal with the HCP?

3. What power do you have to set limits on the HCP?

4. What power does your community have to set limits on the HCP?

5. What effect will your approach to setting limits on the HCP have on you, as the Target of Blame? Will it backfire on you?

6. What effect will your approach to setting limits on the HCP have on your community? Will it make your community's culture of conflict even worse?

In this Tip I address each of these issues. This is not a comprehensive explanation of how to set limits. There are many other books about that (especially parenting manuals). Instead, this is an explanation of the special factors to consider in setting limits with HCPs. I start with a well-known example of HCP logic, from which we can all learn.

1. HCPs Don't Respond with Ordinary Logic or Realistic Self-Interest

Saddam's Logic

In studying terrorists, a former United States agent for the Federal Bureau of Investigation (FBI) suggested that terrorist leaders have an extreme form of narcissistic personality. He mentioned Saddam Hussein, the former dictator of Iraq, in this group (Navarro, 2005).

If Saddam had an extremely narcissistic personality pattern, then his logic would be preoccupied with him *appearing* to be a very superior person, so he would *feel* like no one else could be superior to *him*. For this reason, he would want the world to *think* he had Weapons of Mass Destruction (WMD). He would not be able to accept anyone else's demands of him. He would have to be in charge. He would not be able to stop himself from lying and manipulating to keep up this appearance.

For many years, the United Nations had a program of setting limits on Saddam's ability to produce such weapons, and apparently it was successful. However, he often interfered with UN inspectors, which gave the *appearance* that he still had

WMD to hide. His rhetoric with the rest of the world was highly aggressive, and he refused to appear intimidated by the world's threats and restrictions.

When the United States and a few others invaded Iraq in 2003, they scoured the country for WMD. None were found. Saddam went into hiding. He was found in a tiny room underground. Saddam was tried, convicted of crimes against his own people, and executed.

This *may* be a perfect example of an HCP's Mistaken Assessment of Danger; he was in danger, but he got it wrong. He thought the danger was that he might appear *too weak or inferior*, when the real danger was that he appeared *too strong*. This influenced others to believe he had to be eliminated. Therefore, his actions were totally self-defeating and appeared to make no logical sense. They were driven by his personality-based fear of *appearing* to be inferior or dominated by others.

While this example may seem far removed from everyday neighbor and workplace conflicts, it helps show that the dynamics of HCPs are the same everywhere you go. Remember: The issue's not the issue. The high-conflict personality is the issue.

2. What's Your Goal?

If your goal is to control HCP behavior, or to "make them see the light," you'll be forever frustrated. If your goal is to aggressively eliminate the HCP, you may have a backlash in your community, as I explain below. Of course, it's natural to feel like responding this way, but it just doesn't work.

Containment is the Primary Goal

An HCP's personality is not under your control. Their patterns of thinking, feeling, and behaving are imbedded and unconscious. This is the result of life-long patterns that take years to change—if the HCP wants to change, which most HCPs don't. You're not the cause of their problems, you can't control them, and you're not the cure (as they say in Al-Anon to family members of alcoholics). But you may be able to contain their behavior.

Instead of insight or elimination, think in terms of containment. What you really want is to *stop their Behavior that's Aggressively Defensive.* This behavior against their Targets of Blame may include verbal attacks, rumors, interference with the Target's work, interference with a peaceful home, destruction of property, physical assaults, filing frivolous lawsuits, recruiting Negative Advocates, to name a few. What you want to do is think about containing their misbehavior by setting limits on it rather than eliminating or changing the HCP.

Domestic Violence Example

An example of containment is domestic violence programs to stop spouse abuse. Most chronic domestic violence perpetrators ("batterers") appear to have high-conflict personalities, especially Borderline HCPs and Antisocial HCPs. Research shows that programs that treat batterers are generally effective at significantly reducing battering behavior. Whether it's a 6- or 12-month program, follow-up studies show that one year and even four years later, the batterer has stopped or significantly reduced battering behavior.

So these programs are a benefit to batterers and victims both. However, they don't change the person's personality. Research also shows that these programs don't really change how they think. Instead, their behavior has been contained.

Interestingly, if you talk with batterers (and I've had both victims and batterers as divorce clients) and ask them why they were hitting their spouses or unmarried partners, some still say it's the other person's fault. But after a batterers' treatment program, they'll say they've *learned not to hit* the other person, even if they think it's all their fault.

Another example of domestic violence containment is restraining orders. Today, about 20% of divorce cases involve requests for restraining orders (Eddy & Waldman, 2006). Restraining orders commonly require the alleged perpetrator of domestic violence to stay 100 yards away from the alleged victim. If the restrained person violates the order and shows up at the door of the victim, then the victim can call the police and the restrained person will be picked up and often taken to jail for one or more days. In this manner many HCPs are *restrained from hitting*.

In some cases, batterers spend months or years in jail for serious assaults and battery on their victims. This is another way of containing their behavior and protecting their victims. They are *prevented from hitting*. This doesn't change their personality and it doesn't remove them forever—except in rare cases, like murder. However, jail is a form of setting limits and usually has a lasting impact on a batterer's future behavior, because it's a negative consequence that they want to avoid in the future.

These three methods are ways of containing HCP behavior. They don't rely on insight and they don't eliminate the person. The focus is on the desired behavior, which is that they don't hit anyone. This approach benefits the HCP as well as their Targets of Blame. They all are forms of setting limits on misbehavior.

Treatment May be a Secondary Goal

If you plan to have an ongoing relationship with the HCP, then you may want to consider getting him or her into some form of treatment for personality problems. For example, if you're an employer or a family member, you may have many reasons why you believe the HCP can be a contributing member of your community.

This is similar to substance abuse treatment, which employers and family members will often pay for (although usually only one time), with the understanding that a "recovering addict" can be a good employee and good family member. Research shows that it's less expensive to keep a skilled employee by getting them into recovery than it is to hire a new employee and start over again. Likewise, divorcing a potentially good spouse or kicking out a family member may be more traumatic in the long run than dealing with one who really gets "clean and sober."

Most treatment approaches for treating personality disorders include both cognitive and behavioral treatments. This means they go beyond stopping the HCP's aggressive behavior and help the HCP actually start to change their cognitive distortions, including their high-conflict thinking. One of the most highly regarded treatment approaches for Borderline Personality Disorder is DBT, or Dialectical Behavior Therapy, which was described in Tip #3.

Dialectical Behavior Therapy (DBT) is growing rapidly as a treatment approach for Borderline Personality Disorder. It involves skills training groups for managing emotions and impulsive, self-destructive behavior, as well as individual therapy for changing personal behavior patterns. Such groups and individual therapists may be found through the phone book, on the Internet, or through referrals from other mental health professionals. While this approach has not been applied to the other personality disorders, it may be in the future.

Other approaches include Schema Therapy and Cognitive-Behavior Therapy (CBT), which involve changing thinking and behavior patterns. Again, these may be found through the phone book, on the Internet, or through referrals from other mental health professionals. Individual therapists who are not associated with a specific treatment approach may be helpful, but working with personality disorders and traits is such difficult work that it really helps if the therapist has a consultation group or organization for support and managing difficult issues.

Of course, you may remember that people with personality disorders (including HCPs) generally *don't* believe they have any problems that need treatment. So you may need to use the power of your community (such as your employer or your family) to do an intervention and get them into treatment. Only do this after you've become aware of resources in your area and have prepared a very strong intervention plan with an intervention professional.

3. Setting Personal Limits: Use the Power You Have

Realistically, as the Target of Blame for an HCP, you're in a weak position to set limits on his or her behavior by yourself. In the domestic violence examples above, the community is involved in setting limits out of necessity: police, courts, and treatment programs. However, in many cases of non-violent HCPs, there are many small things you can do with the power you have.

Setting Limits on What You Will Discuss

HCPs are high energy and high drama. Their emotions are all over the place. You can tell an HCP that you won't discuss certain topics, or not for very long.

Pat may have told Alison: "I know you're really angry at your boyfriend, but I'm not willing to talk about him anymore. Let's talk about you, and what you're going to do tomorrow. Anything fun?"

Jason may have told Bob: "Sounds like you had a great weekend. I need to get back to work now. There's a report that's due this week. Talk to you later."

Maria may have told Carlos: "I'm not willing to discuss having you move in with me anymore. It's just not an option. I don't need to explain it any further. Did you find any listings in the paper that I can help you with?"

It's surprising how simple this is with ordinary people, and how hard it is with HCPs. They just don't get it. They just go right on talking about whatever it was, even though you just said you won't discuss it. If you've ever dealt with a High Conflict Person, you know what I am talking about. It's one of the first signs of HCPs—they have a very hard time truly listening to others, especially under stress (which may be often).

This means that you need to be prepared to keep setting the same limits. "Remember, I said I won't discuss that any further. Let's talk about …." Or you might have to start physically moving away from him or her. Rochelle said to Phil: "I really have to get back to this report. Talk to you later."

Try to remain calm and reinforce setting limits with your actions. Resist the urge to give in to HCPs and keep on discussing whatever they want. Resist the urge to get angry with them for not hearing you. They honestly have a hard time stopping themselves. Just be persistent and repetitive.

Setting Limits on Your Contacts

When Alison returned Pat's corkscrew, she said: "Thanks, Pat. Hey, let's get together over a glass of wine again soon ourselves."

Pat responded: "I'll have to check my schedule. Sounds like you had a good time with your new friend."

"Oh yeah," said Alison. "I think he's going to work out really great."

"Well, I gotta go now," Pat replied. "Lots of work to do to prepare for tomorrow."

"Okay, well let me know when you want to get together."

"Okay," Pat replied.

Pat couldn't figure her out. How could Alison be so friendly, then so hateful, then so friendly again? (Remember, Alison was a Borderline HCP.) "What kind of fool does she think I am?" Pat considered marching back over to Alison's condo and telling her how rude and inconsiderate she was, and that she was never going to get together with her over a glass of wine ever again.

Then she thought about Alison's reaction, and how the banging would probably start again. She also realized she was taking it personally. She didn't have to tell Alison anything. Instead, she decided to drop it. She didn't intend to ever have Alison over again for a glass of wine. She would just not bring it up. She didn't think that Alison could handle a direct answer "No" (a realistic assessment).

Over the Thanksgiving holidays, Maria decided not to have her usual family dinner, but to go out of town for a vacation. Carlos and her mother objected, but Maria said, "I fix a big dinner every year, and it's a lot of work. I've decided to take this year off and go on a vacation. There are lots of holiday dinners you can go to or you can make your own. I've been under a lot of stress at work, so this year that's what I'm going to do."

Setting Limits Through Attorneys

When Michael found an attorney to help him with his case, he gave him the letter that Jonathan had sent (see the end of Tip #6). "I want to stop him from sending me letters like this. What can you do?"

His new attorney said, "I would suggest that I write back to the District Attorney, point out how aggressive Jonathan is, and encourage the D.A. to investigate what's in it for him."

The attorney was attempting to set limits on Jonathan through the District Attorney by making it clear that Jonathan should not directly contact Michael. "No contact" is standard procedure between the defendant and witnesses against him, but HCPs ignore standard procedures and try to cut corners all the time. Jonathan may be acting at Darlene's request or on his own initiative, but Michael's attorney's letter will probably inspire the D.A. to stop him. If not, it'll show the D.A. how inappropriate his star witness is.

Avoid Threats

HCPs react extremely negatively to criticisms and challenges. Therefore, threats generally make things worse. Of course, for a brief moment, making a threat may make you feel good, but then the HCP escalates and you're generally worse off.

However, in some situations you might be able to matter-of-factly explain that a consequence will occur if such-and-such behavior continues. But try to say you hope this won't happen and give them some empathy and respect when you tell them this.

Setting Limits on Your Relationship

In extreme cases, you may decide that the only way to set sufficient limits on HCPs is to end your relationship with them. You need to be very careful in doing this. HCPs are generally dependent on others because of their own weak problem-solving skills. If you end the relationship, it'll potentially trigger an extreme crisis for the HCP, who may attack you and blame you for the Internal Upset triggered by this loss. This can lead to spreading rumors, stalking, legal attacks, and violence.

Generally, the way to end a relationship with an HCP is to have a step-by-step plan that either gets you out safely all at once with no chance of retaliation (like moving to a "safe house" for a domestic violence victim), or eases you out of the relationship in small steps (like Pat spending less time with Alison, but not saying she won't be her friend). This is a decision best made in consultation with friends, family and/or professionals (such as therapists or attorneys) who have experience dealing with these situations.

Develop Confidence in Setting Limits

All of this may seem obvious and simple. However, with HCPs nothing is obvious and simple! It can be very unnerving to set limits on an HCP. So many people avoid setting limits and HCPs often gets away with their misbehavior. Most people naturally hesitate to set limits with them. HCPs are highly resistant to any feedback or limits. Ordinary efforts to set limits often fail, so people just give up and give in. Unfortunately, this reinforces their high-conflict behavior.

Therefore, it's very important to have confidence when you're setting limits with HCPs. Some HCPs are extremely sensitive to nonverbal cues. If you seem ambivalent about setting limits, many HCPs will simply ignore the limits. Others will take your ambivalence as a challenge to talk you out of setting limits. If you show confidence, then they're more likely to take you seriously.

If you have doubts about setting limits, consult with friends or professionals to make sure that you're doing the right thing. Then, develop your confidence by practicing with friends or in front of the mirror. If you're prepared for the normal HCP resistance and you keep persisting, then HCPs often back down.

If you lack confidence and just angrily try to set limits, you may make things worse by triggering the HCP's aggressive defenses. In Tip Four, when Jason said to Bob, "We'll see when we get back to the office," he was threatening him without any real plan. This triggered Bob to defend himself by bad-mouthing Jason to the boss. Jason had triggered, rather than soothed, Bob's defenses while setting limits.

If you try to aggressively set limits while you feel upset and haven't thought out what you're doing, you can make matters worse by triggering the other person's defenses—and their awareness of your vulnerabilities. This escalates High Conflict People, who are used to looking for weaknesses in others to help themselves feel less vulnerable. This increases the conflict, rather than setting limits on it. If you don't have confidence in setting limits, don't set limits until you do. Otherwise, your nonverbal behavior demonstrates that you don't really mean it—and you lose credibility and influence.

4. Setting Community Limits: Use the Power Structure You Have

With HCPs and their aggressive behavior, you may need one or more people to work with you in Setting Limits. Your Community may be your workplace: co-workers, managers, and departments designed to assist employees, such as Human Resource (HR) departments and Employee Assistance Programs (EAPs). Your Community may be a neighborhood association or a homeowners association (HOA) with a Board. Your Community may be your extended family: brothers, sisters, parents, grandparents, children, cousins, and others.

Your Community always has a power structure, which may be able to help you in dealing with your HCP—or may be part of the problem. This power structure may include the HCP or several HCPs and Negative Advocates, so you have to be careful to Analyze Your Realistic Options in using the power structure. A key part of effective limit setting is figuring out this power structure so that you understand its potential and its limitations. Remember to use the power structure you have, not one based on wishful thinking!

Maria's Intervention Plans

Maria decided to include her mother in Setting Limits with Carlos because she was a key part of the family power structure. When her mother told Maria to take pity on Carlos, she used her power to undermine Maria. When her mother supported Maria on an issue, Carlos often stopped pressuring Maria as much. Essentially, their mother was a Negative Advocate for Carlos and an important part of their family power structure. Therefore, Maria invited their mother to meet with her and her therapist.

"Mom, thanks for coming to meet with us. I've been trying hard to figure out how to help Carlos, and I can't do much more. But my therapist thinks there's a program that could help Carlos if he would agree to go for at least several weeks. He's never gone to any counseling that I've ever suggested."

Maria's mother responded defensively, "How do you know this is what he needs?"

"From Maria's description, Carlos seems to be stuck in self-defeating ways of solving his problems," said Maria's therapist. "There are some programs with groups to learn about managing his extreme emotions and an individual counselor who can help him become more self-aware. He needs to go to a program like this, just as someone with an alcohol or drug problem can benefit from a counseling program."

"What do you think his problem is?" said Maria's mother.

The therapist replied, "I don't know for sure, because I've never met him myself. I can't diagnosis him, because I'm not his therapist. But I can refer him to programs with professionals who can make an assessment and see if they can help him."

Maria's mother asked, "What do you think his problem might be?"

"Well, he seems to have a problem with his behavior, his thoughts, and how he feels. This program helps people with a pattern of these problems. I mostly want to help Maria get him into some kind of program to see if they can help him. That's where you come in. Maria needs your help, in order to help Carlos. Would you be willing to help?"

After a pause, Maria's mother said, "What do I have to do?"

"I know this will sound real hard, Mom," said Maria, "but you and I need to tell him that we can't help him in any way—in any way at all—unless he gets this help for himself right now. You, me, and my therapist would have a meeting with him and tell him that unless he goes into such a program of individual and group counseling, we can't provide him with any further support. That means we won't give him money, help him find another place to live, not even talk to him. We hope this will push him hard enough to get this help. And, to be honest, if he won't do it, I can't talk to him anymore. I just can't take it. I hope you can agree to do this with me."

"It sounds pretty harsh. Are you sure there isn't something else we could do?" said her mother.

The therapist responded, "This is a type of Intervention. It's worked in many cases to help people get into alcohol and drug treatment programs. It's been done to get other people into other programs. As long as he knows he can keep having your help without changing how he handles problems, he won't change. He has a problem that's very hard to change—but not impossible if he gets the right kind of help. I think committing to an ongoing program of individual and group counseling will give him a good start."

"Will you help us help him, Mom? It's the last chance we have to help him, I think. He's already 38 and really stuck in life. I'm not willing to go down with him. He's got a problem neither of us understands, but there are professionals who may be able to help him. I'll help pay for it, if you'll help pay too."

"I'll have to think about it. Can I call you back about this?" said her mother.

"Why don't you think about it," the therapist said, "then we can meet again. But Maria needs to tell you how strong she feels about this. Maria?"

Maria said, "Mom, it's really hard for me to do this, but I'm not going to have any more contact with Carlos until he gets into a counseling program. So, whether you do this with me or not, I am permanently changing my relationship with Carlos. No more bailing him out. No more late-night crisis phone calls. No more endless drama. But without you, it won't be as strong. Please help me give him this last chance."

"This is upsetting. But I'll think about it. I agree that we have to do something and I want to help Carlos."

"Okay. Let's meet again in a week," said the therapist. "I really appreciate you coming to meet with Maria and me. I know it means a great deal to her. She's really exhausted. You could really help a lot."

"Okay," said Maria's mother. "I'll see you in a week."

It may take several meetings with Maria and her therapist to help Mom understand how important her role is in getting Carlos into some counseling for his self-defeating behaviors—his high-conflict personality. But this will be the key factor in setting limits on him. Otherwise, he'll just complain to their mother when Maria tries to set limits herself. He might convince Mom that it's all Maria's fault. Then it looks like a civil war between Maria and Carlos, or that Maria is being the HCP. If the power structure is unsupportive or against you, setting community limits is extremely difficult, if not impossible, and you may have to focus on setting personal limits as described above.

Community Dispute Resolvers

Many communities have trained individuals to help people resolve conflicts. They may be volunteers or paid professionals with some training or with years of experience. Their availability and procedures have significantly grown over the past few decades, with strengths and weaknesses in each approach. In general, I recommend starting with the least expensive and least strong approach, then moving to the next stronger level if necessary. However, with some HCPs it's clear from the start that they need the strongest approaches. The following is a brief explanation of the pros and cons of each approach.

Mediation

Many businesses and neighborhoods have trained mediators, ombudspersons, and facilitators. These people are trained to help resolve conflicts informally in a way that reduces the conflict and is often confidential. Their role is as a neutral person. They don't take sides, and the people in conflict are usually the decision-makers. You can usually contact a mediator or mediation agency and ask if your dispute sounds appropriate for mediation. They are usually listed in the yellow pages or other local referral services. Mediators can also be found through the national Association of Conflict Resolution, located on the Internet at www.acrnet.org, and can also be found at www.mediate.com.

Usually, a mediator or mediation center will help in contacting the other person and encouraging him or her to show up and participate in good faith. Of course, with an HCP, showing up and good faith are often doubtful. But some disputes can be resolved with a skilled mediator, especially one who has experience with high-conflict people—even if they don't call them that.

Since the decisions are made by the people involved, it may seem odd that I've suggested mediation as a form of Setting Limits with HCPs. However, involving a mediator for the purpose of resolving a dispute gives your situation more attention and more seriousness. Also, the mediator may inform the HCP (and you) about what might happen if you don't reach an agreement to end the dispute (going to court, police involvement, etc.). Most of all, the mediator might actually help you settle the dispute.

HCPs generally want to look good in the eyes of the public. They often have a lot of charm and really care about being respected. As a mediator, I've seen many HCPs who decide to look good by settling their dispute in mediation. Of course, you have to have a more detailed agreement than usual, with highly specific consequences built in to make sure they actually do what they say they'll do—a form of setting limits in advance.

A limitation of mediation with HCPs is that the mediator can't make the HCP do anything, and the mediator doesn't make the decisions. If the HCP drags his or her feet, lies, or won't attend, then you need stronger measures. Also, HCPs often need a Positive Advocate involved in the process, someone who is their very own advocate, such as an attorney or support person. I've had several mediation sessions in which an advocate (a Positive Advocate) also attended the mediation sessions and was very helpful with an HCP.

Collaborative Law

Collaborative law is a fast-growing new development in resolving legal disputes. Collaborative divorce is the most common form, but this method is beginning to be used in other types of disputes, such as business disputes. In this approach, each person has his or her own lawyer and sometimes there is a collaborative coach (a mental health professional not acting as a therapist). The professionals and the parties sign an agreement that they'll negotiate a settlement of their dispute without ever going to court. If negotiations fail, the parties will have to hire new attorneys to go to court, which is a strong incentive for everyone to work hard at settling the case. The beauty of this process for HCPs is that each party has their own Positive Advocate in their separate lawyer and ideally a separate coach. This often makes it possible for the case to be resolved when it might not have been resolved in mediation. Many local bar associations can give you referrals for attorneys involved in collaborative practice, or you can go to the national website at www.collaborativepractice.com for more information or to locate collaborative professionals.

Arbitration

Arbitration is a more formal dispute resolution process. It's built into the power structure for many organizational grievances and conflicts, including those based on labor management contracts, homeowners association procedures, or government agency procedures. While these may also offer neutral mediation, many have arbitration clauses built in to their rules. Arbitration is more formal than mediation, with certain procedures that must be followed, and the decision-maker is the arbitrator, not the people in conflict.

Arbitrators are supposed to be familiar with the laws and rules applying to your dispute. Therefore, going to arbitration may force the HCP to learn about the laws and rules and the potential consequences of not following them. If the HCP loses in arbitration, it usually costs them something important, such as a sizable settlement, their job, or a piece of property. Also, the loser in arbitration often has to pay some or all of the other person's attorney's fees, as well as the arbitration fees.

Simply having to go to arbitration sometimes influences HCPs to change their behavior. The last thing many HCPs want is to have someone else making decisions about their behavior. For example, Narcissists may feel belittled and Antisocials may feel dominated. On the other hand, Histrionics may enjoy the attention and Borderlines may believe that the arbitrator will be "all good" (splitting) and will therefore take their side. So you have to Analyze Your Realistic Options about this. Arbitrators may be found through local organizations or through the American Arbitration Association at www.adr.org. This organization also has mediators. The Association of Conflict Resolution mentioned above (www.acrnet.org) under Mediators also has arbitrators listed on its website.

Litigation

Litigation means having the dispute decided by a judge or a jury. This may be all that stops some HCPs. Courts can impose financial penalties, loss of property, loss of a job, loss of a business, and loss of freedom, including restraining orders and prison. Today only about 5% of cases filed in court actually get decided by a judge or jury. Most litigation cases get resolved before a trial—sometimes just moments before a trial and sometimes over the phone between the people involved or between their attorneys. As with mediation and arbitration, it helps to get a very specific agreement or court order, with very specific consequences for violating it.

Unfortunately, when HCPs are involved, some courts have trouble understanding the true facts of the case. They may get the case backwards. HCPs sometimes mislead the judge or jury into believing that their Target of Blame is really at fault. Darlene is a good example, as she made her false claim with the free assistance of the District Attorney. Michael had hired an attorney to defend himself, with the cost paid out of his own pocket.

Deciding whether to take a case to court can be a difficult decision, and may require consultations with more than one attorney. You can find experienced attorneys most easily through your local county bar association, through the phone book, or on the Internet. Since most courts operate locally by counties, getting a local attorney is often the best approach—at least for a start. Many will offer an initial consultation for an hour without a longer commitment.

Police and other Security Services

Unfortunately, in today's world an increasing number of HCPs are unable to restrain themselves from breaking the law and giving in to their own violent impulses. Therefore, there's a need for the community to restrain them, often through police or other security services. Police are called in more and more to deal with high-conflict custody and visitation exchanges, heated neighbor disputes, and workplace violence. If your situation may need such assistance, it helps to discuss this with law enforcement or security personnel before it reaches a crisis point. You can contact police community service officers in your area by contacting the non-emergency number for your local police.

Remember Your Goal

Remember that your primary goal is usually to contain the HCP. Your efforts to set limits won't cause insight or significant behavior change in most cases, but can still resolve a dispute. Using any of the above dispute resolvers may slow down the HCP or influence the HCP to leave the neighborhood or job, or reduce contact with the family. In many cases, HCPs leave a community rather than accepting the community's authority. They would rather leave than appear to be inferior or dominated in people's eyes.

Also, throughout the dispute resolution process you should continue to treat the HCP with empathy, attention, and respect. This will help keep the HCP from escalating the dispute even more. This may also help the HCP save face—and saving face is extremely important to HCPs. This is particularly important in helping an HCP accept consequences he or she doesn't like. If you gloat, you'll make things worse for yourself. If you prevail, treat your victory in a matter-of-fact manner; the HCP is less likely to take it personally and have it trigger more defensiveness and future trouble for you.

5. Use a Highly Assertive Approach to Set Limits

The approach you use to Set Limits with High Conflict People will largely determine whether you remain a Target of Blame. Setting Limits will help you avoid being a Target if you remember to use a Highly Assertive Approach. Since you will be naturally tempted to use an Aggressive approach or a Passive approach, I want to help you understand the differences among these three approaches.

An **Aggressive** approach means that a person uses his or her power to harm or eliminate the HCP. The thinking behind the Aggressive approach is that harming or eliminating the HCP will keep them from becoming a threat again. There's no concern for the HCP's welfare in the Aggressive approach.

A **Passive** approach means that a person takes no action against the HCP. Instead, the person attempts to protect him or herself by avoiding the HCP. There is no attempt to advance one's own welfare or point of view, but rather an effort to avoid further conflict by not dealing with the HCP. With HCPs, this Passive approach leaves you wide open to being harmed by their naturally aggressive approach.

An **Assertive** approach means the person takes action to assert his or her own welfare and point of view while respecting the other person's welfare and point of view. This approach seeks solutions that allow for a balanced co-existence between the person and the HCP, even though there may still be serious differences. An assertive approach is a protective approach that doesn't necessarily trigger the other person's aggressive approach.

A Highly Assertive Approach to Setting Limits simply emphasizes that you'll need to be as active as the aggressive HCP, which means using more energy to Set Limits than you need in being assertive with the average person. Remember that HCPs have above-average aggressive energy because even in ordinary conflicts they constantly *feel* they are in life-or-death situations.

There are pros and cons to each of these approaches in different situations. However, when it comes to HCPs, you'll automatically *feel* like using an aggressive approach or passive approach. Instead, I strongly recommend taking an assertive approach, for reasons explained below.

An Aggressive Approach Backfires with HCPs

When you're dealing with HCPs, it's natural to *feel* like fighting against them, to attack back in an aggressive manner. Since they regularly engage in highly aggressive behavior themselves, it will trigger your natural defenses, your "flight or fight" response. The "flight" approach is the passive or avoidant approach, which I will discuss below. But if you consider the "fight" approach, you have to remember that it will trigger the highly aggressive fight approach of the HCP. In general, HCPs will be much more experienced at fighting than you are, and especially at fighting dirty without any empathy or respect for ordinary rules of behavior during a conflict.

Also, when you use an aggressive approach, you must remember that you're not just dealing with the person in isolation. Usually, there are other people in your community—your family, your workplace, and your neighborhood—who are all potential Negative Advocates for the HCP. If you aggressively fight with the HCP, you'll appear to be engaged in a "civil war" with the person, and considered equally to blame—if not more so. You may appear to be an HCP as well, or the only HCP! This may inspire some of those in your community to become Negative Advocates against you in an effort to protect the "helpless little" HCP. And HCPs are particularly good at manipulating those around them to see them as victims, while they are actually the perpetrators.

Aggressive behavior by anyone, inside or outside of a community, feels threatening to the community. Communities don't like to see members harmed by anyone, including people from inside the community. Remember, the aggressive approach is focused on harming someone. People will tell you to stop acting aggressively, unless you have a good reason. Otherwise, it puts everyone on edge.

If the HCP who is blaming you can convince others that you're abusing him or her, then you'll be treated with the community's anger. Your aggressive behavior will reinforce the HCP's claim that you're a bully or high-conflict person yourself. Communities don't like aggressive behavior within the community, as it's a potential threat to the entire community's stability. You can quickly become a Target of Blame for a whole community if you act in a manner that's considered too aggressive.

Many HCPs have learned how to put a "spin" on a Target's innocent behavior, to make the Target look guilty of something while the HCP appears to be an innocent victim who deserves the community's protection and assistance. In high-conflict disputes, it's often hard to determine who is acting badly when one person attacks another, be it verbally, financially, or violently.

Was one person simply defending him or herself against an aggressive person? Or was that person the aggressive one? If both are acting aggressively, perhaps it's a battle of equals, who are equally responsible for acting "badly." You could be seen in that light, as are many people in communities who are simply trying to defend themselves against an HCP.

It's difficult to win with an aggressive approach against HCPs because they're usually much more experienced at using an aggressive approach—even while disguising themselves as helpless victims. If you're too aggressive, you may give them the ammunition to convince others, "See, it *is* all his (or her) fault!!"

If you're too aggressive, you may become a Target of Blame for the whole community. You may activate the HCP's defenses—and everyone else's! This appears to be how mob behavior works. It's a rapidly contagious passing of anger in a group that feels a great deal of fear and has suddenly been given a Target of Blame. You don't want to be that Target!

For example, I have seen many divorce cases in which one spouse withdrew all of the money in a bank account because he or she feared that the other spouse will cut him or her off financially. Unfortunately, this triggered the anger of the other spouse—and the court—because it harmed the first spouse. It looked like an aggressive act intended to make a grab for all the money, when in fact the person making the withdrawal thought he or she had to do this to protect him or herself. There is less of a problem if one spouse takes half of an account and keeps it in a new account with good record-keeping. This is less likely to harm the other spouse and less likely to appear to be an aggressive act.

A business example occurs when one partner changes the locks on the doors of the business because he or she fears that the other partner is going to take certain assets without discussion or agreement. Many people do this, thinking they are protecting themselves, while it often looks like a power grab to gain control of the business—an aggressive act that may backfire when the other partner gets to court.

A Passive Approach Backfires with HCPs

A passive approach also backfires with HCPs because your lack of a response reinforces their thinking that they are right and that you really are a source of danger. Remember, they're operating under their Mistaken Assessment of Danger. On their own, HCPs "jump to the conclusion" that you're dangerous. Your passive approach allows them to be aggressive against you without restraint. For many HCPs, just listening and/or being nice (using your E.A.R.) won't stop their life-long aggressive behavior. They can't stop themselves for long, even if they calm down temporarily.

Each year, many people decide just to plead guilty to false legal charges brought by an HCP in order to be free of the HCP and go on with their lives, as Michael considered doing in the theater incident in Tip #6. The tension of fighting against an HCP, going to court, and coping with public opinion intimidates most people. Attorneys advise their clients all the time to settle cases instead of taking the risks of trial. There's a lot of wisdom in this, and in choosing your battles in life.

However, when HCPs are involved, if you accept a court settlement just to end a phony claim or legal charge based on their distorted perceptions, you run a big risk. Your permanent record of being found legally guilty of "bad" behavior in your community makes you *more likely* to be a Target of another HCP in the future. Anyone who has a dispute with you can pull out the court records and

the fact that you were once found guilty of "bad" behavior—bad enough to be found guilty in your community's court systems. This will make it look like *you* have a "history."

I've heard from many people (Targets of Blame) who pled guilty to a minor charge of "disturbing the peace" or "misdemeanor assault and battery" for an incident alleged by an HCP when no such event ever occurred. The Target just thought it would be easier to get it over with by settling, but later regrets it. In many such cases, that was just the beginning—not the end—as more legal action followed. Taking the "passive approach" of ignoring false statements about you or accepting false charges will make you a target in the future just as easily as being too aggressive.

In an interesting historical note, in the early 1950s U.S. Senator Joseph McCarthy held dramatic public hearings in which he questioned over 300 people about being Communists, who he feared would overthrow the government. His behavior was a good example of an HCP who made big headlines for two years, then became fully discredited for "McCarthyism" because of his wild and always dramatic allegations. He ruined many people's lives and careers, in the government and in the arts, with his high-conflict actions. Some even fled the country.

In 2003, 4,000 pages of transcripts from his hearings were released. Apparently, they revealed that he used closed sessions to interview witnesses and didn't call back for public hearings those who *assertively stood up to him*. If he thought they were *passive enough* that he could push them around, he would call them to the public hearings. Even though he threatened people with contempt of court if they didn't answer the way he wanted them to, no one ever went to jail. Eventually, his own political party turned against him (as Negative Advocates often do) and in 1954 they *censured him for his aggressive tactics* (Frommer, 2003).

The message is: don't let your own fear drive you to take an aggressive approach or a passive approach with an HCP. Instead, use a balanced, assertive approach, no matter how strongly you feel like striking back or giving in. Otherwise, you may easily become a Target of Blame for the HCP and your community, whether it's your family, your neighborhood, or your workplace.

A Highly Assertive Approach Can Work

The C.A.R.S. Method described in this book is designed as a Highly Assertive Approach. You should consider responding with as much energy as the HCP's aggressive energy, without trying to harm the HCP. By **Connecting** with Empathy, Attention, and Respect, you are reducing the likelihood of triggering their Mistaken Assessment of Danger by letting them know that you don't intend to harm them. If you don't say anything, they'll spontaneously assume you're an enemy and their "M.A.D. to B.A.D." thinking may proceed on its own.

By putting your energy into **Analyzing Realistic Options**, you're taking an Assertive Approach because you're not reacting impulsively. You're taking time to think it through. You're also fitting your expectations to the specific realities of the HCP's behavior, which usually means not trying to aggressively change the HCP's behavior, but instead trying to contain it. You're not being passive because you're actively generating options and analyzing them.

By **Responding Quickly to Misinformation** in your community and providing factual information in a matter-of-fact manner, you're not likely to be seen as aggressive. Most communities respect calm people who take the "high road" by simply providing non-emotional information, which is a very reasonable approach to problem-solving. Since you're not attacking the HCP personally, you're unlikely to be seen as aggressive. Since you're speaking up and not letting false information go unchallenged, you're not being passive. Of course, if the only person involved is the HCP, you might not be Responding to Misinformation anyway, because the community isn't involved and the HCP may take it as negative feedback.

Lastly, **Setting Limits** is an assertive approach because you're not trying to harm or eliminate the HCP by being aggressive, and you're not allowing the HCP to hurt you by being passive. Instead, the assertive goal of Setting Limits is to stop their aggressively defensive behavior without either of you getting hurt.

There is a huge difference in a community when you appear to be *protecting yourself* (and, perhaps, the community) rather than *threatening to harm another community member*. Most communities will respect you for your efforts and reasonableness.

6. Calming the Culture of Conflict

HCPs often rise in community cultures dominated by fear or passivity. In many ways, it's the same dynamic regarding the three approaches to Setting Limits that we just discussed, but at the community level. Therefore, the manner in which you set limits on one or more HCPs may actually influence your community's culture of conflict. This is especially true if you're in a position of authority, such as corporate upper management, a homeowners association board member, or the patriarch or matriarch of a large family.

If people in your community are afraid, then aggressive action will seem necessary and will be rewarded—until it backfires. Since aggressive behavior is a characteristic of HCPs, they often rise in fearful communities because they're the most aggressive personalities.

If your community has a passive power structure, then HCPs will rise because no one is paying attention or trying to set limits on them and they're the ones who most challenge authority. That is, until things get bad enough that the community finally becomes assertive about setting limits on HCPs. This is particularly true with managers who are avoidant or afraid to enforce the consequences of breaking the rules. Over time, the culture of the workplace tolerates and reinforces high-conflict behavior, and valued employees leave.

However, if your community assertively sets limits, with clear rules and the routine enforcement of consequences, then the culture of conflict won't reinforce the negative behavior of HCPs. Instead, people will feel safe and not worried about fighting to defend themselves or to get ahead. The most successful communities that I've seen have predictable rules and procedures, which are enforced, and a context of empathy, attention, and respect for everyone. Even HCPs like and benefit from an assertive culture because their chronic sense of danger is calmed down and they can focus on the reasonable tasks and responsibilities in their lives.

Workplace Bullying

From my experience and seminar feedback, workplace bullying is a growing international problem. Businesses and government agencies and even "benevolent" organizations such as schools, universities, non-profit organizations, research centers, and hospitals may have one or more department managers who are bullies and who seem untouchable. They've been there for years. They are HCPs, but they consider themselves "special" and the organizations don't set limits on them for many reasons: "With tenure, there's nothing you can do." "His department is financially successful." "He brings in a lot of grants." "She's just irritable, but she's brilliant." "He's related to a major donor." "It would take too much work to remove her." "He's retiring soon, so just live with it and don't take it personally."

Over the past couple of decades, workplace bullying has begun to receive the same kind of attention that schoolyard bullying has received for years. Perhaps it's the same dynamics for people whose personality development has been stuck since childhood. Interestingly, research indicates that 16 to 21% of employees experience health-endangering bullying and that it's four times greater than sexual harassment reports (Yamada, 2007).

These statistics (16 to 21%) are very similar to the statistics for personality disorders described in Tip #1 (approximately 15 to 17%). Since bullies also have *enduring patterns* of *dysfunctional behavior*, many of them may have personality disorders. Research on family violence shows a strong correlation between ongoing domestic abuse and personality disorders (Dutton, 2007).

It's also interesting that the growth of this problem in the workplace seems to parallel the increase in personality disorders in our modern society. They can't seem to stop themselves, and many organizations seem to tolerate them. The definition of workplace bullying does not mean a single incident, but rather an ongoing pattern of incidents. Some define this bullying to include a pattern of intense, repeated negative behavior one or more times a week for at least six months (Lutgen-Sandvik, Tracy, & Alberts, 2006).

Another important identifying feature of workplace bullying is that there's usually a power imbalance. Many examples refer to managers, such as the ones described above who are regarded as untouchable by their organizations. The victim of bullying is typically called the "target" and feels unable to set limits on the bully alone. With this lack of support, victims have experienced symptoms that included depression and even suicide. Many targets simply quit the business or organization. Even witnesses of workplace bullying are affected, although less so than targets (Lutgen-Sandvik et al., 2006).

Most workplace bullies may be HCPs (personality disorders or traits). Realizing this helps understand that the problem is:

- a problem of long duration that won't just go away

- a deep and serious problem, rather than a minor problem

- a problem that must be solved at the community level, rather than putting the burden on the individual target to stop the HCP

Along these lines, organizations and lawmakers are considering ways to set limits on this bullying behavior. For example, some suggest that there be a procedure for reporting bullying that goes around the person's manager, if the manager is the bully, since most problems are supposed to be discussed with the employee's own manager first. Also, training employees and managers in conflict resolution skills that relate to bullying can be helpful (Cohen, 2007). Finally, there are proposed laws, such as the Healthy Workplace Act (Yamada, 2007). As of this writing, bills for this law have been proposed in 13 states, but none have been passed yet. For updated information, see www.bullyinginstitute.com.

The result of this increasing awareness is that communities are setting limits on this behavior that is not controlled by the individual bully. Yet, even bullies are people too, and in many cases their skills are needed by the organization. Therefore, finding ways to effectively set limits on them may make the difference between having a stable, safe culture of conflict and maintaining an aggressive or passive environment that encourages or tolerates bullying while losing good employees—bullies and targets alike.

Bullying is an issue that demonstrates the need for community action rather than placing the burden on the individual. As we are all community members, we should support and promote these efforts at building assertive cultures of conflict and opposing aggressive or passive community cultures.

If you are a Target of a bully, it may help to apply the tips described in this book. Hopefully, this will encourage you to not take their bullying personally, but to get support and consultation on how to deal with this problem. Analyzing your realistic options and responding to misinformation may be particularly helpful.

Cyberbullying Example

As many people around the world have learned, on October 16, 2006, Megan Meier, a 13-year-old girl, committed suicide after a MySpace friend, Josh Evans, and others suddenly posted very mean comments about her. She had a history of depression and struggles with her weight, but she had been feeling better about herself, apparently because Josh Evans said, over the Internet, he liked her. When he and others started attacking her with very mean comments, she became distraught and hung herself in her bedroom.

It turned out that Josh Evans was not a real person, but the creation of two adults in the same neighborhood. Apparently, they created the false MySpace account to try to find out what Megan was saying about the woman's daughter, who had an on-again, off-again friendship with Megan. Apparently, they sent the mean messages to break off the friendship and close the account. The last message was apparently, "The world would be a better place without you."

It's disputed whether these adult neighbors knew she had a history of depression and that she'd once before thought about committing suicide. Megan's parents believe the neighbors did know and should be held responsible for what happened. Others feel that Megan's parents should have had more control of Megan's computer.

As with many news stories, it's hard to know exactly what happened. However, this may be a good example of a community—cyberspace—that has a passive culture about conflict. It tolerates and perhaps encourages high-conflict behavior with few controls. If you read journals and blogs on the Internet about this sad story, there is a lot of judgment of the neighbors and the parents. But in many ways this is a modern problem that no one anticipated. The issue shouldn't be Who to Blame, but What Do We Do Now?

Cyberspace needs to have some limits set. We clearly can't take a passive approach and depend on everyone to restrain themselves from harmful behavior. There are and will be HCPs out there who can't restrain themselves sufficiently. In fact, it'll probably be HCPs who lead the way in harming others with little empathy or insight, which will inspire non-HCPs to set these limits.

Apparently, there was no crime committed by the neighbors, and there was no liability on the part of MySpace for the false account. As many people have commented in response to this tragedy, the Internet is a place where anyone should be free to say anything. Some say that the burden was on Megan and/ or her parents to screen the Internet. But this would be the passive approach to responding to HCPs: doing nothing, and allowing HCPs to escalate hurtful behavior on the Internet.

On the other hand, an aggressive approach would be to attack the neighbors and drive them out of the neighborhood. Some suggested this on the Internet. Megan's father apparently drove his truck on the neighbor's lawn and was charged with a misdemeanor. As I have mentioned throughout this Tip, the aggressive approach often backfires.

The aggressive approach also does not solve the larger problem of changing the culture of conflict on the Internet community so that this does not happen to other young people. Cyberbullying is a much larger problem than this one

tragic case. Many others on the Internet have said the same type of cyberbullying has happened to them.

So, how would you assertively set limits on HCP behavior on the Internet? How would you protect people, especially young people, without aiming to aggressively harm HCPs and making the Internet a more aggressive culture of conflict?

Make cyber-harassment a crime, with jail time and fines? Sure. That would set limits on HCPs, who are oblivious to how harmful their behavior might be, as well as those who purposely harm others. Apparently this is where Megan's parents put their energy to protect other children in the same situation, and apparently they have had some success, as their community has established cyber-harassment laws since her death.

Put warnings up on the MySpace web pages and have better measures for verifying users? Sure. That sets limits to protect people without harming other people.

Tell parents to supervise and limit their children's use of MySpace? Sure, but that's apparently what Megan's parents did. It wasn't enough, somehow. What another commenter has suggested is that MySpace should simply be shut down. That would certainly protect teenagers. Someday, if there is enough harm done on such social networking sites, it may be necessary. Since I believe that HCPs are increasing, and they aggressively push the limits, who knows what limit-setting will be needed in the future if there isn't enough done now.

In summary, the very culture of conflict in a community is affected by HCPs and how people set limits on them. All communities need rules and logical consequences for violating them because there will always be some HCPs who can't stop themselves from harming others. We know that aggressively attacking HCPs or passively ignoring them just makes things worse—for the Target of Blame and the whole community. An assertive approach of setting limits seems to be the most effective and lasting approach, even if it doesn't give a feeling of satisfaction in the moment.

A Question

For our question, let's go back to a more familiar type of bully—the new neighbor in Tip #9 who made noise and dropped a branch into his neighbor's yard. Which of the following alternatives do you believe are good ways to handle him, now that you are thinking about your community's culture of conflict?

A. Throw the branch back into his yard to teach him a lesson.

B. Gather the neighbors together, go over to his house together, and tell him to straighten up or leave the neighborhood.

C. Select one person among the neighbors to speak to him.

D. Call a mediation center and ask the center staff to invite him to a mediation with two or three of the neighbors.

E. Call the police each time he does something that violates even the smallest rule.

I would suggest "D" as the best alternative, as mediation focuses on opening up a dialogue while also bringing the authority and reality of the community into the picture. If the presence of two or three neighbors feels too threatening to him, the mediator can meet with him and just one of the neighbors for part of the mediation session. (I have done this myself in neighbor mediation cases.) During this process (if he attends), the mediator can educate him about the consequences of not resolving these issues—such as going to an arbitration or court, where he could be fined for violating the local zoning rules for how he handles noise, tree branches, etc.

A. *Throw the branch back into his yard to teach him a lesson.* This would probably escalate the dispute, as he would probably throw the branch back again. It's an aggressive approach that generally escalates HCPs rather than giving them insight.

B. *Gather the neighbors together, go over to his house together, and tell him to straighten up or leave the neighborhood.* This might also be perceived as an aggressive approach. Whether in the workplace, the family, or in a neighborhood, HCPs react very badly to group confrontations. They feel too dominated and belittled by this approach, and therefore they escalate their Behavior that's Aggressively Defensive.

C. *Select one person among the neighbors to speak to him.* This is a better solution than "B," but not as good as the mediation in "D," if he'll attend. If he won't attend mediation, then "C" would be the next best answer. If that doesn't work, then filing a legal action for arbitration or court may be necessary.

E. *Call the police each time he does something that violates even the smallest rule.* This would probably not be effective by itself, as it didn't work in the example of the "Hate Thy Neighbor" case in the first Tip. It just escalated into a seven-year battle. However, some police involvement may be necessary and might help, along with the mediation process or court involvement.

Conclusion

Setting Limits is often the most important step in handling HCPs. They often can't stop themselves and need to have others contain their behavior. Reasoning with them usually fails because of their cognitive distortions and chronic defensiveness. Individual aggressive efforts to eliminate them from the community often backfire because they make it look like a civil war between the two of you or make you look like the HCP.

When community leaders engage in blaming behavior and show a lack of empathy, attention, and respect, it creates an aggressive culture of conflict. Such a culture encourages HCPs to rise in the community because they are more skilled at blaming and attacking others without empathy.

A passive culture of conflict allows and encourages HCPs to increase bullying behavior. However, when communities assertively set limits and follow through with logical consequences, many HCPs are able to contain themselves.

Conflict is inevitable. A safe culture of managing conflict is created by continuing to use empathy, attention, and respect *while* assertively setting limits and providing consequences. Such a culture of conflict benefits everyone, including HCPs, who can often be very creative and productive members of communities that sufficiently contain their high-conflict tendencies.

In a sense, HCPs push the limits and are often at the creative, cutting edge in rapidly changing times. We just have to make sure that no one gets cut!

TIP #11 SUMMARY

Set Limits on Misbehavior

The process of setting limits has two simple steps:

Step 1:   You establish rules (policies, procedures, laws).

Step 2:   You provide logical consequences if the rules are violated.

With HCPs, however, there are difficult issues that also need to be considered:

1. HCPs don't respond with ordinary logic or realistic self-interest!

   Their focus is on their chronic, personality-based preoccupations with relationship fears: Fear of Abandonment, Fear of Being Belittled, Fear of Being Ignored, and/or Fear of Being Dominated.

2. What is your goal?

   The primary goal is containment of HCP misbehavior. In cases of ongoing relationships (family or workplace) a secondary goal may be cognitive and behavioral treatment.

3. Set Personal Limits: Use the Power You Have.

   • Limit contact.

   • Limit the subjects you will discuss.

   • Terminate the relationship (very carefully).

   • Leave the community: workplace, neighborhood, or family.

4. Set Community Limits: Use the Power Structure You Have.

- Mediation

- Ombudspersons

- Collaborative Law

- Arbitration

- Litigation

- Law Enforcement

5. Use a Highly Assertive Approach to Setting Limits.

- An aggressive approach backfires.

- A passive approach backfires.

- Match the HCP's level of aggressive energy, but do it assertively.

6. Establish an Assertive Culture of Conflict in Your Community.

- Use empathy, attention, and respect, even while setting limits.

- Regularly create or revise rules with community input.

- Regularly impose consequences that fit the violation of rules.

- Contain the aggressive misbehavior of everyone, including HCPs.

- Welcome the creativity of everyone, including HCPs.

Tip #12: Choose Your Battles

CHAPTER

12

"I'm afraid you've had a paradigm shift."

Tip #12
Choose Your Battles

Congratulations! You've made it to the last Tip of a book that tells you to do the *complete opposite* of what you feel like doing with High Conflict People. I appreciate your patience and willingness to try new approaches. I believe that as you handle the HCPs in your life you'll be rewarded by sleeping better, having more energy, and taking things less personally.

Remember, you're not alone in facing this problem. We'll all benefit when more people learn to logically think ahead rather than to defensively react when handling a High Conflict Person. Since this is easier said than done, this last Tip focuses on how to choose your battles with HCPs.

Support and Consultation

For several reasons, it helps to get support and consultation when you handle HCPs, especially when you're deciding whether to engage in battle with their high-conflict thinking and behavior. One of the worst situations is to feel isolated while you're being attacked by an HCP. Handling HCPs is stressful and it helps to have several people you can turn to for support and consultation so that you don't burn out any one person with your own distress and so that you can get lots of useful ideas.

In my own work dealing with many high-conflict situations, I get a lot of support and consultation from those I work with at the High Conflict Institute and National Conflict Resolution Center. I'm much calmer now, and more effective in handling high-conflict cases, since I understand these disputes are not about me.

However, I still get emotionally hooked once or twice a week. When I tell my colleagues that I'm stuck on a case, one of the first things they ask is, "Bill, are you getting hooked? Are you taking it personally?" That itself usually makes a big difference, because I'll stop and think, "Yeah. I didn't even realize I was hooked. I started taking it personally. I stopped thinking logically and didn't even know I stopped thinking logically! Thanks!"

But you may also benefit from having someone help you think it through. This is when you need consultation, which is more than just support. Anyone, a relative, a neighbor, a co-worker, or a professional, can give you consultation, but you need to be careful that your consultant doesn't become your Negative Advocate.

Negative vs. Positive Advocates

Remember what Tip #7 said about Negative Advocates? It is natural and very common for people to want to help someone in distress. In fact, it's how a lot of people connect these days. This is a good thing, except when they become Negative Advocates. If you're distressed by an HCP, it's very likely that one or more people around you will:

1. Tell you that it's all the HCP's fault.

2. Tell you that you're blameless and there's nothing you can do.

3. Tell you that he or she will fix it for you.

4. Tell you that you should sue the SOB.

5. Spend a lot of time discussing the problems with you.

6. Try to take over your life.

7. Try to tell you what to do.

8. Disappear when the going gets rough.

The first four items are momentarily reassuring, but in the long run they're not helpful and often lead to the next four items. They are all characteristics of Negative Advocates. I'm sure you've met one. I'm sure you've seen HCPs gather Negative Advocates. And, I'm sorry to say, I'm sure you've been a Negative Advocate at some point in time—I know that I have been, until I realized I'd gotten hooked.

What you really need is a consultant who will be a Positive Advocate for you, someone who will:

1. Help you try to understand how the HCP might be thinking.

2. Help you look at what you can do now—to plan ahead, rather than just react.

3. Help you think about the problem without fixing it for you.

4. Help you get information about your legal rights, responsibilities, and options.

5. Schedule time by mutual agreement to discuss the problems with you.

6. Respect your time and priorities, and expect you to respect theirs.

7. Help you find resources and to reach your own decisions.

8. Remain consistent and slightly distant so they don't burn out and leave you.

Using a Positive Advocate

What you really need is a Positive Advocate who is comfortable with conflict. This can include therapists, attorneys, mediators, union stewards, and others. This person may be a paid consultant or a friendly volunteer, depending on the difficulty of your situation. This could be your Aunt Mary, or an elder from your church, synagogue, or mosque, or from another one of your communities. It could be anyone who can work with the following approach:

1. *Find a Positive Advocate:* Find someone who is willing to be a Positive Advocate rather than a Negative Advocate. (You can show the person the two lists above to help them understand their role.) This can be a healthy and well-balanced friend, family member, co-worker, neighbor, or even a professional, such as a therapist, attorney, or person experienced in conflict resolution.

2. *Find a time to discuss your situation patiently:* Make sure it's someone who can schedule time to sit down and discuss your high-conflict situation logically. Tell your Positive Advocate that high-conflict emotions are contagious and that it's more important that he or she gives you a little empathy and respect at first rather than giving you a lot of feedback or advice. Unfortunately, many people jump in and tell you "you should do this," or "you should have done that," when you really need someone who'll listen and give you some empathy and respect first—to give you the energy to deal with a high-conflict dispute.

3. *Use a C.A.R.S. worksheet:* Once your Positive Advocate understands enough about your situation and has given you some empathy and respect, you could ask him or her to go over your C.A.R.S. worksheet with you. (Either fill it out in advance, or fill it out with your Positive Advocate.) Just follow

the format of the worksheet, using as many additional pages as you need. Then discuss your options and ask for additional ideas your Positive Advocate might have for each of the four steps of C.A.R.S. See if your Positive Advocate thinks your ideas realistically fit the situation and the HCP. He or she may be able to help you get a better perspective, especially regarding questions like safety and wishful thinking, and whether you are miscalculating the power you have. Are you being overly optimistic about your ability to impact the HCP (too aggressive)? Or are you not taking the strong steps you could (too passive)? These are the types of questions to ask your Positive Advocate.

4. *Don't focus on analyzing the HCP's personality:* DON'T have your Positive Advocate try to analyze the HCP's personality, unless the consultant is a licensed therapist who's trained and experienced in explaining the patterns of personalities without reaching any conclusions about a person he or she hasn't met. Just knowing the possible personality patterns and how you might deal with them can be helpful. If you're really confused by the HCP, you might meet with a therapist who really understands personality disorders and traits at least once.

5. *Don't ask your Positive Advocate to fight for you:* DON'T try to convince your Positive Advocate to join you on the battlefield (such as attending meetings, going to the HCP's home, speaking for you in mediation, or going to court with you). Instead, their job is to help you prepare for events and, if necessary, to find others to join you, such as attorneys, mediators, administrators, or other conflict resolvers. You want your Positive Advocate to be able to help you in handling yourself and choosing your battles. This may be a continuous process, so it's good to have at least one person who stays on the sidelines, away from the battle itself. A therapist or consulting attorney could be especially good in this role.

When to Fight

HCPs trigger our defensive emotions over and over again. It takes a lot of practice and self-discipline to be able to resist constantly reacting and over-reacting to their outrageous behavior, their intense emotions, and their high-conflict thinking. Instead, you want to be able to think things through with your Positive Advocate and to choose when to assertively respond and when to ignore the HCP. This is more of an art than a science, and you'll get better at it the more you understand HCPs and practice thinking about dealing with them, such as using the C.A.R.S. Method.

There are no absolute answers with HCPs, so you must learn from your own experience as you go along in dealing with them. The more you become self-aware of your own unconscious, emotional, and defensive responses, the easier it'll be to manage them. Remember that managing your own thoughts, emotions, and behavior is the key to managing the HCP. Otherwise, you may be a victim of your own automatic responses, and may be more likely to escalate the behavior of the HCP.

We all have a lot of hidden reactions, but we can generally understand them and control them if we admit they are there and become more self-aware. I've learned a tremendous amount about myself from working with cases involving HCPs. All my buttons get pushed—even ones I didn't know I had!

The more self-aware you are, the easier it is to have the confidence to keep fighting when it makes sense. And the easier it is to let go of a battle when it doesn't. Fear and pride stop being issues when you truly understand HCPs. Because it's no longer about you, you don't need to fight unnecessarily to defend yourself or your self-image.

Be Self-Aware of How It's Going

In a high-conflict dispute, this comes down to two key questions to ask yourself:

Am I being too aggressive? If so, you probably need to back off and analyze your realistic options. If you're too aggressive, it will activate the HCP's defensiveness and possibly turn your community against you.

Am I being too passive? If so, the aggressive HCP is likely to take advantage of you or persuasively convince your community that you're a bad person. You may need to take steps to become more assertive in responding to misinformation and misbehavior.

Sometimes, if you're not sure, it helps to examine whether you're a Target of Blame. Have you become isolated by the HCP? Are you being blamed by your community? Does the way you respond to the HCP bring attention to you? You may be justified in being upset, but the way you handle it makes all the difference. You're probably being too aggressive or too passive if your community has been persuaded to think badly of you. Unless you find the assertive balance, you risk being a Target of Blame.

It's easy to *feel* like you're being too passive, when you're actually being too aggressive. Or to *feel* like you're being too aggressive, when you're actually being quite passive. It's very hard to figure this out on your own, so ask trusted friends for feedback.

For example, I've handled many conflicts in which someone stated, "I'm tired of being pushed around. I'm not going to compromise any further." While this may sound (and feel) like a passive person becoming assertive, it's usually an aggressive person justifying continuing to be aggressive.

This is quite different from the apparently passive person who says, "I'm tired of being pushed around. I'm going to just give up and give in on everything." However, even in this case, the apparently passive person may later change his or her mind and cancel the previous agreements. This may actually be a passive-aggressive person.

This can be very confusing, but the point is to examine what you're doing and whether it's working. It's often not obvious whether you're being too aggressive or too passive, and you risk having your actions backfire. Use your Positive Advocate in trying to figure this out.

When to Let Go

Choosing your battles with HCPs often includes letting go of many conflicts you might otherwise try to resolve with an ordinary person. It also means that it's necessary to end the relationship in many cases because the HCP is unable to change his or her own behavior enough to make the relationship work. Making these decisions is often very confusing because your logical brain and your relationship brain are often in conflict.

For example, Antisocial HCPs can be very good at forming friendships based on promises and logic, "Trust me. I've never hurt you. I've never let you down." Your logical brain may examine the facts of your relationship and determine that this is true. But your relationship brain may be aware of a gut feeling that this is a person who can't be trusted—even though you can't exactly say why. (Remember that Tip #7 described that your right brain operates mostly unconsciously and nonverbally.) This is especially common with Antisocial HCPs because they have no empathy or remorse about hurting you, so your relationship brain may be the one that picks this up while your logical brain is being manipulated and focused on logical reasons to trust the person.

Remember, you need both your logical and relationship brains working together to make the best decisions. Think of your relationship brain as an early warning system that gives you uneasy feelings that you need to logically examine before you make a decision based on those uneasy feelings.

Sometimes, trust your gut. Other times, don't trust your gut. The resolution to this dilemma is to always pay attention to your gut feelings and to always examine them logically before making a decision. Getting feedback from your support system or positive advocate can really help when it's hard to figure this out.

Your Conflict Clock

Be aware of your "Conflict Clock." We all have this. It tells us it's time to get out of a dispute after we have made sufficient efforts to resolve it normally. I became aware that I had a Conflict Clock in my early years as a family law attorney. I would be excited about meeting a new client and taking on his or her case. I would quickly figure out the problems and the solutions in my mind. I would do the legal research, send legal letters, make negotiation phone calls, take depositions, prepare for court hearings, and argue the case before the judge.

But then, after six months to a year, it became clear that some cases might never end. I started to feel resistance—and sometimes dread—about working on the case. I started to delay returning phone calls. I had hopeful fantasies of being fired by my client. I promised myself that it would be over soon—but then it wasn't.

I finally realized that I had this Conflict Clock inside and that all other attorneys did as well. I realized that I could actually outlast my most aggressive opposing attorneys by pacing myself better and not being attached to the outcome of the case.

I started thinking of myself as "helping and protecting my clients along the journey," rather than feeling that I had to control everybody to accomplish a certain outcome, since this was impossible. I became more patient with my clients and more tuned in to their Conflict Clocks. I learned how to calm them down and focus on the next task. I encouraged them to consider how this awful court process would help them become more self-aware and stronger.

I became more comfortable with the Assertive Approach and less concerned about the HCP's Aggressive Approach. I learned to point out the other party's aggressive behavior and judges started to catch on. And my approach worked! My clients got stronger instead of weaker, and we worked together to "chip away" at the case until we reached a satisfactory resolution.

I actually got excited about learning from my high-conflict cases with my clients and writing about what I learned (without using any names). "I wonder how this case will turn out," I asked myself. "What will make it finally get decided correctly?" I became much more effective because I was able to listen to my Conflict Clock and tell it how long this might take. "Be prepared for another year of this," I would tell myself. "And don't feel that you can control the outcome—just do your job assertively and be patient with your client."

With this approach, I saw that many of my most difficult cases were getting resolved. It just took an extra year or two sometimes, but then a good or reasonable result finally occurred—and it lasted. Sometimes it was because the judge finally "got" that my client was acting reasonably and that the other party was stuck in high-conflict behavior. Other times it was because the other attorneys finally "got it" and helped their client lower his or her unrealistic expectations so that we were able to reach a settlement. And occasionally, I "got it" and realized that my own client was too stuck and blaming to make any progress, and I learned how to end those relationships without getting sued.

So be aware of your own Conflict Clock, and pace yourself. These high-conflict disputes will often work out reasonably, but it may take longer than you initially expected. So be persistent and don't give up prematurely.

On the other hand, be realistic. Analyze your realistic options by checking for the HCP's high-conflict thinking—and your own! Some relationships may have to end, especially once you see the pattern clearly and have tried to influence positive changes without any success. Letting go is hard to do, but sometimes it opens up a much better future. When in doubt, use your Positive Advocate in making these difficult decisions.

A Question

Justin is 15 and has gotten involved with some new friends at school who seem to be having a negative influence on him. His good grades have suddenly dropped and his mother, Kristen, thinks she smelled marijuana on him one day after school, but he strongly denied it, and it was just once. He spends a lot of time in his room on his computer, instant-messaging with these friends.

Kristen doesn't want to interfere too much with his daily life and wants him to learn from his own experience. But she's told Justin that if he gets any D's or F's on his next report card, she'll move his desk and computer into the living room, where she can keep an eye on him. He'll have to stop communicating with his friends while he's at home. And she'll take away his cell phone for a month.

Justin got really angry with her about these ideas. He told her, "No one else in my whole school has their desk and computer in the living room. I'll be laughed at by everyone. Besides, I'll go live with Dad. He isn't so controlling. That'll be the end of your 50-50 custody of me!"

Justin's grades came out and he failed one of his courses. What should Kristen do?

A. Give Justin another chance and wait until the next report period ends because her plan might stigmatize him at school, embarrass him with his friends, and hurt his self-esteem.

B. Tell him he has a choice: move the desk and computer himself, or she'll do it for him.

C. Move his desk and computer while he's at school.

D. Talk to Justin's father about supporting her decision.

E. Take him to a drug treatment program for an assessment.

You might think it's unfair to include a teenager in this book, since teenagers naturally have difficult personalities until they're grown up and they learn how to balance their emotions and behavior—and most of them don't develop personality disorders or high-conflict personalities. Besides, this teenager doesn't sound very unusual at all.

But he can be a difficult kid at times, and he's still developing his attitudes and behaviors. The way his mother handles him may make a difference for the rest of his life. Yet today's modern culture includes children having their own rooms and their own computers, TVs, and cell phones. Should Kristen get in the way of that?

I say Yes! I believe that B and D together are the best.

B. *Tell him he has a choice: move the desk and computer himself, or she'll do it for him.* By doing "B" she is setting limits and enforcing them by following through with the consequence of moving the desk and computer, just as she threatened to do. Giving Justin a choice in how it's done helps him develop more responsibility by participating in carrying out his mother's consequence.

D. *Talk to Justin's father about supporting her decision.* Doing this would help Kristen build support for her actions in the power structure of their small community (still two parents). If Justin's father does not support her, and actually supports Justin against her, then it will appear that Kristen is a difficult, insensitive parent. It will appear like a civil war between parent and child. She could actually lose custody, as many family courts give a lot of weight to the child's preferences by this age. Therefore, I believe that Kristen must get support from the other parent before choosing this battle. Ideally, she would have done this before threatening to move the desk.

A. *Give Justin another chance and wait until the next report period ends because her plan might stigmatize him at school, embarrass him with his friends, and hurt his self-esteem.* This would weaken Kristen's ability to set future limits because she's not following through with enforcing the rule she already made. Self-esteem will grow more from learning to follow reasonable rules that have good and bad consequences than from not having rules. If she gives up on her threat, she can expect more bad behavior in the future, rather than good.

C. *Move his desk and computer while he's at school.* This is a good choice, although "B" is much better because teenagers need to practice making decisions and feel in charge of something, as long as they're responsible about it. If Justin opposes his mother's decision and refuses to move his desk and computer, then it would be appropriate for her to move the desk and computer herself (with help, so she doesn't hurt her back), just as she said she would.

E. *Take him to a drug treatment program for an assessment.* This may be unnecessary if there was just one incident suggesting marijuana. Since Kristen is choosing her battles, she may want to save this one for the next incident suggesting marijuana use. Choosing her battle around the school grades and the desk and computer may solve this problem anyway, as Justin learns that she means business. Many teenagers are going to try marijuana one way or the other. This may not be preventable and a parent may never know. The issue is whether this becomes a problem that reaches the parent's attention again, in which case getting an assessment is a good idea and a good consequence. In some cases, getting a drug assessment may be appropriate as the first consequence, even before moving the desk and computer. It's a question of judgment and knowing your child's community. But once Kristen threatened to move his desk and computer, I believe she needed to follow through and stay focused on that one battle for now.

Justin's Reaction

"Then I'm going to go live with my father!" Justin yelled at his mother when she gave him the choice to move the desk himself or she would do it the next day.

"It's too late, Justin," she replied. "I talked with him today and he agrees with me on this. He's going to do the same thing at his house when you go there this weekend."

"Then I'm not talking to either of you. Ever again! Ever, ever, ever!" Justin yelled.

After he silently moved his desk and computer into the living room Justin settled into his chair and scrolled through some pages on his computer. Kristen went about her business in the kitchen, making her lists and getting food ready for them for the next day.

Suddenly, after about 20 minutes, Justin said, "Hey, Mom. Look at this!"

"What is it?" Kristen said, coming over to his desk.

"They've invented a new kind of rocket that you can steer somehow," he explained, showing her some news report on his computer. "I'm studying it for my science class."

"That's amazing! There's always something new," she said, showing great interest and surprise.

"Someday, I want to be a scientist," Justin commented while clicking on his computer screen. "I want to be famous for doing something good."

"That's great!" she replied. "If you study hard, I'm sure you could be. You're certainly smart enough."

"Hmm," he replied distractedly and went back to his homework.

Kristen went back to her work in the kitchen.

A few minutes later, without turning around to look at her, Justin said,

"Thanks, Mom."

In my years as a therapist at a psychiatric hospital, with teenagers, young adults, and their parents, it wasn't unusual for there to be a period of one to two years when there was great warfare between parent and child over school, drugs, drug dealing, sex, petty crime, running away, and so forth. Yet for parents who stuck with it—choosing the battle of setting limits while still caring (tough love)—their children eventually became more responsible and, by age 25 or 30, thanked their parents for caring enough to set limits on their destructive behavior.

I have some personal experience with this subject. When I was growing up, my parents never had a television in our home, from the time I was born until I left for college at age 18. To my knowledge, our family was the only one in our whole school that didn't have a TV all those years. This was in the 1950s and 1960s when television was at the center of the baby boom generation. I begged and pleaded for us to have a television, and at school I felt totally out of it, because I didn't know what happened in the shows everyone had watched the night before. But my father, a scientist, said television was like a car without an engine. "It might look good, but it doesn't take you anywhere." My mother agreed with him on that even though it meant that they were going against what all the other parents were doing.

So I grew up spending a lot of my time reading, writing, and watching real people. Of course, as a child I resented it. I resented being left out of much of the youth culture that my generation enjoyed through television. Even in my 20s I complained to my friends that I was culturally deprived. But by my 30s I began to appreciate my parents for having the strength to be different. I realized that much of what I know today about personalities started when I was very young because I was fascinated by real people and how they really got along. My mother was a volunteer community social worker and introduced me to a lot of different kinds of people. (Perhaps I'm less afraid of people and conflict, because I didn't see the 10,000 murders that most kids reportedly see on television by the time they're 18.) So, this is my way of saying "Thanks, Mom and Dad, for choosing that battle."

TIP #12 SUMMARY

Choose Your Battles

1. **CONNECT** using Your Empathy, Attention, and Respect

2. **ANALYZE** your Realistic Options

3. **RESPOND** to Misinformation

4. **SET LIMITS** on Misbehavior

Don't be a Target of Blame

1. Lower your expectations so that you don't attack the HCP because of wishful thinking that he or she will change lifetime personality patterns.

2. Don't be Aggressive—the HCP's Negative Advocates and your Community will be easily convinced that you're a problem and should be treated as a Target of Blame.

3. Don't be Passive—HCPs will walk all over you, as they can't stop themselves.

4. Take an Assertive Approach, being as assertive as the HCP is aggressive.

5. Practice writing out C.A.R.S. Method worksheets so that it becomes automatic when you're under pressure. This way, you won't slip into being aggressive or passive and become a Target of Blame.

6. Get assistance from Positive Advocates. Avoid Negative Advocates.

7. Make your own decisions. These are tools, not rules.

CONCLUSION

Now you know the basics of the HCP Theory and the C.A.R.S. Method for Conflict Resolution in everyday life. Hopefully, you understand that many of today's "high-conflict" disputes are driven by the Internal Upsets of someone with a High Conflict Personality. In these cases, your actions may have little or nothing to do with the dispute. The "issue" is not the issue. And the question is not "Who do you blame?" It's "What do we do now?"

In many cases there is just one HCP who is driving the high-conflict dispute. In others there are two HCPs going at each other because they each are stuck in a Cycle of High Conflict Thinking, feeding each other the blame that keeps them going. We all risk getting drawn into disputes with High Conflict People. Anyone can be a Target of Blame.

I hope you feel relieved to know that these are worldwide, predictable personality problems and you're not alone in facing them. In fact, your responses to HCPs up to now were probably very normal, just not very effective. Even now, knowing all of this HCP information is the easy part. Practicing it takes a lot of effort because it involves going against your natural impulses.

In using the suggestions in this book, try to resist the "all-or-nothing" thinking that: 1) these tips will be easy to do or 2) these tips will never work. It's not a perfect approach, but I've found it helpful in handling most of the disputes that I couldn't handle before I understood all of this. I still have some disputes I can't resolve, and I still get emotionally hooked sometimes—and I've been teaching this for several years!

In fact, as I am writing this conclusion, I have been interrupted six times by "crisis" phone calls related to a family court issue that I thought was settled two months ago. Is it really a crisis? I'm trying hard to practice the lessons that I've written in this book—and it's still hard to do when I'm stressed and trying to meet a deadline. Am I being too rigid? Am I being too flexible? Is the other attorney paying too much attention to his client's Internal Upsets? Should I be setting firmer limits? Or should we change the plan because of a misunderstanding? Or is it really a calculated manipulation by his client? Can this HCP ever be contained? Setting limits with HCPs can be like a shaky levee, constantly needing to be shored up where you thought it was already solid.

I do believe it gets easier with time and practice. Simply understanding the dynamics of HCP conflicts helps. At least I step back more quickly now and don't take it personally. I can keep empathizing, even when I'm irritated. I start analyzing right away.

Now that I've recovered from those distracting "crisis" phone calls, and you know that we all have these problems, there are a few closing points I want to share with you regarding each part of this book.

Be Wary of Labelers

I have emphasized having empathy and respect for HCPs. They didn't choose to be this way, and many of them have been victims of abuse or trauma, which has triggered overactive high-conflict thinking. I've encouraged you to be sensitive to HCPs, their Negative Advocates, and the Community you're in. However, as knowledge of HCPs grows, some people are already using this knowledge to show disdain for others and to disregard their concerns by openly labeling them. "You're a Borderline." "You're a Narcissist." Or "You're an HCP."

Ironically, the people who openly label others this way tend to lack empathy and remorse. This brings us back to the central message: HCPs get it backwards. You'll find that the people who use this information negatively in public often have the personality traits of HCPs. They just can't see it. I hope that you'll use this knowledge privately, without openly labeling those around you.

On the other hand, I encourage you to share this general information with those around you so that you have more support in your own struggles, and so that more people recognize these patterns and avoid becoming Negative Advocates. You may have an HCP in your neighborhood, workplace, or family, and it can help if you can work together. You can say to others, "We might have an HCP problem," or "So-and-so may be an HCP." If the goal is to help the group and help the HCP, then these phrases are appropriate. If your goal is to put someone down and feel superior, well, you already know what's wrong with that!

Tools not Rules

I have given you four steps to consider in handling the issues of HCPs: Connecting, Analyzing, Responding, and Setting Limits (C.A.R.S.). You can think about applying these steps, one after the other in that order. You can also just do one step or another, without all four, hopefully starting with the first step (E.A.R.) and working your way down through the steps until your dispute has eased up.

These steps are meant to be flexible and adapted to your circumstances, not a rigid approach that must be followed without question. Adaptation is a key principle when dealing with HCPs and in avoiding being an HCP yourself.

Sometimes Setting Limits is clearly needed. This is especially true if the HCP is unable to stop him or herself and you don't have time to analyze things. Call for help, as it's very hard to do alone. At other times, you'll have to decide quickly whether you should be Responding or not! Go ahead and address that issue. You don't have to do these steps in this order if it doesn't fit your situation. These are tools, not rules.

However, the more empathy you have in Responding or Setting Limits, the more effective you'll be. Remember that HCPs do best when they're not feeling defensive. Empathy helps keep their defensiveness to a minimum, while helping you stay focused on solving problems and not blaming the HCP in retaliation.

Also, don't forget to keep it from getting personal. We all have responsibility in solving problems. Don't ask, "Who's to blame for this sorry situation?" Ask, "What do we do now?" Don't forget to ask yourself, "Is this really true?" and, "What's my part in solving this?"

Seeing Patterns

I have given you limited psychological information about the four High Conflict Personalities. You shouldn't attempt to diagnose people. Instead, just recognize that HCP behavior has some predictable patterns in conflict situations.

If you recognize some traits of a particular HCP, you may be able to anticipate other traits, so you won't be as surprised. For example, if you recognize constant lying, manipulation, and lack of remorse, you may realize that you're dealing with an Antisocial HCP and that he or she probably has a legal "history." If you recognize the mood swings of a Borderline HCP, there's a likelihood that anger and chaos are just around the corner, even when things are going well.

But you must be very careful with this information. Otherwise, you'll jump to conclusions about who has which personality patterns, and you may be very wrong. That's why you must always approach these issues with a Private Working Theory that you keep to yourself and only discuss with compassionate others in your community. You must be willing to change your perspective easily. The goal is not to judge people, but to understand them.

Some HCPs are dangerous, so be aware of your internal warning signs. Don't allow yourself to be misled by a fast-talking but abusive person. Stop and think: Am I being manipulated here? Is this charming person really a danger to me? Remember that there are HCPs out there with lifetime skills in manipulation.

On the other hand, you may be over-reacting to an HCP. Histrionic HCPs will hook you into their drama before you even know it. By and large they are sincere, but their emotions are manipulative and persuasive.

And some HCPs can be great workers, neighbors, and friends, even though their personalities are difficult some of the time. Avoid jumping to conclusions that your relationships with them can't work. They just need to be managed more than people who aren't HCPs. They may be more flexible on another day or another week, so you may just need to manage the nature of your contacts, rather than giving up on them completely.

I strongly recommend that you consult with a mental health professional if you're dealing with a specific HCP and you want to understand more about him or her and what to expect in the future. I also recommend meeting with an attorney if you feel that you're in legal or physical danger from an HCP. You can also meet with a mediator in your area to resolve any specific dispute that appears to be escalating. Use your community's resources and power structures.

Are You an HCP?

After reading my books, or attending my seminars, many people think more about their own personality patterns and occasional high-conflict behavior. Some people wonder (or worry) that they have a high-conflict personality. I have three things to say about this.

First, if you're worrying about your own personality and considering ways you might adapt your behavior, then it's unlikely you have a high-conflict personality. Remember, HCPs lack self-awareness. They don't reflect on their own personalities, and they don't believe they have anything that needs changing.

Second, you can always become more self-aware and adapt your behavior to be more effective in your environment. As long as you become increasingly self-aware and try new behaviors, you'll be happier and get into fewer conflicts.

Third, maybe you have some HCP traits or even a personality disorder. I encourage you to meet with a therapist who is skilled at working with personality disorders and traits. Many people with personality disorders have been helped, and many more are working hard on changing their own personality patterns. There is hope! The more people who work on this, the better off we will all be.

Recovering HCPs

It's also very important to recognize that there is a wide spectrum of High Conflict Personalities. You'll be able to resolve disputes easier with some than with others. Some HCPs have learned to recognize their personality problems and are working hard to overcome them. There are "recovering borderlines," for example. Avoid making the assumption that people never change. While HCPs have rigid personality patterns, those who are motivated by real consequences (such as Alison) may surprise you with their ability to change.

In the future, I believe that it's possible that we'll have effective and widely available treatment programs for those with personality disorders and traits (and therefore HCPs), and that these programs will be as widely accepted as recovery is today for addicts and alcoholics. There should not be a stigma, but instead a wide-spread understanding of the HCP problems we all have to deal with in all of our shared communities.

Today, our whole society recognizes that addiction is a problem for which there is empathy, real consequences, and treatment. My hope is that HCPs will receive the same type of social response so that there will be sufficient consequences for their misinformation and misbehavior to get them into recovery.

The HCP Theory

The HCP theory is just that—a theory. You should make your own decisions based on your own best judgment. Use the HCP theory to the extent that it helps you. I can't guarantee the results of using this understanding of people and their personalities. Rather than giving you the results of years of research, I am giving you the results of my thirty-plus years of personal experience.

I would love to have researchers study the C.A.R.S. method to see if it really reduces people's stress and conflicts with HCPs. But that hasn't been studied yet. While I could have waited 10 more years to study this approach, I have decided to share what I believe will help other people now. Since many of my suggestions are based on related mental health research and years of experience, I feel hopeful that they are useful.

I'm also very concerned that people will do what they automatically feel like doing in conflicts with HCPs, unless they are given the information that we have already. If there's one thing I've learned over the past 30 years, it's that you make things much worse when you just react out of your feelings in your dealings with HCPs. I don't believe we have another 10 years to study this before teaching people to stop and think. There is an urgent need to slow down and stop the Cycles of High Conflict Thinking all around us.

The Future

High Conflict People may be like the canaries in the coal mine that dramatically warn of danger when the oxygen is running out in the mine. HCPs appear to have been present throughout history and in all cultures around the world. However, they seem to be increasing in our modern, hi-tech societies. It may be that they're meant to get our attention when our cultures get out of balance.

In communities, for example, HCP's intense emotions and highly aggressive behavior often point directly to areas that may need more attention—such as bullying and blaming in the workplace and over the Internet. Rather than trying to eliminate HCPs, we should contain their negative behavior while listening to them and learning what their behavior is telling us about our communities.

In families, for example, parents of children who appear to be developing high-conflict personalities may need to provide a better balance of setting limits and empathy, attention, and respect. High-conflict personalities seem to develop when there's not enough of both. With all the stresses on parents these days and both parents working, young children may not be getting enough social glue (E.A.R.). With all the technological intrusions into our families (TV, movies, Internet websites, cell phones), children may be getting too many role models against setting limits, which undermines their parents and hurts their life-long personality development. The solution is not to eliminate technology. The solution is to find a better balance.

Between nations, we seem to be getting more HCPs as leaders, many of whom are persuasive blamers and splitters. They loudly promote the elimination of their "all-bad" enemies, while asking to be excused for the harm they do because they're the "all-good" leaders in "exceptional times." All times in history are exceptional. We're still the same human beings with the same basic personalities. These HCP leaders may be more dangerous than the vast majority of people of any country or religion. As citizens, we need to work harder at containing our own leaders and communicate to the world that we're interested in sharing this planet peacefully rather than eliminating "enemies."

Our modern societies need to calm down. We pay too much attention to histrionic electronic media stories about disasters and extremes of human behavior. We need to realize that the images of angry and frightened faces on television play directly to our brain's unconscious fears. It's natural to worry when we hear shrill tones of voice and police sirens, but we hear these many times a day on the radio, television, and Internet. We gladly pay attention to these extremes because they're exciting and our brains are programmed to be riveted by excitement. While much of this may be entertainment for adults, it's role-modeling for our children's personality development.

Repetition and emotional intensity determine where we pay attention, and electronic media has a huge capacity to steal our attention that written news and calm in-person conversations don't have. These are very recent changes that we, as a modern world culture, need to reflect on and adapt to more effectively. Otherwise, we will be completely manipulated by our own inventions. Unfortunately, we haven't yet learned how to pull ourselves away and find a better balance.

We could go for a walk in the morning and greet our neighbors, which reassures our brains that we're at peace and can handle the world around us. Instead, we start our days by rushing to get ready for stressful work while we watch the news of the latest disasters worldwide!

No wonder we're anxious, especially since 9/11. Research shows that when our brains are triggered into anxiety, the "fight-or-flight" chemicals in our bodies remain ready for action for a long time. The next alarm makes us more anxious, even if the previous alarm is no longer a threat. And research shows that when people are anxious they're more likely to absorb the emotional messages of others (Goleman, 2006). Between HCP leaders and constant disaster news, our attention is being stolen from nurturing ourselves and raising children with confident, balanced personalities.

Instead, as nations and people, we need to pay more attention to teaching healthy conflict resolution skills, providing healthy child development, and understanding healthy personality differences and similarities among the world's cultures. We need to realize that many of today's frightening behaviors by different people around the world may be fear-driven behavior in response to our own behavior or the personality-based Internal Upsets of a few leaders who get a lot of attention. They need to be contained, but so do we. We need empathy, attention, and respect, and so do our enemies.

My hope for the future is that with these realizations and greater self-awareness, we may be able to contain HCPs and live as neighbors in a rapidly shrinking world. Because we're all part of the world community and we can't go back. Now we are all neighbors, co-workers, strangers—and family.

GLOSSARY

The following are some of the terms I use throughout this book, some of which may be unfamiliar. Terms I have created to help explain High Conflict People and the dynamics of their high-conflict disputes have an (*) beside them.

Adaptation:

Changing your behavior to fit the situation you are in. For example, when you go outside you might adapt by putting on a coat. People with personality disorders often don't adapt their social behavior to changes in their circumstances, so they often get into conflicts and don't try to adapt to be more successful. Lack of self-awareness (see Self-Awareness and Self-Reflection) and lack of adaptation are primary characteristics of those with personality disorders (see Personality Disorder).

Antisocial Personality Disorder (ASPD):

A personality disorder characterized by the routine violation of social rules and laws, lack of empathy and remorse, a willingness to harm others for personal gain, smooth deception and conscious manipulation.

Antisocials:

Short term for people with antisocial personality disorder or people with some antisocial personality traits but not a disorder.

Arbitration:

A process for resolving disputes in which a neutral person makes decisions for the people in conflict after a hearing that is more formal than mediation (see Mediation), but less formal and less costly than court. The parties usually get to pick the arbitrator and the arbitrator has to follow certain rules in making his or her decision.

Assertive Approach*:

My term for taking strong action in a high-conflict dispute without purposefully harming others and being careful not to make yourself into a Target of Blame. This is in contrast to the Aggressive Approach used by most High Conflict People, and the Passive Approach used by many Targets of Blame before they became aware of the dynamics of High Conflict People.

Behavior That's Aggressively Defensive (B.A.D.)*:

This is behavior that feels necessary to a High Conflict Person in order to defend himself or herself from perceived danger from a Target of Blame. This can include verbal attacks, lawsuits, physical violence, rumors and false accusations, or any other type of aggressive behavior. It is not caused by the Target, but instead is caused by the High Conflict Person's Mistaken Assessment of Danger, which usually comes from inside of himself or herself as a spontaneous Internal Upset or is triggered by a minor or irrelevant action of the Target. This is part of the Cycle of High Conflict Thinking (see Cycle of High Conflict Thinking).

Behavior Therapy:

A mental health treatment method focused on changing one's behavior in small steps for greater success and satisfaction in life. This is a part of many therapy methods for treating many behavior problems. It is included in treating personality disorders in Cognitive-Behavior Therapy (CBT) and Dialectical Behavior Therapy (DBT).

Blamespeak*:

This term describes the flow of negative, blaming comments that High Conflict People so frequently use in private and public conversations about their Targets of Blame. It tends to be emotionally intense, very personal (about the Target's low intelligence, morals, sanity, etc.), absolute (no redeeming comments), and easily shared with others. It appears designed to humiliate or destroy the Target in the eyes of others.

Borderline Personality Disorder (BPD):

A personality disorder characterized by a rigid pattern of difficulties that often includes fear of abandonment, frequent anger, wide mood swings, clinging behaviors, impulsive and self-destructive acts, manipulative behaviors, and an inability to reflect on one's own role in their frequent personal problems and conflicts.

Borderlines (BPs):

Short term for people with borderline personality disorder or people with some traits but not a disorder.

C.A.R.S. Method™*:

A four-step method of conflict resolution that addresses the key issues of High Conflict People, but that can be used in any dispute with anyone. The four steps are: Connect using your E.A.R., Analyze your realistic options, Respond to misinformation, and Set Limits on misbehavior. See the overview and C.A.R.S. worksheet at the beginning of Part II of this book.

Cognitive Distortions:

Spontaneous thoughts that are extreme and inaccurate for the present circumstances. All people have cognitive distortions from time to time. Most people are able to examine their thoughts for current accuracy and to disregard the distortions. However, people with personality disorders or traits tend to have more frequent cognitive distortions, tend to believe in them without examination, and tend to act on them as true. They unconsciously resist new information and instead intensely defend their distortions.

Cognitive Therapy:

A treatment method for reducing cognitive distortions and feeling better by writing down and discussing negative thoughts, negative feelings, and more realistic positive responses. It is a way of dramatically changing your life by changing your own thoughts. It is one method for treating many problems, including depression, anxiety, and personality disorders. It is often combined with behavior therapy (see above) and called Cognitive-Behavior Therapy (CBT).

Collaborative Law (Most often Collaborative Divorce):

A relatively new process of legal dispute resolution in which each party obtains an attorney who agrees to never take the case to court. The process often includes one or two mental health coaches and a financial specialist to assist the process of negotiating a settlement. The goal is to reach a complete legal agreement without the highly adversarial nature of court. If no agreement is reached, the parties must hire different professionals to take the case to court. This strongly motivates reaching an out-of-court settlement.

Cycle Of High Conflict Thinking*:

High Conflict People often feel that they are in life-or-death danger, when they are not. Therefore, they have a Mistaken Assessment of Danger (see below). Even though this *feeling* of danger is inside of them, High Conflict People *think* that it is caused by someone else, whom they *think* they must attack in order to feel safe. Therefore, they attack a Target of Blame using Behavior that's *Aggressively Defensive*. However, their Targets often give them Negative Feedback, which reinforces their Mistaken Assessment of Danger, and the Cycle of High Conflict Thinking continues.

Defense Mechanism:

This is a psychological term for a person's unconscious coping methods. Everyone has defense mechanisms, but we generally cannot see our own. They help us cope with upsetting information that threatens our sense of identity or survival. An example includes "projecting," described below, in which people see their own negative qualities in others but not in themselves.

Dialectical Behavior Therapy (DBT):

A treatment method, developed by Marsha Linehan in Seattle, that has been well-researched as particularly effective in treating BPD (see Borderline Personality Disorder). It includes training to help Borderline patients self-regulate their emotions and behavior, and teaches self-acceptance and tolerance for the co-existence of opposites, such as being angry at someone and still loving the person, or making mistakes and still being a competent person. This DBT approach has been growing rapidly over the past 10 years and shows a lot of promise for the future.

Dysfunctional Behavior:

Behavior that is not functional (not helpful to the person), but the person does not realize it is unhelpful. It is usually a pattern of behavior that keeps interfering with the person's goals and relationships, but the person keeps doing it.

E.A.R.*:

Empathy, Attention, and Respect, as described throughout this book, especially in Tip #8.

Emotional Facts*:

Emotionally generated false information, accepted as true and appearing to require emergency action by others. Similar to rumors. These "facts" are commonly generated from the emotional reasoning of a High Conflict Person (HCP), to whom they *feel true*, therefore they are accepted as true. These emotional facts are often highly persuasive in court or other settings in the short term, because of the unconscious transfer of the HCP's high-intensity emotions. The High Conflict Person may adamantly believe these emotional facts, even when no one else does.

Emotional Reasoning:

A cognitive distortion recognized by therapists for many years. The person feels that something is true and therefore *believes* that it is true, without any logical examination of the reality of this belief. For example, a skinny person might *feel* fat and therefore stop eating regardless of the logical reality of the situation.

Emotionally Hooked*:

This means that someone has become emotionally upset in their contact with a High Conflict Person and is now emotionally reacting rather than logically deciding his or her next actions. This usually occurs when the HCP's high-intensity fear and anger are transferred unconsciously and nonverbally to the other person, who often becomes the HCP's Negative Advocate (see below). Once you are aware of this unconscious ability to get emotionally hooked, you can often recognize it when it is happening and remain logical without getting emotionally hooked. This doesn't mean you don't have emotions. It just means that your logical mind is clear and not dominated by upset emotions.

Empathy:

The ability to understand and feel similar uncomfortable feelings that another person *might* be feeling, and to communicate to the other person that you can understand and care about how they *might* feel.

Fight, Flight, Or Freeze Responses:

These are automatic responses in your body that can be triggered in a fraction of a second by any strong indication of fear, anger, or other signs of danger. Your heart rate goes up; your body is flooded with adrenaline and other hormones for quick, strong defensive action; and your muscles tense in readiness. Before you know it, you may be hitting someone, running away, or freezing in place. Once the danger has passed, your body takes a little while to calm down again.

High Conflict People (HCPs)*:

Plural for High Conflict Person (see High Conflict Person).

High Conflict Person (HCP)*:

Usually someone with a high-conflict personality (see High Conflict Personality). Some people with other mental health problems may also be high conflict people, such as those with alcoholism, bipolar disorder, and schizophrenia. However, many of those do not stay in long-term conflicts with a Target of Blame, as they may be too dysfunctional to stay focused or their problems may be successfully treated. High-conflict people usually have a life-long pattern of high-conflict behavior unless they get sufficient treatment—which they usually avoid because they believe that it is everyone's problem but their own.

High Conflict Personality*:

Usually someone with the long-term traits of a Cluster B personality disorder listed in the Diagnostic and Statistical Manual of the American Psychiatric Association—presently the DSM-IV-TR (APA, 2000). Cluster B includes borderline, narcissistic, histrionic, and antisocial personality disorders. These four are best known for their frequent and dramatic personal conflicts and crises. Their personality characteristics often bring them into disputes that involve many other people, and sometimes the courts. Not all of those with a Cluster B personality disorder or traits have a High Conflict Personality, just those who also focus on a specific Target of Blame and engage them in an ongoing, intensely personal dispute.

High Conflict Thinking*:

Frequent thinking that is highly defensive and distorted because of an unrealistic sense of life-or-death danger. It is characterized by a Mistaken Assessment of Danger based on cognitive distortions and unconscious defense mechanisms (see Cognitive Distortions and Defense Mechanism). When a person is in life-or-death danger, the brain automatically shuts down ordinary logical thinking and focuses instead on fast, defensive action. Common examples of cognitive distortions and defense mechanisms associated with High Conflict Thinking include:

all-or-nothing thinking, jumping to conclusions, personalization, emotional reasoning, mind reading, wishful thinking, tunnel vision, exaggerated fears, projecting, and splitting.

Histrionic Personality Disorder (HPD):

A personality disorder characterized by constant drama, a lot of emotional reasoning, fear of being ignored, extreme efforts to be the center of attention, superficial relationships, and difficulty solving one's own problems.

Histrionics (HPs):

Short term for people with histrionic personality disorder or people with some traits but not a disorder.

Internal Upset (IU)*:

The painful feeling that a High Conflict Person often feels inside (internal distress) but thinks is caused by a person or event outside of himself or herself, often their Target of Blame. This often occurs spontaneously and is related to early life negative experiences that were too traumatic or too early in life to be consciously understood. Therefore, the High Conflict Person mistakenly thinks that someone nearby must have caused the feeling in the present and they blame a Target of Blame: " think it's who made me feel this way."

Maladaptative Personality Traits ("Traits"):

These are the traits of personality disorders that cause people to remain stuck in ways of thinking and behaving that interfere with their lives and the lives of people around them. They are "maladaptive" because they do not adapt to changes around them. For example, one maladaptive trait of people with borderline personality disorder (see Borderline Personality Disorder) is frequent anger, even when it will get them in trouble. They have a hard time adapting to situations in which frequent anger hurts them, therefore it is a maladaptive trait of their personality. When a person has enough of these traits, he or she has a personality disorder.

Mediation:

In mediation, a neutral person helps two (or more) people in conflict to sit down and talk in a step-by-step way. The mediator helps them understand each other's point of view and to make agreements. The mediator doesn't make the decisions, but directs the discussion so the people in conflict can reach their own agreements. This can be done informally at any time by a third person acting as a mediator, or this may be a formal process with specific rules and several meetings.

Mistaken Assessment Of Danger (M.A.D.)*:

The feeling of danger that High Conflict People often get when they are under stress or experiencing an Internal Upset (see Internal Upset). This is usually based on cognitive distortions and unconscious defense mechanisms (see Cognitive Distortions and Defense Mechanism). Common examples of cognitive distortions and defense mechanisms associated with Mistaken Assessment of Danger include: all-or-nothing thinking, jumping to conclusions, personalization, emotional reasoning, mind reading, exaggerated fears, projecting, and splitting. When the person thinks this feeling is caused by a Target of Blame, they attack the Target with Behavior that's Aggressively Defensive, which leads to the Cycle of High Conflict Thinking (see Cycle of High Conflict Thinking).

Narcissistic Personality Disorder (NPD):

A personality disorder with a rigid pattern of social difficulties, including fear of being belittled or seen as inferior, extreme self-centeredness, disdain and disrespect for others, expectations of special treatment, lack of empathy, manipulative behaviors, and an inability to reflect on their own role in their frequent personal problems. Narcissism (believing in yourself) in small doses is a healthy characteristic that helps people through hard times, but those with NPD have too much narcissism and their excessive belief in themselves prevents them from connecting with others in a meaningful way.

Narcissistic Injuries:

This is the extreme sense of devastation that happens to any person from time to time when caught by surprise by a setback they thought would never happen to them. This could be failing to get the job you expected, a breakup, or even a small criticism from a respected friend. It feels like there is something wrong with you as a person. Narcissists constantly feel narcissistic injuries from life events, even routine life events. In reality, there is no one to blame, but the narcissist feels so devastated that he or she repeatedly finds someone else to blame because it "must be somebody else's fault." This can lead to disputes from breach of contract obligations in business, to domestic violence, and even to murder.

Narcissistic (NPs):

Short term for people with narcissistic personality disorder or people with some traits but not a disorder.

Negative Advocate*:

This is a term for anyone who advocates for a High Conflict Person's negative thinking, feelings, and behaviors. This is similar to an "enabler" for an alcoholic or addict who covers up, apologizes for, and generally reinforces the behavior problems of the alcoholic or addict. However, Negative Advocates often go beyond being enablers and become emotionally hooked into fighting the battles for the High Conflict Person at many levels, including court, and may be more persuasive than the HCP. Anyone can become a Negative Advocate: family members, co-workers, neighbors, and even professionals such as attorneys and therapists. In many cases, once they become fully informed they stop advocating and may abandon the HCP.

Negative Feedback (N.F.)*:

This is the third step in the Cycle of High Conflict Thinking (see Cycle of High Conflict Thinking). This occurs when a Target of Blame or anyone else responds to a High Conflict Person by suggesting in any way that the HCP's past behavior was not completely appropriate. HCPs take Negative Feedback very personally, defend vigorously against it, and it tends to increase their Mistaken Assessment of Danger. While criticism would obviously be considered Negative Feedback, it can be any form of feedback about past behavior. Even "constructive feedback" in the form of positive suggestions can have the same effect on an HCP, as it is interpreted as criticizing the HCP's past behavior. The best approach is to avoid any direct feedback about past behavior and use the steps described in Part II of this book instead.

Peripheral Persuasion:

This is a term identified in negotiation theory and advertising. It is the unconscious process of persuading people to buy things, vote for candidates, or settle a dispute. It is in contrast to direct or "central route persuasion," which is identified as conscious and logical. The dynamics of peripheral persuasion seem to explain why High Conflict People are able to persuade people to become their Negative Advocates (see Negative Advocates). Since High Conflict People have intense negative emotions, peripheral persuasion may be why people become Negative Advocates without even realizing it or logically knowing why.

Personality Disorder:

Mental health professionals consider a person to have a personality disorder when he or she has a significant pattern of long-term emotional distress and/or ongoing serious dysfunction in their relationships with others. These disorders usually started in early childhood, but they are not diagnosed until adulthood in most cases. This pattern will continue throughout their lives in many different settings and with many different people. In a sense they are stuck behaving the same way throughout their lives. They are not able to reflect on their own behavior and make changes accordingly. There are 10 personality disorders listed in the Diagnostic and Statistical Manual (DSM-IV-TR) of the American Psychiatric Association (APA, 2000). More recently, there has been increased interest in understanding and treating personality disorders, which seem to be increasing for the reasons described in the first Tip of this book. Mental health research indicates that approximately 15% of the United States population has one or more personality disorder(s).

Persuasive Blamers*:

This is a term which describes High Conflict People when they are able to persuade others that their Targets of Blame are at fault for their problems. Usually they convince others because of their high-intensity fear and/or anger, their charm, and the sheer volume of complaints they have against their Targets. The people they persuade usually become their Negative Advocates (see Negative Advocates), although this often doesn't last after the Negative Advocate becomes fully informed. Therefore, High Conflict People constantly use their skills as persuasive blamers to obtain new Negative Advocates.

Projecting:

More formally known as "projective identification" by mental health professionals, this term describes the unconscious defense mechanism of seeing one's own negative qualities in others but not in oneself. For example, if a person grew up learning that it was bad or dangerous to show any sign of weakness, he or she might get angry at another person for being too weak whenever he or she felt weak. He or she might even physically or legally attack the other person to relieve the "bad" feeling inside. This is a common factor in domestic violence and many high-conflict court cases.

Social Glue Bits*:

This is based on the term "social glue," which some brain researchers use to describe the social nature of brain and personality development. It appears that healthy children need thousands or millions of positive social interactions while they grow up to really develop an adaptable brain and a healthy personality. I call each of these little positive social interactions a "social glue bit." I believe that children are growing up with less and less social glue bits these days, with so much emphasis on electronic devices and the weakening of family ties in modern urban societies. This may be one reason children have grown up with more personality disorders or traits in recent generations.

Target Of Blame (TOB)*:

When a High Conflict Person blames another person for problems that are more of the HCP's own making, I call the wrongly blamed person a Target of Blame. The dispute is not really about the Target, although it may look that way at first from the outside. High Conflict People have frequent Internal Upsets (see Internal Upsets), which they don't understand so they believe that these upsets are caused by the people close to them or by people in positions of authority. Therefore, anyone can become a Target of Blame just by being in a close relationship or being an authority figure in the High Conflict Person's life. There are many things described in this book that a Target can do to manage or ease out of the situation.

Self-Awareness and Self-Reflection:

These are general terms for knowing what you are thinking and feeling and recognizing your effect on other people and their effect on you. This is also known as being "conscious" of yourself. Most of the time, we are only aware or conscious of a small portion of what we are thinking, feeling, and doing. If we focus some attention on ourselves (self-reflect) we can usually become more aware. However, deep thoughts, confusing feelings and self-defeating behaviors are usually harder to identify or understand, so we need someone else to help us look at ourselves. This is part of human nature. Most of us learned to be basically self-aware while we were growing up. However, people with personality disorders seem to particularly lack this ability to be self-aware or to self-reflect, so that they don't realize that much of their behavior is self-defeating and socially inappropriate.

Splitting:

Splitting is an unconscious defense mechanism most frequently associated with borderline and narcissistic personality disorders. The person "splits" people into all-good and all-bad. While most people realize that people are a mix of good and bad qualities, borderlines and narcissists often experience people as absolutely all-good or all-bad. When they see themselves as all-good, then their Target of Blame is all-bad. With this type of thinking, the HCP believes it is all right to attack and even injure the all-bad Target. When several people are involved in a high-conflict dispute, the HCP may see some people as perfect all-good allies and other people as all-bad enemies.

Unconcious:

This is another word for lack of self-awareness (see Self-Awareness and Self-Reflection). Most of our thoughts, feelings, and behaviors are unconscious, but we can become conscious of them if we pay attention to them. People with personality disorders are generally not conscious of their troublesome behavior for psychological reasons, so they don't try to change it. It may be because of abuse, other trauma in their past, or other reasons. You can't "make" other people conscious of their own internal dynamics.

REFERENCES

American Psychiatric Association. (2000). Diagnostic and statistical manual of mental disorders (4th ed.). Washington, DC.

Baumeister, R. F. (2006, August/September). Violent pride: Do people turn violent because of self-hate, or self-love? Scientific American Mind, 17(4).

Beck, A., & Freeman, A. (1990). Cognitive therapy of personality disorders. New York: Guilford Press.

Beck, A. T., Rush, A. J., Shaw, B. F., & Emery, G. (1979). Cognitive therapy of depression. New York: Guilford Press.

Bleiberg, E. (2001). Treating personality disorders in children and adolescents. New York: Guilford Press.

Borelli v. Borrelli. (2000) 77 Cal. App. 4th 703; 91 Cal. Rptr. 2d 851.

Braun, G. (2007, February 28). Motorist's rampage a chilling reminder. The San Diego Union-Tribune.

Burns, D. (1980). Feeling good: The new mood therapy. New York: Morrow.

Cavaiola, A., & Lavender, N. (2000). Toxic coworkers: How to deal with dysfunctional people on the job. Oakland, CA: New Harbinger.

Ceci, S. & Bruck, M. (1995). Jeopardy in the courtroom. Washington, DC: American Psychological Association.

Cohen, C. (2007, Fall/Winter). Taking the bull(y) by the horns: Workplace bullies and conflict resolution. ACResolution.

Dadds, M. R. et al. (2006, December). Failure to recognize fear in others—a marker for psychopathy? The Brown University Child and Adolescent Behavior Letter, 22(12).

Davis, K. (2007, May 13). Neighborhood watcher or video vigilante? The San Diego Union-Tribune.

Dutton, D. (1998) The abusive personality: Violence and control in intimate relationships. New York: Guilford Press.

Dutton, D. (2007) The abusive personality: Violence and control in intimate relationships (2nd ed.). New York: Guilford Press.

Eddy, W., & Waldman, E. (2006). Unpublished survey of 131 family law attorneys. San Diego, CA.

Ford, C. (1996). Lies! Lies!! Lies!!! The psychology of deceit. Washington, DC: American Psychiatric Association.

Friedman, M. (2004). The so-called high-conflict couple: A closer look. The American Journal of Family Therapy, 32, 101-117.

Frommer, F. J. (2003, May 6). Hearing transcripts show McCarthy's bully tactics. The San Diego Union-Tribune.

Gladwell, M. (2005). Blink: The power of thinking without thinking. New York: Little, Brown.

Goleman, D. (1998). Working with emotional intelligence. New York: Bantam.

Goleman, D. (2006). Social intelligence: The new science of human relationships. New York: Bantam.

Grant, B. F., Hasin, D. S., Stinson, R. S., Dawson, D. A., Chou, S. P., Ruan, W. J. et al. (2004, July). Prevalence, correlates, and disability of personality disorders in the United States. Journal of Clinical Psychiatry, 65(7).

Gross, G., Moran, G., & Hughes, J. (2003, September 6). A tragic ending to custody fight. The San Diego Union-Tribune.

Hoffine, B. (2003, August 28). Letters to the editor: Families must help students with math. The Beacon.

Hudson, J. (2006, October). Coworker Conflict Drives Up Employee Stress Levels. From the ComPsych website: http://www.compsych.com/jsp/en_US/content/ pressRelease/2006/coworkerConflict.jsp

Jones, H. (2004, April). Defendant decided to testify, and thus became a target. The San Diego Union-Tribune.

Jones, J. (2003, August 28). 'Hate thy neighbor' fight gets to court. The San Diego Union-Tribune.

Khamisa, A. (2007). TKF. From the Tariq Khamisa Foundation website: http://www.tkf.org

Kirbens v. Wyoming State Board of Medicine. (1999). 992 P. 2d 1056.

Kotowski v. DaimlerChrysler. (2007). 2007 U. S. Dist. LEXIS 85581, 1.

Kreger, R., & Gunn, E. (2007). The ABC's of BPD. Milwaukee, WI: Eggshells Press.

Lawson, C. (2002). Understanding the borderline mother: Helping her children transcend the intense, unpredictable, and volatile relationship. Northvale, NJ: Jason Aronson.

Lawson, C. (2004). Treating the borderline mother: Integrating EMDR with a family systems perspective. Family Treatment of Personality Disorders. New York: Haworth Clinical Practice Press.

Linehan, M. (1993). Cognitive-behavioral treatment of Borderline Personality Disorder. New York: Guilford Press.

Lutgen-Sandvik, P., Tracy, S. J., & Alberts, J. K. (2006, November 2). Burned by bullying in the American workplace: Prevalence, perception, degree, and impact. Journal of Management Studies.

Maki, A. (2007, September 21). He was used to being on camera—but not 24/7. The Globe and Mail.

Meloy, J. R. (1997). Violent attachments. Northvale, NJ: Jason Aronson.

Navarro, J. (2005). Hunting terrorists: A look at the psychopathology of terror. Springfield, IL: Charles C. Thomas.

Parker, I. (2004, January 26). Victims and volunteers. The New Yorker.

Rice-Oxley, M. (2006, January 23). R-E-S-P-E-C-T, find out what it means to England. The Christian Science Monitor.

Rieke, R., & Stutman, R. (1990). Communication in legal advocacy. Columbia: University of South Carolina Press.

Schore, A. (2007, February). The science of the art of psychotherapy. Two-day workshop on right brain attachment and affect regulation. Los Angeles, CA.

Siegel, D. J. (1999). The developing mind. New York: Guilford Press.

Smith, A., & Mattingly, S. (2005). Unlikely angel: The untold story of the Atlanta hostage hero. Grand Rapids, MI: Zondervan.

State Civil Litigation Notes. (2005, November). California. Lesbian/Gay Law Notes.

Thernstrom, J. (2003, August 24). Untying the knot. New York Times Magazine.

Toobin, J. (2005, January 17). Annals of law. Killer instincts: Did a famous prosecutor put the wrong man on death row? The New Yorker.

Twenge, J. (2006). Generation me: Why today's young Americans are more confident, assertive, entitled—and more miserable than ever before. New York: Free Press.

U.S. Journal Training. (2007, May). Intervention Conference, Las Vegas, NV.

Weber, D. (2004, September-October). Poll results: Doctors' disruptive behavior disturbs physician leaders. The Physician Executive.

Weigert v. Georgetown University. (2000). 120 F. Supp. 2d 1.

Wekerle, C., Miller, A. L., Wolfe, D. A., & Spindel, C. B. (2006). Childhood maltreatment. Cambridge, MA: Hogrefe & Huber.

Yamada, D. (2007). The "Healthy Workplace" Bill: A model act to provide legal redress for targets of workplace bullying, abuse, and harassment, without regard to protected class status. From the Bullying Institute website: http://www.bullyinginstitute.org

Yi, D. (2006, April 3). Homeowners associations: Many consider them fighting words. Los Angeles Times.

ABOUT THE AUTHOR

William A. ("Bill") Eddy is President of the High Conflict Institute, LLC, in Scottsdale, Arizona, and Senior Family Mediator at the National Conflict Resolution Center in San Diego, California.

He is a Certified Family Law Specialist in California with 15 years' experience representing clients in family court and a Licensed Clinical Social Worker with 12 years' experience providing therapy to children, adults, couples, and families in psychiatric hospitals and outpatient clinics.

Since 1983, Bill has also been a part-time mediator with the National Conflict Resolution Center (formerly San Diego Mediation Center), at first as a volunteer and then as a paid mediator. He has mediated neighbor disputes, workplace disputes, landlord-tenant disputes, small business and consumer disputes, school disputes, business disputes, and personal injury cases.

He taught Negotiation and Mediation at the University of San Diego School of Law for six years. He provides seminars on mental health issues for judges, attorneys, and mediators, and seminars on law and ethics for mental health professionals. His articles have appeared in national law and counseling journals. He is the author of several books, including High Conflict People in Legal Disputes and SPLITTING: Protecting Yourself While Divorcing a Borderline or Narcissist.

Bill is a co-founder of the High Conflict Institute and has been a speaker in 20 states, 4 provinces in Canada, and France and Australia. He has become an authority and consultant on the subject of high conflict personalities for legal professionals, employee assistance professionals, human resource professionals, ombudspersons, healthcare administrators, college administrators, homeowners associations, and others.

Bill obtained his law degree in 1992 from the University of San Diego, a Master of Social Work degree in 1981 from San Diego State University, and a Bachelors degree in Psychology in 1970 from Case Western Reserve University. He began his career as a youth social worker in a changing neighborhood in New York City and first became involved in mediation in 1975 in San Diego. He considers conflict resolution the theme of his varied career.

Bill Eddy's website is www.HighConflictInstitute.com.

About High Conflict Institute, LLC

High Conflict Institute LLC was co-founded by William A. ("Bill") Eddy, LCSW, Esq., and Megan L. Hunter, MBA, to provide education and resources to professionals handling high conflict disputes. The Institute provides training and consultation for handling High Conflict People in a wide variety of settings: legal, workplace, healthcare, education, government, business, and others.

For more information about high conflict seminars, consultation, the C.A.R.S. Method™ or other resources with Bill Eddy, Megan Hunter, and their associates, go to www.HighConflictInstitute.com.

About National Conflict Resolution Center

The National Conflict Resolution Center is a not-for-profit corporation that provides mediation, arbitration, facilitation, and training for community, business, and legal clients. With more than 20 years of experience and over 10,000 cases resolved, NCRC has come to be recognized as an international leader in mediation instruction and conflict resolution.

For more information about mediation services and mediation training, go to www.ncrconline.com.

Continuing Education for Mental Health Professionals

Bill Eddy provides continuing education courses on working with high conflict people and alienated children in divorce at www.ContinuingEdCourses.net.

CPSIA information can be obtained
at www.ICGtesting.com
Printed in the USA
JSHW011141111219
2923JS00004B/10

9 781936 268023